THE AMERICAN QUARTERLY REVIEW, NO. 18, JUNE 1831

LECTOR HOUSE PUBLIC DOMAIN WORKS

THE AMERICAN QUARTERLY REVIEW, NO. 18, JUNE 1831

VARIOUS

ISBN: 978-93-90145-01-0

Published: -

LECTOR HOUSE LLP
E-MAIL: lectorpublishing@gmail.com

THE AMERICAN QUARTERLY REVIEW,
NO. 18, JUNE 1831

VOL. IX.

CONTENTS

AMERICAN QUARTERLY REVIEW.

NO. XVIII.
JUNE, 1831.

ART. I.

COLLEGE-INSTRUCTION AND DISCIPLINE.

1.—*Journal of the Proceedings of a Convention of Literary and Scientific Gentlemen, held in the Common Council Chamber of the City of New-York. October, 1830. New-York: pp. 286. 8vo.*

2.—*Catechism of Education, Part 1st, &c. By William Lyon Mackenzie. Member of the Parliament of Upper Canada. York: 1830. pp. 46. 8vo.*

3.—*Address of the State Convention of Teachers and Friends of Education, held at Utica. January 12th, 13th, and 14th, 1831. With an Abstract of the Proceedings of said Convention. Utica: 1831. pp. 16. 8vo.*

4.—*Oration on the advantages to be derived from the Introduction of the Bible and of Sacred Literature as essential parts of all Education, in a literary point of view merely, from the Primary Schools to the University: delivered before the Connecticut Alpha of the ΦBK Society. On Tuesday, September 7th, 1830. By Thomas Smith Grimke, of Charleston, S. C. New-Haven: 1830. pp. 76. 8vo.*

5.—*Lecture on Scientific Education, delivered Saturday, December 18th, 1830, before the Members of the Franklin Institute. By James R. Leib, A. M. Philadelphia: 1831. pp. 16. 8vo.*

The subject of practical education has always been one of intense interest with every reflecting individual in this Union. It is a universally received axiom, that the foundation of a republic must be in the information of its people; and that whilst the monarchical governments of other countries may be successfully administered by an oligarchy of intelligence, a government like our own cannot be carried on without an extensive diffusion of knowledge amongst those who have to select its very machinery. The political circumstances of a country will also modify, most importantly, the course of instruction; and that system which is adopted in the old Universities of Oxford, Cambridge, and Dublin, in a nation in which the law of primogeniture exists, where wealth is entailed in families, and where the colleges themselves are richly endowed, may be impracticable or impolitic in a country not possessing such incentives. Education must, therefore, be suited to the country; and a long period must elapse before we can expect to have individuals as well educated as in those universities, although the mass of our community may be much more enlightened. We have no benefices, no fellowships with fixed stipends, to offer for those who may devote themselves to the profound study of certain subjects. In England and Ireland, it is by no means uncommon for a student to remain at college until he is twenty-two or twenty-three years of age, in the acquisition of his preliminary education, or of those branches that are made to precede a professional course of study—the whole period of his academic residence being consumed in the study of these departments. In this country, such a course would be as unadvisable as it is generally impracticable. The equal division of property precludes any extensive accumulation of wealth in families. The youth are compelled to launch early into life: the more useful subjects of study have to be selected, and the remainder are postponed as luxuries, to be acquired should opportunity admit of indulgence.

In no country are the colleges or higher schools so numerous, in proportion to the population, as in the United States.

In France there are three universities; in Italy, eight; in Great Britain, eight; in Germany, twenty-two; and in Russia, seven: whilst in the United States, we have thirteen institutions bearing the title of universities, and thirty-three that of colleges; making in all forty-six higher schools capable of conferring degrees: yet a very wrong inference would be drawn, were we to affirm that the education of a nation is always in a direct ratio with the number of its higher schools. Such would be the fact, did these institutions assume an elevated standard in the distribution of their highest honours, and were the condition of the intermediate schools such that the youth could be sent to the university so prepared as to be able to cultivate his studies there to the greatest advantage. Unfortunately, in many parts of the United States the condition of the intermediate schools and academics has been grievously neglected; and the authorities of the universities have been compelled to lower their standard, and to admit students totally unprepared for more advanced studies. In this way many of the higher schools have degenerated into mere gymnasia, or ordinary academies. This circumstance, with the multiplication of institutions capable of conferring degrees, has been attended with the additional evil, that, in some, the highest honours have been, and are conferred for acquirements, which would scarcely enable the possessors to enter the lowest classes in others.

It seems, indeed, that the real or fancied insufficiency of most of our existing institutions, gave occasion to the proposition for establishing a university in New-York, and to the Convention, a review of whose proceedings will enable us to offer some practical considerations and reflections, deduced from some experience and meditation on this momentous subject. "Much as our country," observes the Rev. *Dr. Mathews*, in his opening address in behalf of the committee of the university, "owes to her excellent colleges, the sentiment seems to be general, that the time has arrived when she calls for something more; when she requires institutions which shall give increased maturity to her literature, and also an enlarged diffusion to the blessings of education, and which she may present to the world as maintaining an honourable competition with the universities of Europe." p. 14.

The establishment of a university in the city of New-York having been determined upon, and "an amount of means" pledged to the object, which would place the institution at its commencement on a liberal footing, its friends, "believing it to be desirable, and that it would prove highly gratifying to all who feel an interest in the important subject of education, that a meeting should be convened of literary and scientific men of our country, to confer on the general interests of letters and liberal education," appointed a committee, with powers to invite, as far as practicable, the attendance of such individuals in behalf of the university. Accordingly, on the 20th of October last, a number of literary and scientific gentlemen assembled from various parts of the United States, when President Bates, of Middlebury College, Vermont, was appointed president of the convention; and the Honourable Albert Gallatin, and Walter Bowne, Esq. Mayor of the City, were named vice presidents. The convention sat daily until the 23d inclusive, when it adjourned *sine die*; but not without having provided for the perpetuation of its species at a future period.

In an assemblage so constituted, it was not to be expected that, excepting the notoriety occasioned by it, any great advantage could accrue to the university or to the public from its deliberations; the most discordant sentiments on almost all points of discipline and instruction;—the views of the experienced and inexperienced—the *experientia vera*, and the *experientia falsa*—of the contemplative and the visionary, were to be anticipated; but we must confess, that humble as were our expectations from the results of its labours, the published record of its proceedings proves that we had pitched them too high. The committee appear to us to have had no definite object—no system—in bringing many of the subjects before the convention; every discussion is arrested, without our being able to decide what was the conclusion at which the meeting arrived: and

> "Like a man to double business bound,
> They stand in pause where they shall first begin,
> And both neglect."

Of these debates the "Journal" is, doubtless, a faithful record, so far as regards their succession; the brevity, however, of the minutes, published by the secretary, renders the work very unsatisfactory; and scarcely elevates it above the character of a log-book, if we make exception of one or two excellent addresses—such as that of Mr. Gallatin—which are reported at length; and of some (generally indifferent) communications transmitted by their authors.

The first topic presented for the consideration of the convention, was:—"*As to the universities of Europe; and how far the systems pursued in them may be desirable for similar institutions in this country.*" On this subject, Dr. Lieber read a communication of interest in relation to the organization, courses of study and discipline of the German universities, which was referred to the committee of arrangements. Mr. Woolsey, of New-York, gave an account of the French colleges; their system of instruction and discipline; a few desultory observations are next made by Mr. W. C. Woodbridge. Mr. Hasler flies off at a tangent, and offers "a few remarks on the appointment of professors," and is followed by Professor Silliman on the same subject. Mr. Sparks presents a few observations and alludes to the organization of Harvard College. President Bates gives the plan of choosing professors adopted at the college over which he is placed; and Mr. Keating, of Philadelphia, puts a *finale* to the proceedings of the day and to the question at the same time, by the expression of his views. After this, we hear no more of this "topic," and we are left in the dark whether the system or any part of the system of the universities of Europe be desirable for similar institutions in this country.

It is a mere truism to remark, that the success of an institution must be greatly dependent upon the character of its professors; hence, in all universities, the best mode of selecting them has been a point of earnest and careful inquiry. In some countries, they are appointed by the government; in others, the office is obtained *au concours*. The candidates being required to defend theses of their own composition, and the most successful receiving the office; whilst in others, the faculty have the power of supplying vacancies in their own body. In our own country, no uniformity exists on this point. Harvard, by the scheme of organization, is under the supervision and control of two separate boards, called the *Corporation*, and *Board of Overseers*. The former is composed of seven persons, of whom the president of the college is one, by virtue of his office; the other six being chosen from the community at large. The board of overseers consists of the governor and lieutenant-governor of the state, the members of the council and of the senate, the speaker of the house of representatives, and the president of the college *ex-officio*; and, also, of fifteen laymen and fifteen clergymen, who are elected, as vacancies occur, by the whole board. This board has a controlling power, which, however, is rarely exerted over the acts of the corporation.

The professors are all chosen, in the first instance, by the corporation, or rather nominated for the approval or rejection of the board of overseers: "but as a case has rarely, if ever been known, in which such a nomination has been rejected by the overseers, the election of all the professors and immediate officers, may be said to pertain in practice to the corporation alone. It is probable, however, that this is seldom done without consulting the members of the faculty into which a professor is to be chosen." *Journal*, p. 82.

In the generality of our institutions, the appointing power is vested in a board of trustees, who have no controlling body placed over them. In almost all, however, we find from the Journal of the Convention—that the faculty are consulted—"that" according to Dr. Bates, "experience had proved the wisdom of consulting the faculty on any contemplated appointment of a professor; and that, in fact, though not professedly, yet in effect, professors are appointed by the instructers or faculty,—and thus by securing their good will towards the new incumbent, amity was enforced." P. 83.

The great difficulty exists in becoming acquainted with the qualifications of the candidate, especially if he has not been previously engaged in teaching. There can be no better mode of testing the capacity of a teacher, than in the class room;

but if this be not available, the recommendation of *sufficient* individuals, with us, has always to be taken; and in this, a certain degree of risk must necessarily be incurred. It is never, however, a matter of so much moment to procure a professor, who is pre-eminently informed upon the subject of his department, as one that is capable of communicating the knowledge he possesses, is systematic, has a mind that can enable him to improve and to take part as a member of the faculty in the management of the university, in which the greatest firmness, good sense, and ability are occasionally demanded. "A man," says the illustrious Jefferson, "is not qualified for a professor, knowing nothing but merely his own profession. He should be otherwise well educated as to the sciences generally; able to converse understandingly with the scientific men with whom he is associated, and to assist in the councils of the faculty on any subject of science in which they may have occasion to deliberate. Without this he will incur their contempt and bring disreputation on the institution."[1]

Young professors are, on the above accounts, *cæteris paribus*, preferable to old. They have not had time to acquire any bad system; are energetic in the acquisition of information, and become attached to the occupation. In institutions where the faculty live within the same walls, it is, likewise, important that the disposition of the individual should be taken into the account, in order that every thing may go on harmoniously. A kind, conciliating deportment, will also gain the respect of the student, and tend materially to discipline.

The best system for the appointment of professors, perhaps, would be—that the faculty should nominate, and the trustees approve or reject. It is improbable, that they would ever be guided by any feelings which would be counter to the prosperity of the institution; whilst they would generally have better opportunities of becoming acquainted with the qualifications of individuals than the board of trustees. This course appears to us less objectionable than any other; and we are glad to find that it was suggested by Mr. Sparks, in the convention.—

> "No good policy," he remarks, "would introduce an efficient member into a small body, where such a step would be likely to endanger the harmony of feeling and action. For this reason, it may be well worthy of consideration, whether, in the scheme of a new constitution, it is not better to provide for the nomination of a professor by the members of the faculty, with whom he is to be associated. Such a body would be as capable as any other, to say the least, of judging in regard to the requisite qualifications of a candidate, and much more capable of deciding whether his personal qualities, traits of character, and habits of thinking, would make him acceptable in their community. It seems evident, therefore, that something is lost and nothing gained by referring this nomination to another body of men, who have no interest in common with the party chiefly concerned. It is enough that the electing or sanctioning power dwells in a separate tribunal." P. 83.

Much diversity of opinion has prevailed on the subject of remuneration to

[1] Memoir, Correspondence, &c. Vol. IV. P. 387.

professors. In some universities they are paid entirely by fees from the students. The objection urged against this, is, that the professor is too much dependent upon the student, and that this feeling may materially interfere with discipline. To those who consider that there ought to be no discipline in our universities—and strange as it may seem, such views were expressed in the convention—this plan of remuneration can be liable to no objection. Nor to institutions in which there are no resident pupils, like the one proposed in New-York, would the objection apply. On the contrary, the mode in which the professor receives his remuneration entirely from the students, the stimulus which is thus excited, and the feeling that his emoluments may be proportionate to his energy and success in conveying instruction, may have the most beneficial effect upon his exertions. Accordingly, we find the most meritorious application on the part of the professors in our great medical schools; and a degree of enthusiasm aroused, which might not be elicited were the mode of recompensing them other than it is.

On the other hand, it has been maintained, that the professor should be in no wise dependent upon the student; that he should receive no fees, but be paid by a fixed salary. The objection urged against this system is, that there is here no stimulus, and that as the professor feels his income altogether independent of his exertions, he will relax in his efforts, neglect his duties, become inattentive to his own improvement, and uncourteous in his behaviour to the pupil. This is plausible in theory, and doubtless, has occasionally been found to be the fact. It is not likely to occur, however, if the professor be held rigidly responsible, and if the tenure of his office be on good behaviour, instead of for life. It is to be calculated, likewise, that every professor is a gentleman, and that the honour of the situation is a part of the emolument. These should be a sufficient guarantee that his duties will be performed energetically, and that his behaviour will be courteous. Should this not be the case, he is unfit for his situation, and the trustees should have moral courage enough to remove him. Experience, too, has, we think, sufficiently proved, that the evils of fixed salaries, under the tenure *dum bene se gesserit*, are more imaginary than real: some of the very best institutions are conducted upon this system, in various parts of Europe and of this country. On the whole, perhaps, where the students reside within the precincts, a combination of a fixed salary, of a sufficient amount to enable the professor to be, to a certain extent, independent of the student, with the payment of a fee from the student for tuition, is the most politic and satisfactory mode of remuneration. In this manner, he receives a certain stimulus to exertion, whilst other objections to both exclusive systems are obviated. Experience, however, shows, that although the zeal and industry of a professor may occasion a slight fluctuation in the numbers that resort to his school, this influence is very limited in its action. It is the character of the study which attracts followers; and whilst one department will be crowded to excess, independently of the merits or demerits of the professor, others will be almost entirely neglected. This will occur in all institutions in which professional, or extremely advanced, or unusual studies are taught. Every student, whether he may be intended for one of the learned professions, or for any other pursuit, considers it absolutely necessary to attend certain academical departments;—those of ancient languages and mathematics for example;—whilst comparatively few can be expected to attend the professional chairs, or the higher branches of study, notwithstanding the subjects may be taught in the most attractive and sufficient manner. Unless the manners of a professor are strikingly obnoxious, but little effect will be produced in the numbers frequenting his school: and if they are so, it is a sufficient ground for removal.

In those universities in which the professors are remunerated by a fixed salary, this inequality of attendance is not felt; but it is a serious evil, where the emolument accrues wholly or in part in the form of tuition fees. The greatest inequality may prevail in the compensation; and those teachers who are engaged in the most abstruse departments, will necessarily be worse paid than those who are engaged in superintending the elementary branches. Suppose the department of mathematics to be divided into the elementary and transcendental: if each be remunerated by an equal fee from his students, the latter cannot expect to have an income of more than one-twentieth part of that of his colleague. This we know is a ground of much dissatisfaction in many institutions, and attempts have been made to obviate it. Meiners,[2] a reflecting writer on the subject of universities, thinks it would be proper to correct this inequality by making a portion of the fees received common stock: but if we admit that the abilities and attention of the professors are equal, and that the same number of hours is employed in teaching the various branches, there seems to be no reason why the remuneration of one professor should be permitted to exceed that of his colleague. On this subject, some pertinent remarks were made by Dr. Lieber, in which he agrees, in many respects, with his countryman, *Meiners*.

> "Now I ask," says he, "how much even Professor Gauss, *le plus grand des mathematiciens*, as *La Grange* called him, has realized from his lectures? Mathematics, at least the higher branches of them, never can be very popular; I mean, it is impossible that they should be generally studied, and it would be to consign a professor to absolute indigence, if government should leave professors of mathematics dependent on the honorarium paid by their students. I studied mathematics under the celebrated Pfaff at Halle, whom *La Grange* called *un des premiers mathematiciens*, and we were never more than twenty in his lecture room, of whom I fully believe not much more than half paid the *honorarium*, which was very small." P. 58.

And again, —

> "Yet I believe, that generally speaking, it is better for professors and students to have fees paid for their lectures, for various reasons, although it would be unsafe to let professors be solely or chiefly depending upon them, for it would be unsafe to settle such annuities upon persons intended to live for science, or guarantee them, forever, an easy life. It has besides been found, that generally, students attend those lectures more carefully for which they pay. With the different branches of instruction, the principle upon which professorships are to be established, ought to vary.

[2] Ueber die verfassung und verwaltung deutscher universitaten. Göttingen, 1801-2.

> In a city, in which many students of medicine always will be as-
> sembled, it may be safe to let the professor greatly depend upon
> the fees of the students, whilst a professor of Hebrew ought to be
> provided for in such a way, that he may follow the difficult study
> of Oriental languages, without the direct care for his support, in
> case the number of students would be too small for this purpose,
> as it generally will prove." P. 65.

In most of our colleges, the president has some control over the course of education in the schools of the institution; and, consequently, over the professors.
Such a plan is, however, impolitic. No control whatever ought to be exerted over
the teacher. If qualified—and if not he is not fitted for his situation—he ought to be
left to himself, and to follow that system which he conceives best adapted to develop the intellect of his pupils; at the same time he should be held rigidly responsible
for his free agency. In the University of Virginia, as well as in other of the higher
schools of the country, the professor is required to send in a weekly report of the
number of lectures he has delivered; the daily examinations instituted; the length
of time occupied in each; and this report of the mode in which his duties have been
executed, is laid before the board of visitors at their next meeting. In this manner
delinquencies can be detected, and the appropriate corrective be applied.

Occasionally, however, it may happen, that a professor may be indolent, and
inaccurate in his reports; and it may be a question, whether it is not advantageous
that the presiding officer should have authority to attest how often a professor really does meet his class, with the length of time expended, and the precise course
of instruction adopted; and then to report to the trustees, but not to interfere himself in the rectification of abuses.

In the discussion of this subject in the Convention, Mr. Keating has committed
a blunder, regarding the University of Virginia.

> "He would like to see the president, in truth, the head of
> the university, occupying a distinguished station in the board of
> trustees, controlling all the faculties, superintending all the de-
> partments. It should be a situation such as an experienced and
> retiring statesman would be proud to fill. A good example had
> been set by the new University of Virginia." P. 86.

Now, the rector of that institution is merely a member of the board of visiters,
chosen from out the body to preside over them, has no delegated authority, but
meets the other visiters once a year, and presides over their deliberations, without,
however, having a casting vote. The chairman of the faculty, chosen annually by
the board of visiters, from amongst the professors, is the real president, and possesses the powers usually granted to the presidents of colleges. We are surprised,
by the bye, to observe from the journal of the Convention, that the University of
Virginia was entirely unrepresented there. It has now been established six years,
and has been proceeding on a tide of successful experiment. It is the first effort that
has been made in this country to cast off the trammels that have fettered practical
instruction; to suffer each to take the bent of his own inclination in the selection of

his studies, requiring for the attainment of its highest honours, *qualifications* only, and rejecting *time* altogether. Although the first attempt in this country on a large scale, the plan has been long adopted in other countries, particularly in Germany, which has been so justly celebrated for the novelty and excellence of its academic instruction; yet in no country can such an experiment be regarded with more interest than in the United States, where, for the reasons already assigned, the youth are compelled to attain, if practicable, the strictly useful, and to strive for their own support at a very early period of their career.

In the debates of the Convention, we find few allusions to that institution, and wherever it is referred to, the most lamentable ignorance of its economy is exhibited, and the greatest errors are committed. In it there is an entire separation of the legislative from the executive power; the board of visiters exercising the former—the board of professors, or faculty, the latter. This has its advantages and inconveniences. In many of our colleges for resident students, the president is, *ex officio*, presiding officer of the board of visiters, so that he forms a part of the two *powers*. Where the president is at the same time a professor this is apt to create heart burnings and jealousies, and gives him a decided, and often unfair preponderance in any dispute with his brother professors, in which the decision of the board of trustees may be requested; whilst, if the executive power have no voice in the deliberations of the superior board; and especially if the visiters reside at a distance from the institution, laws are apt to be enacted, which create great dissatisfaction and confusion, which have not been suggested by experience, and which, consequently, are either wholly inoperative, unfeasible, or impolitic. To obviate these evils the executive might have a delegate at the meetings of the legislative body, who, even if he had no vote, might be expected to take part in those deliberations which regarded the rules and regulations of the university, or the interests of the body to which he belonged; but in the discussion of other topics, his attendance might be dispensed with. In this manner, the legislative body would have the advantage of the voice of experience, and the faculty, by choosing their own delegate, could always be represented, should discussions arise between them and their presiding officer. Nothing is more certain, than that laws which seem easy of execution, and admirably conceived, are often found, in practice, to be wholly unavailable and injudicious. But the mischief does not end here. The respect of the student is any thing but increased towards the board that conceives, or the executive which attempts to fulfil such regulations. By the enactments lying before us, of almost all the well regulated institutions of this country, we find, that the board of professors are requested by the trustees to suggest to them such laws as experience may indicate; this is wise; the faculty are unquestionably the best judges, and no non-resident can possibly have the necessary experience.

Well adapted rules are the best safeguards for the success of any university, where the students reside within the precincts especially. They should be simple, yet not trivial; efficient, yet not unnecessarily rigorous, and should be drawn up, if not perspicuously, at least intelligibly. What shall we say to such cases as the following, which we copy from the published laws of one of the oldest colleges of this Union?

"No person, other than a student or other member of the college, shall be admitted as a boarder at the college table. No liquors shall be furnished or used at table, *except* beer, cider, toddy, or *spirits and water!*"

"No student shall be permitted to lodge or board, or without permission from the president or a professor, go *into* a tavern."

And again,—

> "If offences be committed in which there are many actors or abettors, the faculty may select *such of the offenders for punishment as may be deemed necessary to maintain the authority of the laws, and to preserve good order in the college, &c.*"

It is always found more easy to make laws, than to have them well executed. This is, in fact, usually the great difficulty, and formed, very properly, a subject of deliberation in the Convention. No light was, however, shed upon it, and the most visionary sentiments were elicited, denying the necessity of any discipline whatever in the higher schools. Whenever a number of youths are thrown together within a small compass, other rules become necessary besides those of the land. The *esprit du corps*, the influence of bad example afforded by a few, lead to the commission of offences that demand interposition; accordingly, in every intelligent and sound thinking community, certain transgressions, such as gambling, drinking, disorderly behaviour, habits of expense and dissoluteness, and incorrigible idleness, have been esteemed to merit serious collegiate reprehension.

Of the different kinds of government adopted in universities, we shall mention those only which prevail in the United States. The authority is generally vested in a president and faculty, the former having the power of inflicting minor punishments; the major punishments requiring the sanction of the latter. With the president the power is vested of deciding whether any case is deserving the one or the other. An objection has been urged against this system, that if the president be of a timid, vacillating disposition, he may keep every case from the faculty, and in this there is some truth; he is, however, responsible to the trustees, and hence it can rarely happen that he will exercise ill-judged lenity; this danger too, is greatly abated, provided the faculty be allowed collateral jurisdiction, and can act on cases of which he has not taken cognizance. If he has already acted, it would be obviously improper that any additional jurisdiction should be exercised—in accordance with the common law maxim—that no man can be put in jeopardy twice for the same offence.

If such discretionary power be not granted to the presiding officer, he will have to carry every case before the faculty; and thus his office will be merely nominal, for it would be utterly impracticable to define, with any accuracy, the cases that must fall under his dominion, distinctly from those to be assigned for the animadversion of the faculty.

It has been fancifully presumed, that the students themselves might be induced to form a part of the government—to constitute a court for the trial of minor offences, and to inflict punishment on a delinquent colleague; and, further, that their co-operation might react beneficially in the prevention of transgressions. The scheme has a republican appearance, but experience has sufficiently shown that it is impracticable. In the first printed copy of the enactments of the University of Virginia, (1825) we find the following.

"The major punishments of expulsion from the university, temporary suspension of attendance and presence there, or interdiction of residence or appearance within its precincts, shall be decreed by the professors themselves. Minor cases may be referred to a board of six censors, to be named by the faculty, from among the most discreet of the students, whose duty it shall be, sitting as a board, to inquire into the facts, propose the minor punishment which they think proportioned to the offence, and to make report thereof to the professors for their approbation or their commutation of the penalty, if it be beyond the grade of the offence. These censors shall hold their offices until the end of the session of their appointment, if not sooner revoked by the faculty." But in the next edition of the enactments, (1827) we find that no such law exists; hence we conclude, that the experiment had met with the usual unsuccessful issue. So long, indeed, as the *esprit du corps* or *Burschenschaft* prevails amongst students, which inculcates, that it is a stigma of the deepest hue to give testimony against a fellow-student, it is vain for us to expect any co-operation in the discipline of the institution from them. This "loose principle in the ethics of schoolboy combinations," as it has been termed by Mr. Jefferson, has indeed led to numerous and serious evils. It has been a great cause of the combinations formed in resistance of the lawful authorities, of intemperate addresses at the instigation of some unworthy member, and to repeated scenes of commotion and violence, and cannot be too soon laid aside. Sooner or later, it must yield to the improved condition of public feeling; and we cannot but regret to see the slightest and most indirect sanction given to it in the regulations of a university, which has made so many useful innovations in systems of instruction and discipline, that have been perpetuated by the prejudices of ages. The law to which we allude is the following:—"When testimony is required from a student, it shall be voluntary and not on oath, and the obligation to give it, shall be left to his own sense of right."

No youth hesitates to depose in a court of justice touching an offence against the municipal laws of his country, committed by a brother student. The youth and the people at large, are, indeed, distinguished for their ready attention to the calls of justice. Yet it is esteemed the depth of dishonour to testify when called upon by the college authorities, against the grossest violator not only of collegiate but municipal law, as if it could be less honourable to give the same testimony before one tribunal than another; or the morality of the act differed in the two cases.

This erroneous principle, which leads to the separation of so many promising individuals from the universities, threatens their reputation and prosperity, injures the cause and saps the very foundation of education, prevails in some countries, and in some portions of this country more than in others. In some of the most respectable of our own colleges, it is made a duty to give evidence under pain of the highest punishments; and in some of those in which the *esprit du corps* has prevailed to the greatest extent, it has given occasion to the adoption, by the faculty, of the monstrous alternative of selecting persons on bare suspicion, or at random, and punishing them under the expectation that the real delinquent might exhibit himself. A law of this kind prevails in the college of William and Mary, in Virginia. "In any case of disorderly conduct within the college, in which students are concerned, every student in college at the time, whether he be a resident therein or not, shall be considered as a principal and treated accordingly, unless he can show his innocence." It has also been proposed to get over this difficulty, with regard to testimony, by establishing a law court at the university, of which the law professor, for example, might be judge, and the jury be constituted of the inhabitants of the vicinity. This tribunal to possess the ordinary jurisdiction of courts of law, and of course, empowered to require testimony on oath from the student. Such might be a valuable adjunct to the powers ordinarily possessed by the faculties of our colleges.

The majority of the convention, seem manifestly to have been in favour of what they term *Parental Discipline*; but we are left to conjecture how much this embraces. If it be meant, in the language of Meiners, that "the academical authorities should bear to the students the relation of fathers as well as of judges; that they should not only punish, but entreat, admonish, advise, warn, and reprove"—no one will dispute the propriety of the system. It is, in fact, that which is introduced into our best institutions.

"The governors and instructors," say the laws of Harvard, "earnestly desire that the students may be influenced to good conduct and literary exertion, by higher motives than the fear of punishment; but when such motives fail, the faculty will have recourse to friendly caution and warning, fines, solemn admonition, and official notice of delinquency to parents or guardians; and where the nature and circumstances of the case require it, to suspension, dismission, rustication, or expulsion." But important as may be the reformation of an offender, and interesting as it is to see the wild and the thoughtless restored to the paths of rectitude, it is obvious, that the prime object of discipline is less such reformation than the advantage to others; and if in the collegiate, as in the corporeal economy, an offending member should endanger the safety of the whole fabric, it will have to be removed. A man is not sent to the penitentiary merely because he has stolen a sheep, but in order that sheep may not be stolen. The term parental discipline, in fact, is most undefined; it includes the most discrepant and the most heterogeneous modes of correction. Solitary confinement, sitting in a corner, whipping, are used according to circumstances; but we presume none of these punishments were contemplated by the Convention.

Most of the speakers seem to have been of opinion, that the parental system of intercourse, such as a wise father would maintain with his son, is best adapted for instruction and discipline in our colleges. Such a course would be manifestly impracticable where the number of students is considerable, and is of doubtful policy in all. The professor should, indeed, be kind, courteous, and affable; conciliating and ready to afford every information; but we doubt whether either discipline or instruction is aided by constant and familiar intercourse. There should be a certain distance maintained between pupil and preceptor; but no presumption, no affected dignity on the part of the latter; and under such circumstances every thing will be better effected than where the communication is closer and less unrestrained.

But the great dread entertained by these gentlemen, has been towards the infliction of disgrace; yet no punishment, whatever, can be awarded, without more or less of this. It is a disgrace to an offender to be reprimanded; to be dismissed from the schoolroom for a time; to be sent away from the institution; the good, however, of the rest requires it, and it is pseudo-philanthropy to repine. One point canvassed in the Convention and connected with this subject, requires notice. "Whether a student who has been dismissed from one institution ought to be refused admittance into any other? There is a general understanding amongst the colleges of the United States, that no student thus separated from one, shall be received into another, unless he be so far restored to favour as to be able to obtain from his college what is termed a regular dismissal." (Journal, p. 145.) Unconditional refusal to admit, appears to us to be a rule which can allow of but little justification. Meiners observes, that "those who come from other universities ought to bring certificates that they have not been expelled. If merely dismissed, they may be admitted,—but then they should be narrowly watched." It would, however, be barbarous to exclude even an expelled student, provided he could produce satisfactory evidence of his return to rectitude. It is a good practice to make the matriculation, under such circumstances, difficult; and to require a sufficient period of probation before he is permitted to join the university. The University of Virginia, has no comity in this respect with the other institutions of the Union. It has followed the only rational plan; ordaining—"that no person who has been a student at any other incorporated seminary, shall be received at that university, but on producing a certificate from such seminary, or *other satisfactory evidence*, to the faculty, with respect to his general good conduct." A no less important regulation would be, to exclude those of notoriously idle or dissolute habits, and yet who had never been at any incorporated seminary.

But Mr. Hasler is of opinion, and in this he is joined by Dr. Wolf, and, so far as we can judge, from the published speech of Mr. Woodbridge, by that gentleman also,—that little or no control is necessary over the students who resort to universities. The paper from the pen of that gentleman, in the Journal before us, bears the stamp of visionary enthusiasm; exhibits, we think, clearly a total deficiency of experience, and is

> "A fine sample, on the whole,
> Of rhetoric, which the learn'd call rigmarole."

> "Against this liberal discipline," he remarks, "the example of the Virginia university has very erroneously been alleged by way of disapprobation, or as a failure: it affords no proof of that kind. The erroneous system of collegiate life has been preserved in it. The locality is insulated, and the constant sameness of the company, of fellow-students only, produces the bad results of tedious and too close influence between the student, even with the professors. Besides that, the architect of that building, the well informed, philosophical, and amiable Jefferson, died before it was finished; for the construction of such an institution is not finished,

> with the walls that enclose its lecture rooms, or the dwellings; the organization can only be the result of several years actual activity of the institution, particularly when the plan is novel in the place where it is established. To this is still to be added, that the professors appointed there, were all accustomed to the collegiate life, and therefore not likely of such dispositions as to be proper secundents to the liberal plans of the original founder." P. 265.

Without pointing out the numerous minor errors that pervade this paragraph, we may remark, that Mr. Hasler is manifestly uninformed regarding the condition of the institution to which he alludes. We have every reason for believing, that the discipline of the University of Virginia, is equal to that which prevails in any institution of the Union. The evils of bad discipline, occasioned by the want of sufficient and efficient rules, were speedily experienced there. The objections felt by the board of visiters to over-legislation, led to an opposite error; whilst undue dependence was placed upon the effect that might be produced from the participation of the students themselves in the judicial power. Accordingly, we find, from the supplement to the printed enactments, that it became necessary to tighten the reins of authority during the very first session.

It has often been remarked, that owing to the feeble domestic discipline which ordinarily prevails in the United States, the youth, particularly of the southern parts of the Union, require a different mode of management from those of other countries. There does not appear to be the slightest foundation for this vulgar error. Young men, as well as adults, are much alike over the whole civilized globe; and if it be found that mild measures are ineffectual, recourse must be had to more severe every where: and in all cases, the laws, where needed, must be executed temperately, unhesitatingly, and firmly.

It has been said, that certain offences are esteemed as such in all institutions: of these, perhaps the most fatal are gambling and drinking. Both exert their baneful effects upon the morals, habits, and application of the student; and it is difficult to say, which is the most to be deprecated. The general evils produced upon society by their indulgence, it is as unnecessary as it would be out of place, to depict. It is only as regards their influence on college life and discipline, that they concern us at present.

Habits of gambling should lead to immediate separation of the offender; they are rarely abandoned; whilst they are as pernicious to the student himself, as they are likely to be by evil example to others. Gaming is one of the offences that require a collegiate, in addition to the municipal law. Under this head are included all those, which, from their seductive character, are apt to engross the time of the student, or to lead to parental loss and inconvenience, as cards, dice, billiards, &c.

Serious, however, as we must necessarily esteem the offence of gambling, it is, if possible, less so than habits of drinking. The latter is not an evil which entails with it so much pecuniary difficulty, but it is apt to lead to the former, and to every other loathsome vice. Few professed drunkards are reclaimed; and even should they be, the valuable time lost in youth in these indulgences, renders the youth subsequently unfit for the reception of moral and intellectual culture; hence he remains in after life debased and vicious, exhibiting merely the wreck of his previous intellect. Both these weighty offences may, in some measure, be checked by wisely devised sumptuary laws. In all well regulated universities, such endeavours have been directed to restrain the expenditure of the students.

The *Credit Gesetre* of Göttingen occupy a space of twenty-two octavo pages in the work of Meiners. At Harvard, (and we take this in our references to institutions on the old system of instruction, as being one of the longest established of those that receive resident students,) every student who belongs to places more than one hundred miles distant from Cambridge, is compelled to have a patron, appointed by the corporation, who has charge of all his funds, and disburses them under the regulations of the establishment. For this duty, he receives from the student six dollars a year as a compensation. In the University of Virginia, the proctor is the patron; and it is enacted, that "no student, resident within the precincts, shall matriculate, till he shall have deposited with the proctor all the money, checks, bills, drafts, and other available funds, which he shall have in his possession or under his control, in any manner intended to defray his expenses whilst a student of the university, or on his return from thence to his residence." On this the proctor is allowed a commission of 2 per cent. To ensure a more faithful compliance with this and other enactments on the subject, each student, about to leave the university, is required to sign a written declaration that he has made such deposit; or if not, to state the sum withheld, and the proctor is entitled to the same commission upon that sum as if it had been deposited. But if the student refuses to give such written declaration, the proctor is entitled to demand and receive from him so much as, with the commission on the money actually deposited, will make the sum of twelve dollars. Moreover, in all cases in which the student fails to make such written declaration, or in which it may appear that he has not deposited the whole of his funds with the proctor, that officer is required to report the fact to the chairman of the faculty, in order that it may be communicated to the parent or guardian of the student, be laid before the faculty and visiters, and otherwise properly animadverted upon.

The contraction of debts by students has, also, been made liable to the severest collegiate penalties; but, notwithstanding, the offence is always committed to a greater or less extent. The tradesman will give credit, and the student escape detection. The last and best resource is in the public spirit of the parent or guardian, who ought, unhesitatingly and firmly, to refuse to discharge any debt of an unauthorized nature, which his son or ward may have contracted, and especially those of the tavern-keeper or confectioner. The censures which he may incur from the exercise of his public spirit, can proceed only from the interested and sordid; whilst he will receive the applause of all those, whose favourable opinion it is desirable to possess. He will, moreover, have the gratifying conviction, that, by such a course, he is contributing to the annihilation of a system which is the cause of much public and domestic mischief.

The legislature of Massachusetts, to aid in the prevention of expense and dissoluteness, have patriotically enacted "That no inn-holder, tavern-keeper, retailer, confectioner, or keeper of any shop or boarding-house, for the sale of drink or food, or any livery-stable-keeper, shall give credit to any under-graduate, of either of the colleges within the commonwealth, without the consent of such officer or officers of the said colleges, respectively, as may be authorized to act in such cases, by the government of the same, or in violation of such rules and regulations as shall be, from time to time, established by the authority of said colleges respectively."

The example might be advantageously followed in other states. The objection, that, in a free country, every one ought to be protected in the exercise of his avocation, provided it be honest, is nugatory. They who are receiving their education at our universities, are to form the future strength, — and, in many cases, the pride and ornament of the state; and the pecuniary detriment that might accrue to a few individuals by the enactment of such a law, must be reckoned as nothing, compared with the overwhelming evil which results where unlimited indulgence is permitted.

One of the most prevalent sources of expense is in the article of dress. They, whose pecuniary means will admit of ostentatious display, will frequently attempt to exceed others in this fancied evidence of superiority. This excites a spirit of emulation in such as are but ill able to afford it, and is the origin of much idle extravagance.

To rectify this evil, as well as to aid in the more ready detection of offences, a uniform style of dress has been adopted in many of the universities of this country, and of Europe.

In some, this consists merely of a gown thrown over the clothes: which latter may be as costly as the wearer chooses.

In others, as in the universities of Harvard and Virginia, cloth of the cheapest colour, and of a determinate quality, has been selected; and the uniform dress, made from this, has been directed to be worn, whenever the student is out of his room. The plan pursued at those colleges, is the most advantageous, both in a sumptuary and penal point of view: the fashion of the dress being such as to distinguish readily the student from others, and thus to admit of the discovery of transgressors.

As a general system, the adoption of a uniform is attended with the most beneficial results: although, in particular cases, it may clearly and necessarily add to the expenditure, where, for instance, the student purposes to remain at an institution for a single session only. He leaves home provided with his ordinary apparel, which he is compelled to abandon, on becoming a matriculate. The prescribed uniform must, of course, be laid aside, on his quitting college at the end of the collegiate year; and, by this time, his ordinary apparel has become too small for him. For this reason, a law requiring a uniform dress, is obviously more beneficial in such institutions as prescribe a particular course and term of study, than where no such regulations exist. In the laws of the University of Virginia, we find that boots are proscribed, and this may seem to be descending to unnecessary minutiæ; but they who are practically conversant with university discipline, are aware that this article of dress is objectionable on other grounds than expense. It is one of the contraband methods, often had recourse to, for the introduction of forbidden liquors. The boot is sent apparently to the shoemaker, containing an empty bottle, which returns, by the same conveyance, filled with the prohibited article.

On the important topic of practical instruction, the Convention appear to have entered at some length; but, seemingly, with the same discursive irregularity, that characterizes all their other deliberations. We observe no method,—no lucid exposition, and no evident conclusion. A great part of their discussion was connected with the question, "whether students should be confined to their classes, or allowed to graduate, when found prepared, on examination?" On this subject, again, we find the most discordant sentiments. The majority, perhaps, are in favour of what they term *"classification,"* and adherence to "tried and well-known courses;" whilst others, from the same premises, have arrived at opposite conclusions:—the courses having been, in their opinion, tried and found inadequate.

The most conflicting sentiments have been indulged on this point for ages: whether, for example, it be advisable to permit a student to select his own studies, or to compel him to enter and proceed with his class: to pass a definite period at college, if desirous of attaining honours, and to offer himself for graduation only in company with his class.

Most of the older universities adhere to the system, which requires a fixed course to be followed, and for a certain time. Many of the more modern, on the other hand, permit a free choice; and some allow the student to become a candidate for graduation, whenever he feels himself competent to offer.

In the United States, with but one or two exceptions, we believe, the antiquated system, with more or less modification, is adopted; and, in most, the distinctions into freshman and sophomore, junior and senior classes, prevail: the sciences only becoming predominant objects of the student's attention in the two last. The course of study in each of these continues for a year, and is the same for every student, whatever may be his capacity or tastes. To be received into any of those upon the old system, it is made indispensable, that he should be acquainted, to a certain extent, with the Greek and Latin languages.

"No boy," says Mr. Gallatin, in an address characterized by the same comprehensive and enlightened views, which we mark in every thing emanating from that distinguished individual—"who has not previously devoted a number of years to the study of the dead languages; no boy, who, from defective memory, or want of aptitude for that particular branch, may be deficient in that respect, can be admitted into any of our colleges. And those seminaries do alone afford the means of acquiring any other branch of knowledge. Whatever may be his inclination or destination, he must, if admitted, apply one-half of his time to the further study of those languages. It is self-evident, that the avenue to every branch of knowledge is actually foreclosed by the present system, against the greater part of mankind." *Journal.* P. 175.

Mr. Gallatin does not seem to have been aware that there is one university in the Union to which his strictures do not apply—the University of Virginia. In it the student, except in the schools of ancient languages, mathematics, and natural philosophy, is subjected to no preliminary examination; and, moreover, he is required to pass through no definite course or term of study; to attend no particular classes, but is left free to select his own studies. When he has once embraced them, however, he is not permitted to relinquish them, unless by request of his parent or guardian, and by the permission of the faculty; and whenever he esteems himself sufficiently informed on the subject taught in any one of his schools, he is permitted to become a candidate for graduation in it. This system, which, so far as it goes, will bear the test of rigid and philosophical examination more than any other, prevails more or less in the German universities, and has been adopted, we believe, in the new London University.

Professor Vethake of Princeton, New-Jersey—a communication from whom was read to the convention, and which exhibits sound practical sense, and ingenious and discriminating reflection—has exhibited the prevalent inaccuracy of information, regarding the system adopted at the southern university, to which, from its novelty, we have so frequently alluded. "I see no objection," he remarks, "to render it obligatory on them (the students) to attend at the same period of time, a certain number of courses, unless specially exempted for sufficient reasons, as is now the arrangement in the University of Virginia." *Journal*, P. 30. No such arrangement exists in that institution. The professor has been guilty of an *error loci*; the plan is pursued at the old college of William and Mary, in Virginia.

In canvassing the comparative merits of the two systems, and, indeed, of every point of college discipline and education, it is necessary to take into consideration the age at which the students are received. In most of our colleges they are admitted when mere boys, and the course of instruction is necessarily made more elementary. In the University of Virginia, on the other hand, no student is received under the age of sixteen, and when, whatever may be the fact, it is to be presumed, that the more elementary portion of his education has been completed, and that he is now prepared for the prosecution of more advanced academic, or for professional, studies. To adopt a rigid rule, that students of this age should be compelled to pass a period of four or more years at college, before they can offer themselves for honours; or that they should be confined to classes, with boys, to whom a few years is a matter of comparatively little moment, would be manifestly unreasonable. This much is certain, that in this country few can spare the time in the mere attainment of academical or preliminary information. The truth is, our universities are, like those of Scotland now, and Oxford and Cambridge in former times—both schools and colleges. The under graduate course, in those venerable seats of learning, seems at first to have corresponded precisely, in point of age, with that of the modern schools. Many of the statutes, still in force at Oxford and Cambridge, respecting the discipline of students, sufficiently attest the boyhood of those for whom they were enacted. One of these directs corporal chastisement for those who neglect their lessons. Another, at Cambridge, prohibits the undergraduates from playing marbles on the steps of the senate house. In process of time, excellent schools arose, at which the ordinary preliminary education was obtained, and the period of resorting to college became thus postponed. The dislike to innovation, which augments in intensity according to the age of the establishment, prevented, however, any modification in the course of scholastic instruction, and thus it would seem was occasioned the length of time consumed there in preliminary education.[3]

It will be manifest, that the objections to the system of classification are not so numerous or so weighty in those colleges into which mere boys are received. It has been repeatedly urged, that by such a system they are compelled to study subjects foreign to their inclinations and capacities; but, until the age of sixteen or seventeen, the mind cannot, perhaps, be better employed than in the acquirement of such knowledge as forms part of the course prescribed in the generality of our universities. The great objection is, that those of all ages are subjected to the same restrictions.

The opposite course, as it at present prevails at the University of Virginia, is also liable to animadversion; the less, however, as the students are not received under sixteen years of age. It will most generally happen, that neither the youth, nor his parent nor guardian, is sufficiently acquainted with the course he ought to adopt with the view of being well educated; and if the youth be left solely to the exercise of his own discretion, which is often a negative quantity, he will be apt to select those schools that require the least application, and are the most interesting, to the exclusion of more severe and elementary subjects. The best system is that which turns out the greatest number of well instructed individuals, or which holds out the greatest amount of incentives to regular study. This cannot be accomplished by any plan which leaves the student, or the parent or guardian—often less competent than the student—to be the sole judge of what should be the course of instruction in all cases. The University of Virginia, which admits this system to the full extent—in no wise controlling the choice of the student—affords us some elucidation of the comparative value attached to different subjects of university instruction, by the student, or by parents and guardians, and of the disadvantages of this unrestricted plan. From the report of the rector and visiters of that university for 1830, we find that there were attending the

School of	Ancient Languages	-	52
	Mathematics	-	60
	Natural Philosophy	-	47
	Moral Philosophy	-	16

We have selected those subjects only, which constitute the usual course of academic instruction; and which, we think, ought to constitute it. The school of chemistry we have omitted, because it was composed of both academic and professional students, with the ratio of which to each other we are unacquainted. The probability also is, that some of those attending the departments of natural and moral philosophy, were students of law or medicine. From this list we find, that whilst the schools of ancient languages, of mathematics, and of natural philosophy were well attended, that of moral philosophy—one of eminent importance in forming the youthful mind—was comparatively neglected. The two first departments, as

---

[3] Quarterly Review, Vol. XXXVI. P. 229.

taught in most of our colleges, are the subject of the first years' attention; the latter are esteemed more advanced studies, and, where free agency is allowed the pupil, he will generally prefer the study of matter, with the advantage of the beautiful and diversified elucidations afforded by the advanced state of physical science, to that of mind, with all its arid, but by no means sterile investigations.

We have said that, in the University of Virginia, the selection of studies by the student is free and uncontrolled. An indirect influence is, however, exerted by the graduation of the fees paid to the professors. If the student attends but one professor, he is required to pay $50; if two, $30 to each; if three or more, $25 to each. A similar effect is produced by the enactment which requires that the student shall enter three classes, unless his parent and guardian shall authorize him, in writing, to attend fewer. Such regulations are favourable only to diffusion of studies over three subjects; the evil remains—of permitting the student to employ his own unassisted judgment in the choice. Such a rule must, however, be generally inoperative. If the collegiate regulation be known, the student will take care to provide himself with the necessary authorization from his parent or guardian; and if not known, it would be hard that the rule should apply. But let us suppose that he arrives at the university without any such authorization, and desires to join the elementary departments of ancient languages and mathematics. When he discovers that he is required to attend three schools, he will necessarily select one that may afford the greatest attractions, and the attention to which may be esteemed recreation rather than study. In such a case, the law, independently of being productive of no clear advantage except that of adding to the emolument of a greater number of professors, has the evil of compelling an elementary student to adopt a more advanced subject of study, or, at all events, an additional study to the disadvantage of the main object for which he joined the university. Less objection would have existed, if the regulation had required the student to attend *two* schools under such circumstances. He might then devote himself exclusively to elementary studies; or, if more advanced, he could readily find a collateral subject, which would not distract his attention from the main department, and might form an agreeable and useful alternation.

The truth is, however, that the law is liable to all the objections which apply to the old collegiate regulations, which make time the only element of qualification for distinction. The board of visiters of that university should have gone a step further, and instead of stating the *number* of schools which a pupil should be compelled to attend, unless his parent or guardian wished otherwise, they should have recommended, not enforced, a particular system of study for those desirous of attaining high literary distinction, or of becoming well educated; still retaining the valuable feature, that they, whose opportunities, tastes, or capacities, do not admit of their following the recommendation, may choose their own subjects.

What this system ought to be, we will now inquire into. It will enter naturally into the consideration of the latter part of the question canvassed before the Convention—"ought students to be confined to their classes, or *allowed to receive degrees when found prepared on examination?*" The affirmative of the proposition, as regards graduation, seems to be the natural view; yet there are few institutions at which this course is permitted. If the pupil be constrained to follow a prescribed and unbending series of studies, as is the case in most of the universities of this country and of Europe, it would appear to result as naturally that the negative view should be adopted.

In the Convention, the most opposing sentiments were here again elicited; and, as on other topics, they seem to have arrived at no fixed conclusion; all that we are informed being, that "the discussion of the topic was discontinued."

As regards the requisites for graduation in the different colleges of the Union, they are as various as the colleges themselves. This circumstance has, indeed, given occasion to the little estimation in which the degrees are in general held. It often happens, in truth, that the degree of Bachelor of Arts is conferred at one institution, on such as would be utterly incapable of acquiring it at another; and, at the close of his college career,—which differs in length in different institutions,—every individual receives the first degree in the arts: the examinations instituted being a matter of form, and, too often, of farce. We cannot be surprised, then, that a degree, thus obtained, should be contemned; and that, even in legislative assemblies, members should be found to declare themselves totally unworthy of the honours thus conferred upon them. This is not the case in the universities of Europe. In the English universities, the Baccalaureate is made the test of severe devotion to particular studies; and, whatever objections may be made to the plan followed in those institutions, of requiring accurate classical and mathematical knowledge, to the exclusion of every thing else, the degree is, at all events, an evidence that the possessor is unusually well instructed in those matters. Hence, we find in that country the initials B. A. and M. A. proudly appended to the names of the Bachelor or Master, and received by all as emblems of literary distinction. How rarely do we see the title thus added in this country? This comes from the causes already alluded to;—the degree is too easily attained; and, when attained, is such an insufficient evidence of learning, that it is discarded; and the parchment and the seal and riband, and the pomp and ceremony of the day for the distribution of honours, which excited so much juvenile exultation, are, in after life, esteemed no criterion of literary distinction. We cannot, then, be surprised, that one of the topics which engaged the Convention, was, "whether the title of B. A. should be retained?"

To the title *Bachelor of Arts*, unmeaning as it derivatively is, we have but little objection, provided certain definite ideas are attached to it. In the University of Virginia, the term *graduate* seems to be considered more appropriate. We do not think it an improvement upon the ancient appellation:—

> "Sound them, it doth become the mouth as well—
> Weigh them, it is as heavy."

But few appellatives, in their received acceptation, would be found to correspond with their derivative meaning. The French have their "Bachelors" and "Masters of Sciences," but these terms are not more significant; whilst "Doctor" too often means any thing rather than *doctus*—"Qui dit Docteur ne dit pas un homme docte, mais un homme qui devrait être docte."

Every well devised system of education should combine an attention to language; to the sciences relating to magnitude and numbers; and to those that embrace the phenomena of mind and of matter.

Little doubt, we think, can exist in the minds of the intelligent, that the ancient languages should form one element. Much has been said, and much will continue to be said, on both sides of this question, into which we do not propose to enter: admitting, however, that the Latin language, for example, is less necessary now than when it was the exclusive language of the learned, and that the modern languages have emerged from their then *Patois* condition, and risen in relative importance, a certain knowledge of that tongue, as well as of the Greek, ought still to form part of the education of every gentleman. The mind of youth cannot be better engaged, during the early period of their university career, than in becoming acquainted with the classic models of antiquity, and practised in the habits of discrimination which the study engenders. Whether it should be prosecuted to the extent inculcated at the English universities, and to the comparative exclusion of other subjects, is another question. In this country, at least, the course would be injudicious and unfeasible, and has been canvassed by Mr. Gallatin with that gentleman's usual felicity of exposition. The illustrious founder of the University of Virginia appears, however, to have had different views on this subject from those we have expressed; and views which appear somewhat inconsistent with freedom of graduation in the separate schools.

In the earliest copy of the enactments, (1825,) we find it stated, amongst other matters relating to the attainment of honours, that "the diploma of each shall express the particular school or schools in which the candidate shall have been declared eminent, and shall be subscribed by the particular professors approving it. But no diploma shall be given to any one who has not passed such an examination in the Latin language as shall have proved him able to read the highest classics in that language with ease, thorough understanding, and just quantity. And if he be also a proficient in the Greek, let that too be stated in the diploma; the intention being that the reputation of the university shall not be committed but to those, who, to an eminence in some one or more of the sciences taught in it, add a proficiency in those languages which constitute the basis of a good education, and are indispensable to fill up the character of a 'well educated man.'"

Without dwelling on the unreasonableness of denying a diploma to one who has sufficient knowledge of mathematics, or chemistry, or of natural or moral philosophy, because he may not be thoroughly acquainted with Latin, we cannot avoid expressing our surprise that it should not have struck that philosophic individual, and his respectable colleagues, as being a total prohibition to graduation in certain departments. To be able "to read the highest classics in the Latin language with ease, thorough understanding, and just quantity," would, of itself, require as much time as the majority of our youths are capable of devoting to their collegiate instruction. Accordingly, we find, from the printed enactments, that the faculty judiciously suggested a modification of the rule relating to graduation, which was confirmed by the board of visiters. As it now stands, it merely requires that every candidate for graduation, in any of the schools, shall give the faculty satisfactory proof of his ability to write the *English language* correctly.

For a *university degree*, then, the subject of ancient languages should certainly be one element. This, we believe, is conceded in all colleges: at least, the only exception with which we are acquainted, is that of William and Mary, in Virginia.

As little doubt can there be, with regard to mathematics; which has, in some institutions, been esteemed the study of primary importance. The utility of a certain acquaintance with numbers and magnitude, is obvious in every department of life; but the greatest advantage from the study, is the precision and accuracy which it gives to the reasoning powers. When the student has attained this more elementary instruction, he is capable of undertaking, satisfactorily, the study of physics, and of becoming acquainted with the bodies that surround him, and the laws that govern them, as well as of entering upon the science of moral philosophy, and of comprehending the interesting subject of his own psychology.

These seem to be the only departments that need be acquired for a university degree. They embrace an acquaintance with the ancient classics, and the philosophy of language, as well as with mathematical, physical, and metaphysical facts and reasonings; and their acquisition enables the student to enter upon professional or political life with every advantage.

We have said nothing, it will be observed, of the modern languages. The valuable stores to be drawn from these, especially from the French and German, are, of themselves, attractions which render unnecessary collegiate restraint or recommendation. No one can now be esteemed well educated, who is thoroughly ignorant of them.

It has been remarked that the student is permitted, in the University of Virginia, to graduate in the separate schools; and that an evil exists there, in no course of study being advised. The consequence of this is, that few can be expected to remain, for any length of time, at that institution. We would by no means interfere with this graduation in the schools; but, in addition to this, there ought, we think, to be some goal of more elevated attainment, which might excite the attention and emulation of those whose opportunities admit of their being well educated. Let it bear the title of *Bachelor of Arts*, or *Master of Arts*, or *graduate*, and, if a definite meaning be affixed to it by the college authorities, it cannot fail to be as well understood as the unmeaning terms, sophomore, freshman, senior-wrangler, &c. and let the requisites for this higher honour be graduation in, or a sufficient knowledge of ancient languages, mathematics, natural philosophy, and chemistry and moral philosophy. If this plan were universally adopted, a certain degree of uniformity might exist amongst the different colleges: the degree would be received as the test of literary merit, and the possessor be proud of appending the title to his name. At present, as Mr. Sparks has correctly observed, the "diplomas of this country, as they are now estimated in the United States, appear to be of little value."

The only other topic on which we shall pause, relates to the mode in which instruction should be conveyed, and to the examinations to be instituted, with the view of ascertaining comparative merit, and of exciting emulation. On this subject, as is well known, the English universities of Oxford and Cambridge, and that of

Dublin, differ essentially from the Scotch and many others: the latter teaching, solely, by lectures delivered orally. The most successful plan is that which combines both lectures and examinations. It is but rarely, that a text book can be found to suit the views of the professor, and no student pays the same degree of attention to a written composition. Even in the departments of ancient languages and mathematics, where the combination of lectures with examinations would appear most difficult, a prælection, explaining the various points of the subsequent examination, may be, and often is, premised with striking effect. In the ordinary method of teaching the classics, little attention is paid, except to the vocabulary; and many a student has thumbed his Horace for the fourth or fifth time, without being aware of the import of the philological, geographical, historical, and other allusions, with which the inimitable productions of the satirist abound. The vocabulary is but the key, that unlocks these various treasures. In a well devised prælection, *things* can be thought as well as *words*. We do not, indeed, know any department of science or literature, in which a union of prælections and examinations may not be employed with advantage. There is, however, another and a more serious objection to confining a student, in most branches at least, to a text book:—the professor is not stimulated to keep pace with the rapidly improving condition of science. If indolent and devoid of enthusiasm, he confines the youth closely to the text,—takes no pains to advance him farther,—and the student leaves the institution with the most insufficient instruction on the subject. The text books which are used at this time, in some of our colleges, and have been so for the last fifty years, are melancholy evidences of the imperfect mode in which particular studies are taught there, and of the absence of all progress on the part of the teachers.

We believe the very best system of instruction, where it can be adopted, is:—to recapitulate the subject of the preceding lecture, and, after the lecture of the day, to examine the class thoroughly on the last lecture but one. In this manner, the facts and theories of a science are impressed three times, upon the memory of the pupil; and if, after this, he is unable to retain them, he must be pronounced incorrigible. This plan we conceive to be the superlative; and to this conclusion we are led, not from theory simply, but from practice.

The nature of certain subjects, and the shortness of time appropriated, in some institutions, to lecture, may, occasionally, preclude its fulfilment: the nearer it can be accomplished, the better. Under this plan, the text book becomes a matter of comparatively trifling moment,—as the student will, of course, be understood to come prepared for examination on the subject of the lecture, as delivered *ex cathedrâ*.

With regard to *public examinations*, we need not dwell on the question of their policy. All well-regulated universities in this country and Great Britain, at least, have a system of rewards, as well as of punishments; and this uniformity may be esteemed a fair criterion of the opinions of the wise and reflecting of those countries on this topic. However desirable it may be, that mankind should do their duty without fear or expectation, every day's experience testifies that the hope of reward, or the dread of punishment, powerfully influences their exertions, not only for temporal, but eternal purposes.

In the German universities, there are neither daily, nor semi-annual, nor annual examinations; and, accordingly, we are not much surprised to find them objected to by some who had received their education in that country. The difference, however, which prevails upon this point in the best colleges of different parts of the globe, ought to have suggested some slight qualification of the sweeping censures that were passed upon the system in the Convention. "The semi-annual examinations," says Dr. J. Leo Wolf, "as recommended by some of the gentlemen of the Convention, lower the student to the rank of a schoolboy, while, being a man, as he ought to be, they are useless, for he will know that it is for his own good, to be assiduous in his studies. Moreover, the result of his studies is proved at the time when he desires to graduate, and to be licensed for the practice of his profession. Then he must pass a strict rigid and public examination; and this I should warmly recommend. In Prussia, these examinations are particularly severe, but quite impartial and recorded." P. 251. So far as we can judge from the involved and almost unintelligible twaddle contained in the address of Mr. Woodbridge on the subject of discipline, we should conceive him opposed to these as well as to all other means, which would excite the *emulation* of the student; thus discarding, on faulty metaphysical speculation, one of the most powerful stimuli to all literary and honourable distinction; and which, if rightly directed, can never, in collegiate life, act otherwise than beneficially. Granting, then, that annual, or semi-annual public examinations are of excellent policy in all higher schools, it remains to inquire into the best mode of conducting them. The oral system is that received into most of our colleges. In it the students are necessarily interrogated on different subjects, so that it becomes a matter of difficulty, nay of impracticability, to determine, with any accuracy, their relative standing. Added to this, if the class be numerous, it is impossible to put a sufficient number of questions to each individual; and the bold and confident, will ever exhibit a manifest advantage over the timid and retiring. In every respect, the oral, seems to us to be inferior to the written examination, where either is practicable. In the departments of the languages—ancient and modern—an admixture of the two would always be requisite, for the purpose of determining the student's acquaintance with quantity or accent, etymology, syntax, &c.

The plan universally adopted into the higher schools of England, is that by written answers. The students of a class are all furnished with the same questions; and the answers to these are written in the examination room. All communication between the examinants is prevented; and no book allowed to be brought into the apartment. After the expiration of a certain time the answers are collected.

The English method has, so far as we know, been received into one of our universities only—the University of Virginia. It has now been practised there for five years; and, we have reason to believe, the results have been such, as to satisfy the faculty of its pre-eminence over the methods usually practised. The following is its arrangement as published in the *Virginia Literary Museum*.

> "1. The chairman of the faculty shall appoint for the examination of each school, a committee consisting of the professor of that school, and of two other professors. 2. The professor shall pre-

pare, in writing, a series of questions to be proposed to his class, at their examination, and to these questions he shall affix numerical values, according to the estimate he shall form of their relative difficulty, the highest number being 100. The list, thus prepared, shall be submitted to the committee for their approbation. In the schools of languages, subjects may also be selected for oral examination. 3. The times of examination for the several schools shall be appointed by the chairman. 4. At the hour appointed, the students of the class to be examined shall take their places in the lecture room, provided with pens, ink, and paper. The written questions shall then, for the first time, be presented to them, and they shall be required to give the answers in writing with their names subscribed. 5. A majority of the committee shall always be present during the examination; and they shall see that the students keep perfect silence, do not leave their seats, and have no communication with one another or with other persons. When, in the judgment of the committee, sufficient time has been allowed for preparing the answers, the examination shall be closed, and all the papers handed in. 6. The professor shall then carefully examine and compare all the answers, and shall prepare a report, in which he shall mark, numerically, the value which he attaches to each: the highest number for any answer being that which had been before fixed upon as the value of the corresponding question. For the oral examinations, the values shall be marked at the time by the professor, with the approbation of the committee, but the number attached to any exercise of this kind shall not exceed 20. 7. This report shall be submitted to the committee, and if approved by them, shall be laid before the faculty, together with all the papers connected with it, which are to be preserved in the archives of the university. 8. The students shall be arranged into three separate divisions, according to the merit of their examinations as determined by the following method. The numerical values attached to all the questions are to be added together, and also the values of all the answers given by each student. If this last number exceeds three-fourths of the first, the student shall be ranked in the first division; if it be less than three-fourths, and more than one-fourth, in the second; and if less than one-fourth, in the third."

This scheme combines the advantages of affording both the *positive* and *relative* standing of the pupil. And as those in the separate divisions are arranged alphabetically, it does not necessarily expose the lowest in the third division to the degradation and mortification, to which, however, they are often richly entitled.

The plan of examinations for honours and prizes, in the University of London, resembles the above essentially; differing from it, indeed, in few particulars. It comprises one regulation, however, which might be advantageously appended to the other. We copy it from the printed "Regulations" — Session, 1828-29.

"The paper containing the answers must not be signed with the student's own name, but with a mark or motto; and the name of the student using it, inclosed in a sealed envelope, inscribed with the mark or motto must be left with the professor, to be opened after the merit of the answers shall have been determined." This prevents the possibility of favouritism, in all classes, which are so large that the professor does not become acquainted with the autographs of his students. The examinants are there also placed, according to the merits of their answers, in classes, denominated the *first*, *second*, and *third*; provided the sum of their answers be equal to a certain amount; all below this point are not classed.

We have now touched upon the most important topics presented by the committee for the consideration of the Convention. Several others were propounded, but they seem to have fallen still-born from their authors. As regards the 11th, 12th, and 14th, "whether any religious service, and, if any, what may with propriety be connected with a university?" — "Whether any course of instruction on the evidences of Christianity will be admissible?" — And, "Is it proper to introduce the Bible as a classic in the institutions of a Christian country?" We shall gladly follow the example of prudence exhibited by the Convention, and pass them over. The affirmative view of the last topic, meets with an enthusiastic supporter in the author of one of the works, whose titles are placed at the head of this article.

One proposition only remains, on which, in conclusion, we may indulge a few remarks: — "The importance of adding a department of English language, in which the studies of rhetoric and English classics shall be minutely pursued." This subject, we regret to see, experienced the fate of others, more deserving of neglect, and was not discussed.

We have long felt impressed, that the organization of our colleges is defective in this respect. Into many of them the student is received, after having been employed in scraping together a few Greek and Latin words and phrases; yet lamentably ignorant of the literature, structure, and even of the commonest principles of the orthography of his own tongue. Such a chair ought to be established in all our universities, and a certain degree of proficiency in the subjects embraced by it, should be a preliminary to every collegiate attainment. It would be an instructive and delightful study to trace back, as far as possible, the language of Britain to its aboriginal condition, and to follow up the changes impressed upon it, by the Celtic, Gothic, Roman, Saxon, Belgic, Danish, and Norman invaders;. the investigation being accompanied with elucidative references to the literature of the different periods. The poetry, romances, and the drama would constitute inquiries of abundant interest and information. To these might be added didactic and rhetorical exercises for improving the student in the practice of writing — not merely accurately, but elegantly and perspicuously.

Such a professorship has been wisely established in the University of London; and we trust the new University of New-York will follow the good example. If we may judge, indeed, from the ungrammatical and inelegant Journal of the Convention, an attention to this subject is as much needed there as elsewhere; and were the professorship in the hands of an accomplished individual, it could not fail to improve the literary taste and execution of the community.

ART. II.

CROLEY'S GEORGE THE FOURTH,

The Life and Times of His Late Majesty, George the Fourth: with Anecdotes of distinguished Persons of the last fifty years. By the Rev. George Croly, A. M. London: 1830.

C'est un métier que de faire un livre comme de faire une pendule—it is a trade to make a book just as much as to make a watch—is a remark which was never better exemplified, than by the manner in which the craftsmen of the book-making trade in London, have compressed the Life of His Late Most Sacred Majesty, within the two covers of a volume. That exalted personage may have descended to the tomb unwept and unhonoured, in reality, however numerous the tears shed upon his bier, or gorgeous the ceremonies attending his interment; but he certainly has not gone down to it unsung, as the above work is only one of several, if we are not much mistaken, in which his requiem has been chanted with becoming loyalty. We have seen none of its fellows, though the advertisement of them has met our eye. Judging, however, from the reputation of its author, there is not much literary boldness in pronouncing it the best which has appeared about its kingly subject.

Mr. Croly is well known as a candidate of considerable pretensions, as well for the honours of Parnassus, as for those which an elevated seat on the prosaic mount, whatever may be its name, can confer. But, in concocting this last production, it is beyond doubt, that the main object he had in view, was one of a more substantial kind than a mere increase of fame. "The Life, &c." is, in fact, a bookseller's job, executed, we allow, by a man of genius. There are evident marks about it of hasty and careless composition,—of a desire to make a book of a certain number of pages, with as little trouble and delay as possible. The style is often deficient in purity and correctness, and overloaded with glittering tropes and ornaments, not always in good taste; the arrangement wants consecutiveness and perspicuity; and attention is sometimes bestowed upon topics comparatively unimportant, to the detriment of such as are of more moment. But it is, on the whole, a work of undeniable talent, containing much powerful writing, richness and beauty of diction, graphic delineation of character, interesting information, and amusing anecdote. Some of the author's sentiments are obnoxious to censure, and we shall venture to disagree with him, occasionally, as we proceed.

It was on the 8th of September, 1761, that His Majesty, George the Third, espoused Sophia Charlotte, daughter of the Duke of Mecklenburg Strelitz; and, on the twelfth of August, in the following year, she presented him with a son and heir, to his own great delight, and the universal joy of the British empire. Ineffable as is the contempt which is expressed at the present day, for the superstitious trust reposed in omens by the heathen ancients, yet nothing of any consequence occurs, without being attended by signs in which the Christian multitude discern either fortunate or disastrous predictions. It has thus been carefully recorded and handed down, that the birth of the royal infant happened on the anniversary of the Hanover accession, and that the same day was rendered trebly auspicious, by the arrival at London of wagons containing an immense quantity of treasure, the fruits of the capture of a Spanish galleon off Cape St. Vincent, by three English frigates. A few days after his appearance in this world, His Royal Highness was created Prince of Wales, by patent, and would have been completely crushed under the load of honours that devolved upon him, had their weight been of a kind to be physically felt; Duke of Cornwall, hereditary Steward of Scotland, Duke of Rothsay, Earl of Carrick, and Baron of Rothsay, were his other titles,—being those to which the eldest son of the British throne is born. There is no harm in this, perhaps, as things are constituted in England, but we have never been able to think of one of the titles to which the second son is heir, without feeling an inclination to smile;—the Duke of York is Bishop of Osnaburgh;—nothing more ridiculous than this, can be discovered even amid the nonsense that is inseparable from regal institutions;—born a bishop!

At the time of the Prince of Wales's birth, George the Third was at the height of popularity,—the reasons for which, Mr. Croly has detailed at some length. In depicting the character of this monarch, he certainly has not employed the pencil with which it was darkened, as our readers may recollect, by Mr. Coke of Norfolk, on a recent occasion, who thus brought upon his own head a torrent of abuse. It was shocking, was it said, to disturb the repose of one who had so long been slumbering in the tomb, in the same way as it had been pronounced monstrous to say aught in disparagement of His Majesty, when he had just been gathered to his forefathers; as if kings were like private individuals, the effects of whose acts either expire with themselves, or are of contracted influence. It is far, however, from our wish, to dispute the fidelity of Mr. Croly's portrait; and we are perfectly willing to believe, that "no European throne had been ascended for a hundred years before, by a sovereign more qualified by nature and circumstances, to win golden opinions from his people, than George the Third," though, we must be allowed to think, that circumstances did not qualify him to win "golden opinions" from us Americans. "Youth, striking appearance, a fondness not less for the gay and peaceful amusements of court life, than for those field sports, which make the popular indulgence of the English land-holder, a strong sense of the national value of scientific and literary pursuits, piety unquestionably sincere, and morals on which even satire never dared to throw a stain, were the claims of the king to the approbation of his people;" but all these claims were neutralized, by the appointment of Lord Bute, as his prime minister. The odium that resulted from this measure, was carefully fomented by the arts of demagogues, the most conspicuous of whom was Wilkes. It was ascribed to an unworthy passion entertained for the handsome nobleman by the princess dowager, and to arbitrary principles in the monarch; and, such was the effect produced upon the latter, by the opposition and virulence which he encountered, that he is said to have conceived the idea of abandoning England, and retiring to Hanover. At one time, his inclination to take this step was so great, that he communicated it to the Lord Chancellor Thurlow, who honestly told him, that, "though it might be easy to go to Hanover, it might be difficult to return to England."

In December, 1765, when not quite three years of age, the Prince of Wales received a deputation from the Society of Ancient Britons, on St. David's day, and, in answer to their address, said,—"he thanked them for this mark of duty to the king, and wished prosperity to the charity,"—an early development of that talent for public speaking, which he is said to have possessed! In the same year, he was invested with the order of the garter, along with the Earl of Albemarle, and the hereditary Prince of Brunswick.

When the Prince had attained an age at which it was deemed necessary for his education to commence, it was determined that it should be conducted on a private plan; and Lord Holdernesse, "a nobleman of considerable attainments, but chiefly recommended by dignity of manner and knowledge of the court," was appointed his governor, and Dr. Markham, subsequently archbishop of York, and Cyril Jackson, were named preceptor and sub-preceptor. This measure excited a violent outcry; it was said that the heir to the throne should receive a public education at one of the great schools; and this opinion Mr. Croly strenuously advocates. It did not, however, produce any effect, and the whole course of instruction which the Prince underwent was private, though the preceptorship was twice changed. The Duke of Montague, Hurd, Bishop of Litchfield, and the Rev. Mr. Arnold, formed the last preceptorial trio.

In January, 1781, when the Prince was but a little more than eighteen, he was declared of age, "on the old ground that the heir-apparent knows no minority;" and a separate establishment, on a small scale, having been assigned to him, he now became, in a measure, his own master. In 1783, when about to take his place in the legislature, arrangements were commenced for supplying him with an income, and at the instigation of the king, the parliament voted him an annual revenue of £50,000, besides an outfit of £100,000. The sum of £60,000 for the outfit had been originally proposed by the king, but it was increased in consequence of the demand of the cabinet, known by the name of the Coalition Cabinet, some of the members of which, especially Fox, insisted for a time upon making the grant £100,000 a year. This, however, the king resolutely refused to allow, "for the double reason of avoiding any unnecessary increase to the public burdens, and of discouraging those propensities which he probably conjectured in the Prince." He accordingly demanded *but* the sums we have mentioned. Can any one read the sentence just quoted from Mr. Croly, without a smile? The precious fruits of royalty!—they even reduce a man of sense to write what is ludicrous from its absurdity. It is, without doubt, an admirable method of avoiding any unnecessary increase of the public burdens, and discouraging the evil propensities of a young man, to deprive the people of five hundred thousand dollars at once, and half that sum every year, in order to bestow it upon the individual who has no other use for it than to gratify those propensities. But, we shall be told, the heir to a throne must support his dignity. In that phrase is comprised as unanswerable an argument against royal institutions, as can be desired. The people must be heavily burthened, to enable the person by whom they are to be governed, to indulge in all sorts of excesses, and thus disqualify himself for that duty, in order that he may support the dignity of his station! Thank Heaven we live in a land in which there is no such dignity to be supported,—where the time of the great officers of state is never occupied in wrangling about the extent of the facilities which shall be afforded the successor to the administration of affairs, of bringing disgrace upon himself, and the country,—where the people are infinitely better governed, at an infinitely less expense, both of money and honour!

"Now, fully," says Mr. Croly, "began his checkered career,"—which, properly interpreted, means, that now he fully plunged into that reckless course of profligacy and folly, which terminated only with his life, and which should render his name odious to all who are friends of decency and virtue. We were afraid when we saw the announcement of the work we are reviewing, that its author would allow himself to be blinded by the regal blaze which surrounded its subject, and would endeavour to palliate those violations by a king, of the most sacred ordinances of the religion of which he is a minister, which he would have branded with indelible infamy in a private individual. Our fears, unfortunately, have not proved groundless. "There are no faults that we discover with more proverbial rapidity, than the faults of others,—and none that generate a more vindictive spirit of virtue, and are softened down by fewer attempts at palliation, than the faults of princes in the grave. Yet, without justice, history is but a more solemn libel; and no justice can be done to the memory of any public personage, without considering the peculiar circumstances of his time." Such is the sophistry with which he enters upon the task of extenuation. The first part of the first period in the above extract, is certainly undeniable—"fit nescio quomodo," says Cicero, "ut magis in aliis cernamus si quid delinquitur, quam nobismet in ipsis;" but, though the second part may also be indisputable as a general position, it is not at all applicable to this case. The historian or biographer, who is discussing the character of a monarch long since "fixed in the tomb," will doubtless find it an easy matter to make

> "His virtues fade, his vices bloom,"

should he be so inclined: no other considerations but those of conscience operate then to influence his pen. But the case is quite different when he is writing about a king scarcely yet cold in the grave, when a species of popular infatuation commands that grave to be strewn with flowers, when it is necessary, as it were, to sail with the stream or sink; and when the brother of the deceased monarch has just ascended the throne, and, for the sake of appearances, may deem himself called upon to consider every thing said concerning his predecessor as touching himself. How many motives combine here to warp the judgment and the conscience, and convert sober history into funeral panegyric! Thus, if Mr. Croly had undertaken the task of delineating the moral features of Richard the III., or of James the II.—we adduce James the II., because our author seems to regard Catholicity as so monstrous a crime that this prince would, we are sure, not be drawn by him in the most flattering colours—he would have found, to use his own words, that there are no faults which generate a more vindictive spirit of virtue, than those of princes in the grave; but in depicting George the IVth., he has proved the reverse of this to be the fact. It is amusing, although at the same time melancholy, to contrast the virtuous indignation with which he pours out his anathemas against those who committed the tremendous crime of advocating and effecting the emancipation of the Catholics, with the gentle terms in which he comments upon the wanderings of the Prince of Wales from the proper path, and the glosses with which he softens their obliquity. One might be induced to suppose that his creed holds religious liberality as the crime of deadly dye, and dissipation of the lowest kind as a vice merely venial in its character.

"Without justice," he continues "history is but a more solemn libel, and no justice can be done to the memory of any public personage, without considering the peculiar circumstances of his time." This remark is true with regard to those public personages whom he has so severely taken to task for their conduct respecting the Catholic question; had not his mind's eye been covered with a film, he would have perceived that the "peculiar circumstances of the time" fully warranted that change in the course pursued by Mr. Peel, the Duke of Wellington, and others, with reference to that important question, which has drawn from him such expressions of horror; but it is far from being equally admissible where he has applied it. That less tenderness should be extended towards the vices of princes than to those of subjects is, we think, undeniable, when the weightier (secular) reasons they have for keeping a strict control over their passions, are considered, — reasons which should completely counterbalance any greater temptations they may be obliged to undergo.

> "A sovereign's great example forms a people;
> The public breast is noble or is vile,
> As he inspires it."
>
> "The man whom Heaven appoints
> To govern others, should himself first learn
> To bend his passions to the sway of reason."

Surely these two considerations—the potent effect of his example, and the almost impossibility of governing others when not able to govern himself—without referring to that paramount one which operates for all men alike, ought to have been sufficient to counteract the tendency of "the peculiar circumstances of his time," to inflame the "propensities" of the Prince; or, at least, should be enough to prevent an extenuation on that ground, of his unrestrained indulgence of them, by the historian of his life. What those circumstances were, we will let Mr. Croly relate.

"The peace of 1782 threw's open the continent; and it was scarcely proclaimed, when France was crowded with the English nobility. Versailles was the centre of all that was sumptuous in Europe. The graces of the young queen, then in the pride of youth and beauty; the pomp of the royal family and the noblesse; and the costliness of the fêtes and celebrations, for which France has been always famous, rendered the court the dictator of manners, morals, and politics, to all the higher ranks of the civilized world. But the Revolution was now hastening with the strides of a giant upon France: the torch was already waving over the chambers of this morbid and guilty luxury. The corrective was terrible: history has no more stinging retrospect than the contrast of that brilliant time with the days of shame and agony that followed—the untimely fate of beauty, birth, and heroism,—the more than serpent-brood that started up in the path which France once emulously covered with flowers for the step of her rulers,—the hideous suspense of the dungeon,—the heart-broken farewell to life and royalty upon the scaffold. But France was the grand corruptor; and its supremacy must in a few years have spread incurable disease through the moral frame of Europe.

"The English men of rank brought back with them its dissipation and its infidelity. The immediate circle of the English court was clear. The grave virtue of the king held the courtiers in awe; and the queen, with a pious wisdom, for which her name should long be held in honour, indignantly repulsed every attempt of female levity to approach her presence. But beyond this sacred circle, the influence of foreign association was felt through every class of society. The great body of the writers of England, the men of whom the indiscretions of the higher ranks stand most in awe, had become less the guardians than the seducers of the public mind. The 'Encyclopédie,' the code of rebellion and irreligion still more than of science, had enlisted the majority in open scorn of all that the heart should practise or the head revere; and the Parisian atheists scarcely exceeded the truth, when they boasted of erecting a temple that was to be frequented by worshippers of every tongue. A cosmopolite, infidel republic of letters was already lifting its front above the old sovereignties, gathering under its banners a race of mankind new to public struggle,—the whole secluded, yet jealous and vexed race of labourers in the intellectual field, and summoning them to devote their most unexhausted vigour and masculine ambition to the service of a sovereign, at whose right and left, like the urns of Homer's Jove, stood the golden founts of glory. London was becoming Paris in all but the name. There never was a period when the tone of our society was more polished, more animated, or more corrupt. Gaming, horse-racing, and still deeper deviations from the right rule of life, were looked upon as the natural embellishments of rank and fortune. Private theatricals, one of the most dexterous and assured expedients to extinguish, first the delicacy of woman, and then her virtue, were the favourite indulgence; and, by an outrage to English decorum, which completed the likeness to France, women were beginning to mingle in public life, try their influence in party, and entangle their feebleness in the absurdities and abominations of political intrigue. In the midst of this luxurious period the Prince of Wales commenced his public career. His rank alone would have secured him flatterers; but he had higher titles to homage. He was, then, — one of the handsomest men in Europe: his countenance open and manly; his figure tall, and strikingly proportioned; his address remarkable for easy elegance, and his whole air singularly noble. His contemporaries still describe him as the model of a man of fashion, and amusingly lament over the degeneracy of an age which no longer produces such men.

"But he possessed qualities which might have atoned for a less attractive exterior. He spoke the principal modern languages with sufficient skill; he was a tasteful musician; his acquaintance with English literature was, in early life, unusually accurate and extensive; Markham's discipline, and Jackson's scholarship, had given him a large portion of classical knowledge; and nature had given him the more important public talent of speaking with fluency, dignity, and vigour.

"Admiration was the right of such qualities, and we can feel no surprise if it were lavishly offered by both sexes. But it has been strongly asserted, that the temptations of flattery and pleasure were thrown in his way for other objects than those of the hour; that his wanderings were watched by the eyes of politicians; and that every step which plunged him deeper into pecuniary embarrassment was triumphed in, as separating him more widely from his natural connexions, and compelling him in his helplessness to throw himself into the arms of factions alike hostile to his character and his throne."

Our readers may compare the above portrait of his royal highness, with that which Mr. Jefferson draws of him in one of his letters.

In 1787, the Prince had involved himself in debt to such an amount, that it was found necessary to solicit Parliament, not only for a sum sufficient to liquidate his obligations, but also for an increase of his income, the salary first granted having proved quite inadequate for his royal propensities. The following account of his debts and expenditure was laid before the House of Commons, and furnishes a teeming commentary on the blessings of hereditary government. In considering this matter, one might be tempted to regard Parliament as a species of eleemosynary institution, for the relief of insolvent royalty.

Debts.

Bonds and debts,	£13,000
Purchase of houses,	4,000
Expenses of Carlton House,	53,000
Tradesmen's bills,	90,804
	£160,804

Expenditure from July 1783, to July 1786.

Household, &c.,	£29,277
Privy purse,	16,050
Payments made by Col. Hotham, particulars delivered in to his majesty,	37,203
Other extraordinaries,	11,406
	£93,936
Salaries,	54,734
Stables,	37,919

Mr. Robinson's,   <u>7,059</u>

£193,648

The debate upon the grant was of a highly animated character, and in the course of it the Prince was not spared. He was befriended by the opposition, with Fox at its head, having thrown himself into the arms of that party, who were endeavouring in every way to drive Pitt from his ministerial seat. But in this instance, as in most others, the latter succeeded in carrying his point; in consequence of which, £161,000 were issued out of the civil list to pay the Prince's debts, and £20,000 for the completion of Carlton House, but no augmentation of his income was allowed. "Hopeless of future appeal, stung by public rebuke, and committed before the empire in hostility to the court and the minister, the Prince was now thrown completely into Fox's hands."

Perhaps the two most interesting chapters in Mr. Croly's book, are those entitled "the Prince's friends," in which he has brought into review most of the principal characters of that period of intellectual giants, whose renown continues to shed increasing lustre around the political and literary horizon of England. The world is never tired of reading whatever has reference to those personages, and a book that professes to speak respecting them, may be said to possess a sure passport to public favour at the present day. Well may the old man now living in England, the prime of whose life was passed in that time, be allowed to be a "laudator temporis acti," without having it imputed to the fond weakness of senility. We shall make copious extracts from this portion of our author's work.

"England had never before seen such a phalanx armed against a minister. A crowd of men of the highest natural talents, of the most practised ability, and of the first public weight in birth, fortune, and popularity, were nightly arrayed against the administration, sustained by the solitary eloquence of the young Chancellor of the Exchequer.

"Yet Pitt was not careless of followers. He was more than once even charged with sedulously gathering round him a host of subaltern politicians, whom he might throw forward as skirmishers,—or sacrifices, which they generally were. Powis, describing the 'forces led by the right honourable gentleman on the treasury bench,' said, 'the first detachment may be called his body-guard, who shoot their little arrows against those who refuse allegiance to their chief.' This light infantry were of course, soon scattered when the main battle joined. But Pitt, a son of the aristocracy, was an aristocrat in all his nature, and he loved to see young men of family around him; others were chosen for their activity, if not for their force, and some, probably, from personal liking. In the later period of his career, his train was swelled by a more influential and promising race of political worshippers, among whom were Lord Mornington, since Marquess Wellesley; Ryder, since Lord Harrowby; and Wilberforce, still undignified by title, but possessing an influence, which, perhaps, he values more. The minister's chief agents in the house of commons, were Mr. Grenville (since Lord Grenville) and Dundas.

"Yet, among those men of birth or business, what rival could be found to the popular leaders on the opposite side of the house,—to Burke, Sheridan, Grey,

Windham, or to Fox, that

> "'Prince and chief of many throned powers,
> Who led the embattled seraphim to war.'"

Without adopting the bitter remark of the Duke de Montausier to Louis the Fourteenth, in speaking of Versailles:—'Vous avez beau faire, sire, vous n'en ferez jamais qu'un favori sans mérite,' it was impossible to deny their inferiority on all the great points of public impression. A debate in that day was one of the highest intellectual treats: there was always some new and vigorous feature in the display on both sides; some striking effort of imagination or masterly reasoning, or of that fine sophistry, in which, as was said of the vices of the French noblesse, half the evil was atoned by the elegance. The ministerialists sarcastically pronounced that, in every debate, Burke said something which no one else ever said; Sheridan said something that no one else ought to say, and Fox something that no one else would dare to say. But the world, fairer in its decision, did justice to their extraordinary powers; and found in the Asiatic amplitude and splendour of Burke; in Sheridan's alternate subtlety and strength, reminding it at one time of Attic dexterity, and another of the uncalculating boldness of barbarism; and in Fox's matchless English self-possession, unaffected vigour, and overflowing sensibility, a perpetual source of admiration.

"But it was in the intercourses of social life that the superiority of Opposition was most incontestable. Pitt's life was in the senate; his true place of existence was on the benches of that ministry, which he conducted with such unparalleled ability and success: he was, in the fullest sense of the phrase, a public man; and his indulgences in the few hours which he could spare from the business of office, were more like the necessary restoratives of a frame already shattered, than the easy gratifications of a man of society: and on this principle we can safely account for the common charge of Pitt's propensity to wine. He found it essential, to relieve a mind and body exhausted by the perpetual pressure of affairs: wine was his medicine: and it was drunk in total solitude, or with a few friends from whom the minister had no concealment. Over his wine the speeches for the night were often concerted; and when the dinner was done, the table council broke up only to finish the night in the house.

"But with Fox, all was the bright side of the picture. His extraordinary powers defied dissipation. No public man of England ever mingled so much personal pursuit of every thing in the form of indulgence with so much parliamentary activity. From the dinner he went to the debate, from the debate to the gaming-table, and returned to his bed by day-light, freighted with parliamentary applause, plundered of his last disposable guinea, and fevered with sleeplessness and agitation; to go through the same round within the next twenty-four hours. He kept no house; but he had the houses of all his party at his disposal, and that party were the most opulent and sumptuous of the nobility. Cato and Antony were not more unlike, than the public severity of Pitt, and the native and splendid dissoluteness of Fox.

"They were unlike in all things. Even in such slight peculiarities as their manner of walking into the house of commons, the contrast was visible. From the door Pitt's countenance was that of a man who felt that he was coming into his high place of business. 'He advanced up the floor with a quick firm step, with the head erect, and thrown back, looking to neither the right nor the left, nor favouring with a glance or a nod any of the individuals seated on either side, among whom many of the highest would have been gratified by such a mark of recognition.' Fox's entrance was lounging or stately, as it might happen, but always good-humoured; he had some pleasantry to exchange with every body, and until the moment when he rose to speak, continued gaily talking with his friends."

* * * * *

"Of all the great speakers of a day fertile in oratory, Sheridan had the most conspicuous natural gifts. His figure, at his first introduction into the house, was manly and striking; his countenance singularly expressive, when excited by debate; his eye large, black, and intellectual; and his voice one of the richest, most flexible, and most sonorous, that ever came from human lips. Pitt's was powerful, but monotonous; and its measured tone often wearied the ear. Fox's was all confusion in the commencement of his speech; and it required some tension of ear throughout to catch his words. Burke's was loud and bold, but unmusical; and his contempt for order in his sentences, and the abruptness of his grand and swelling conceptions, that seemed to roll through his mind like billows before a gale, often made the defects of his delivery more striking. But Sheridan, in manner, gesture, and voice, had every quality that could give effect to eloquence.

"Pitt and Fox were listened to with profound respect, and in silence, broken only by occasional cheers; but from the moment of Sheridan's rising, there was an expectation of pleasure, which to his last days was seldom disappointed. A low murmur of eagerness ran round the house; every word was watched for, and his first pleasantry set the whole assemblage in a roar. Sheridan was aware of this; and has been heard to say, 'that if a jester would never be an orator, yet no speaker could expect to be popular in a *full house*, without a jest; and that he always made the experiment, good or bad; as a laugh gave him the country gentlemen to a man.'

"In the house he was always formidable; and though Pitt's moral or physical courage never shrank from man, yet Sheridan was the antagonist with whom he evidently least desired to come into collision, and with whom the collision, when it did occur, was of the most fretful nature. Pitt's sarcasm on him as a theatrical manager, and Sheridan's severe, yet fully justified retort, are too well known to be now repeated; but there were a thousand instances of that 'keen encounter of their wits,' in which person was more involved than party."

* * * * *

"Burke was created for parliament. His mind was born with a determination to things of grandeur and difficulty.

> "'Spumantemque dari, pecora inter inertia, votis
> Optat aprum, aut fulvum descendere monte leonem.'"

Nothing in the ordinary professions, nothing in the trials or triumphs of private life, could have satisfied the noble hunger and thirst of his spirit of exertion. This quality was so predominant, that to it a large proportion of his original failures, and of his unfitness for general public business, which chiefly belongs to detail, is to be traced through life. No Hercules could wear the irresistible weapons and the lion's skin with more natural supremacy; but none could make more miserable work with the distaff. Burke's magnitude of grasp, and towering conception, were so much a part of his nature, that he could never forego their exercise, however unsuited to the occasion. Let the object be as trivial as it might, his first instinct was to turn it into all shapes of lofty speculation, and try how far it could be moulded and magnified into the semblance of greatness. If he had no large national interest to summon him, he winged his tempest against a turnpike bill; or flung away upon the petty quarrels and obscure peculations of the underlings of office, colours and forms that might have emblazoned the fall of a dynasty."

* * * * *

"Erskine, like many other characters of peculiar liveliness, had a morbid sensibility to the circumstances of the moment, which sometimes strangely enfeebled his presence of mind; any appearance of neglect in his audience, a cough, a yawn, or a whisper, even among the mixed multitude of the courts, and strong as he was there, has been known to dishearten him visibly. This trait was so notorious, that a solicitor, whose only merit was a remarkably vacant face, was said to be often planted opposite to Erskine by the adverse party, to yawn when the advocate began.

"The cause of his first failure in the house, was not unlike this curious mode of disconcerting an orator. He had been brought forward to support the falling fortunes of Fox, then struggling under the weight of the 'coalition.' The 'India Bill' had heaped the king's almost open hostility on the accumulation of public wrath and grievance which the ministers had with such luckless industry been employed during the year in raising for their own ruin. Fox looked abroad for help; and Gordon, the member for Portsmouth, was displaced from his borough, and Erskine was brought into the house, with no slight triumph of his party, and perhaps some degree of anxiety on the opposite side. On the night of his first speech, Pitt, evidently intending to reply, sat with pen and paper in his hand, prepared to catch the arguments of this formidable adversary. He wrote a word or two; Erskine proceeded; but with every additional sentence Pitt's attention to the paper relaxed; his look became more careless; and he obviously began to think the orator less and less worthy of his attention. At length, while every eye in the house was fixed upon him, he, with a contemptuous smile, dashed the pen through the paper, and flung them on the floor. Erskine never recovered from this expression of disdain; his voice faltered, he struggled through the remainder of his speech, and sank into his seat dispirited and shorn of his fame.

"But a mind of the saliency and variety of Erskine's, must have distinguished itself wherever it was determined on distinction; and it is impossible to believe, that the master of the grave, deeply-reasoned, and glowing eloquence of this great pleader, should not have been able to bring his gifts with him from Westminster-hall to the higher altar of parliament. There were times when his efforts in the house reminded it of his finest effusions at the bar. But those were rare. He obviously felt that his place was not in the legislature; that no man can wisely hope for more than one kind of eminence; and except upon some party emergency, he seldom spoke, and probably never with much expectation of public effect. His later years lowered his name; by his retirement from active life, he lost the habits forced upon him by professional and public rank; and wandered through society, to the close of his days, a pleasant idler; still the gentleman and the man of easy wit, but leaving society to wonder what had become of the great orator, in what corner of the brain of this perpetual punster and story-teller, this man of careless conduct and rambling conversation, had shrunk the glorious faculty, that in better days flashed with such force and brightness; what cloud had absorbed the lightnings that had once alike penetrated and illumined the heart of the British nation."

The following investigation of the authorship of Junius will be read with interest.

"The trial of Hastings had brought Sir Philip Francis into public notice, and his strong Foxite principles introduced him to the prince's friends. His rise is still unexplained. From a clerk in the War-office, he had been suddenly exalted into a commissioner for regulating the affairs of India, and sent to Bengal with an appointment, estimated at ten thousand pounds a-year. On his return to England he joined Opposition, declared violent hostilities against Hastings, and gave his most zealous assistance to the prosecution; though the house of commons would not suffer him to be on the committee of impeachment. Francis was an able and effective speaker; with an occasional wildness of manner and eccentricity of expression, which, if they sometimes provoked a smile, often increased the interest of his statements.

"But the usual lot of those who have identified themselves with any one public subject, rapidly overtook him. His temperament, his talents, and his knowledge, were all Indian. With the impeachment he was politically born, with it he lived, and when it withered away, his adventitious and local celebrity perished along with it. He clung to Fox for a few years after; but while the great leader of opposition found all his skill necessary to retain his party in existence, he was not likely to solicit a partisan at once so difficult to keep in order and to employ. The close of his ambitious and disappointed life was spent in ranging along the skirts of both parties, joining neither, and speaking his mind with easy, and perhaps sincere, scorn of both; reprobating the Whigs, during their brief reign, for their neglect of fancied promises; and equally reprobating the ministry, for their blindness to fancied pretensions.

"But he was still to have a momentary respite for fame. While he was going down into that oblivion which rewards the labours of so many politicians; a pamphlet, ascribing Junius's letters to Sir Phillip, arrested his descent. Its arguments were plausible; and, for a while, opinion appeared to be in favour of the conjecture, notwithstanding a denial from the presumed Junius; which, however, had much the air of his feeling no strong dislike to being suspected of this new title to celebrity. But further examination extinguished the title; and left the secret, which had perplexed so many unravellers of literary webs, to perplex the grave idlers of generations to come.

"Yet the true wonder is not the concealment; for a multitude of causes might have produced the continued necessity even after the death of the writer; but the feasibility with which the chief features of Junius may be fastened on almost every writer, of the crowd for whom claims have been laid to this dubious honour: while, in every instance, some discrepancy finally starts upon the eye, which excludes the claim.

"Burke had more than the vigour, the information, and the command of language; but he was incapable of the virulence and the disloyalty. Horne Tooke had the virulence and the disloyalty in superabundance; but he wanted the cool sarcasm and the polished elegance, even if he could have been fairly supposed to be at once the assailant and the defender. Wilkes had the information and the wit; but his style was incorrigibly vulgar, and all its metaphors were for and from the mob: in addition, he would have rejoiced to declare himself the writer: his well-known answer to an inquiry on the subject was, 'Would to Heaven I had!' *Utinam scripsissem!* Lord George Germaine has been lately brought forward as a candidate; and the evidence fully proves that he possessed the dexterity of style, the powerful and pungent remark, and even the individual causes of bitterness and partisanship, which might be supposed to stimulate Junius: but, in the private correspondence of Junius with his printer, Woodfall, there are contemptuous allusions to Lord George's conduct in the field, which at once put an end to the question of authorship.

"Dunning possessed the style, the satire, and the partisanship; but Junius makes blunders in his law, of which Dunning must have been incapable. Gerard Hamilton (Single-speech) might have written the letters, but he never possessed the moral courage; and was, besides, so consummate a coxcomb, that his vanity must have, however involuntarily, let out the secret. The argument, that he was Junius; from his notoriously using the same peculiarities of phrase at the time when all the world was in full chase of the author, ought of itself to be decisive against him; for nothing can be clearer, than that the actual writer was determined on concealment, and that he would never have toyed with his dangerous secret so much in the manner of a school-girl, anxious to develop her accomplishments.

"It is with no wish to add to the number of the controversialists on this blue-stocking subject, that a conjecture is hazarded; that Junius will be found, if ever found, among some of the humbler names of the list. If he had been a political leader, or, in any sense of the word, an independent man, it is next to impossible that he should not have left some indication of his authorship. But it is perfectly easy to conceive the case of a private secretary, or dependent of a political leader, writing, by his command, and for his temporary purpose, a series of attacks on a ministry; which, when the object was gained, it was of the highest importance to bury, so far as the connexion was concerned, in total oblivion. Junius, writing on his own behalf, would have, in all probability, retained evidence sufficient to substantiate his title, when the peril of the discovery should have passed away, which it did within a few years; for who would have thought, in 1780, of punishing even the libels on the king in 1770? Or when, if the peril remained, the writer would have felt himself borne on a tide of popular applause high above the inflictions of law.

"But, writing for another; the most natural result was, that he should have been *pledged* to extinguish all proof of the transaction; to give up every fragment that could lead to the discovery at any future period; and to surrender the whole mystery into the hands of the superior, for whose purposes it had been constructed, and who, while he had no fame to acquire by its being made public, might be undone by its betrayal.

"The marks of *private secretaryship* are so strong, that all the probable conjectures have pointed to writers under that relation; Lloyd, the private secretary of George Grenville; Greatrakes, Lord Shelburne's private secretary; Rosenhagen, who was so much concerned in the business of Shelburne house, that he may be considered as a second secretary; and Macauley Boyd, who was perpetually about some public man, and who was at length fixed by his friends on Lord Macartney's establishment, and went with him to take office in India.

"But, mortifying as it may be to the disputants on the subject, the discovery is now beyond rational hope; for Junius intimates his having been a spectator of parliamentary proceedings even further back than the year 1743; which, supposing him to have been twenty years old at the time, would give more than a century for his experience. In the long interval since 1772, when the letters ceased: not the slightest clue has been discovered; though doubtless the keenest inquiry was set on foot by the parties assailed. Sir William Draper died with but one wish, though a sufficiently uncharitable one, that he could have found out his castigator, before he took leave of the world. Lord North often avowed his total ignorance of the writer. The king's reported observation to Gen. Desaguiliers, in 1772, 'We know who Junius is, and he will write no more,' is unsubstantiated; and if ever made, was probably prefaced with a supposition; for no publicity ever followed; and what neither the minister of the day, nor his successors ever knew, could scarcely have come to the king's knowledge but by inspiration, nor remained locked up there but by a reserve not far short of a political error.

"But the question is not worth the trouble of discovery; for, since the personal resentment is past, its interest can arise only from pulling the mask off the visage of some individual of political eminence, and giving us the amusing contrast of his real and his assumed physiognomy; or from unearthing some great unknown genius. But the leaders have been already excluded; and the composition of the letters demanded no extraordinary powers. Their secret information has been vaunted; but Junius gives us no more than what would now be called the 'chat of the clubs;' the currency of conversation, which any man mixing in general life might collect in his half-hour's walk down St. James's Street: he gives us no insight into the *purposes* of government; of the *counsels* of the *cabinet* he knows nothing. The style was undeniably excellent for the purpose, and its writer must have been a man of ability. If it had been original, he might have been a man of genius; but it was notoriously formed on Col. Titus's letter, which from its strong peculiarities, is of easy imitation. The crime and the blunder together of Junius was, that he attacked the king, a man so publicly honest and so personally virtuous, that his assailant inevitably pronounced himself a libeller. But if he had restricted his lash to the contending politicians of the day, justice would have rejoiced in his vigorous severity. Who could have regretted the keenest application of the scourge to the Duke of Grafton, the most incapable of ministers, and the most openly and offensively profligate of men; to the indomitable selfishness of Mansfield; to the avarice of Bedford, the suspicious negotiator of the scandalous treaty of 1763; or to the slippered and drivelling ambition of North, sacrificing an empire to his covetousness of power?"

Mr. Croly has recorded a quantity of the "good things" that were said by the wits of the day at the table of the Prince, who used the facilities which his rank afforded him, of collecting around him all that was most distinguished in intellect, with praiseworthy zeal. Had his companions been chosen only from among that highest class, we might have quoted with regard to him, the sentence of Cicero—"facillime et in optimam partem, cognoscuntur adolescentes, qui se ad claros et sapientes viros, bene consulentes rei publicæ, contulerunt: quibuscum si frequentes sunt, opinionem afferunt populo, eorum fore se similes quos sibi ipsi delegerint ad imitandum"—but unfortunately his intimacy was habitually shared by far less worthy associates—persons whom it was contamination to approach. Many of these *jeux d'esprit* are of respectable antiquity; we transcribe a few which are attributed to the Prince himself, as specimens of royal humour.

"The conversation turning on some new eccentricity of Lord George Gordon; his unfitness for a mob leader was instanced in his suffering the rioters of 1780 to break open the gin-shops, and, in particular, to intoxicate themselves by the plunder of Langdale's great distillery, in Holborn. 'But why did not Langdale defend his property?' was the question. 'He had not the means,' was the answer. 'Not the means of defence?' said the prince; 'ask Angelo: he, a brewer, a fellow all his life long at *carte* and *tierce*.'"

"Sheridan was detailing the failure of Fox's match with Miss Pulteney. 'I never thought that any thing would result from it,' said the prince. 'Then,' replied Sheridan, 'it was not for want of sighs: he sat beside her cooing like a turtle-dove.'

"'He never cared about it,' said the prince; 'he saw long ago that it was a *coup manqué*.'"

"Fox disliked Dr. Parr; who, however, whether from personal admiration, or from the habit which through life humiliated his real titles to respect—that of fastening on the public favourites of the time, persecuted him with praise. The prince saw a newspaper panegyric on Fox, evidently from the Dr.'s pen; and on being asked what he thought of it, observed, that 'it reminded him of the famous epitaph on Machiavel's tomb,'—

"'Tanto nomini nullum *Par* elogium.'"

"If English punning," says Mr. Croly, "be a proscribed species of wit; though it bears, in fact, much more the character of the 'chartered libertine,' every where reprobated, and every where received; yet classical puns take rank in all lands and languages. Burke's pun on 'the divine right of kings and toastmasters,'—the *jure de-vino*—perhaps stands at the head of its class. But in an argument with Jackson, the prince, jestingly, contended that trial by jury was as old as the time of Julius Cæsar; and even that Cæsar died by it. He quoted Suetonius: '*Jure* cæsus videtur.'»

In October, 1788, George the III. was afflicted with a mental disease, which totally incapacitated him for the duties of government. We do not wish to be unjustly harsh, but when we consider the irritability which, as may be inferred from the anecdote we have related of the King's intention to retire from England, must have formed a prominent trait in his character, and the displeasure he could not help manifesting in his communications to Parliament respecting the Prince's debts, it is impossible to reject the idea that the conduct of the latter was a main cause of his affliction.

He recovered, however, before the preliminary arrangements for the entrance of the Prince upon the regency had been completed. From this period up to the moment when the King became again a victim of the same dreadful malady, from whose grasp he never afterwards was freed, the Prince mixed no more with politics, but "abandoned himself," in the words of our author, "to pursuits still more obnoxious than those of public ambition." The course of his life was only varied by his disastrous marriage with the unfortunate Caroline, Princess of Brunswick. One of Mr. Croly's chapters is headed "the Prince's Marriage," the next, "the Royal Separation." We need not occupy much space with a subject which must be familiar to all of our readers, and of which the details are as disgusting as they are pitiful. Of all the foul stains upon the character of the royal profligate, it has stamped the foulest. Every principle of honour, of virtue, of humanity, was violated in the grossest manner.

That the Prince of Wales was morally guilty of the crime of bigamy in marrying the Princess Caroline, we have no hesitation in asserting. No one can doubt that Mrs. Fitzherbert had the claims of a wife upon him previously to his entering into this second engagement, however it may be attempted, as has been done by Mr. Croly, to deny such claims, upon the ground that the connexion was void by the laws of the land, although the ordinances of religion may have been complied with. If it can be supposed, that the Prince was determined, whilst binding himself at the altar of God by the most sacred vows, to take advantage of the laws of the land to cast aside the solemn obligations he thus assumed, as soon as it suited his convenience, in what a despicable situation is he placed! Deceit, perjury, sacrilege, would be terms too weak for the act. But Mr. Croly's own words are sufficient to prove that the lady was, and is, considered to have been connected with him by other ties than those of a mistress. He says, "she still enjoys at least the gains of the connexion, and up to the hoary age of seventy-five, calmly draws her salary of ten thousand pounds a year!" Would that salary be continued to a mistress? It is evident from the English papers that Mrs. Fitzherbert is treated with the greatest consideration by the present king and royal family, and that she is received by them on the most intimate footing; her name is recorded amongst those of the constant guests at the royal table and social assemblages of every kind. On what other ground can this circumstance be accounted for, than that she is regarded as a sister-in-law by the sovereign, and as a reputable relative by his family?

It is singular enough that Mr. Croly seems to consider a violation of the laws of God less reprehensible than a violation of the laws of man. Such at least is the unavoidable inference to be drawn from his remarks on this matter. He is quite indignant at the idea of his Royal Highness having married a woman of inferior rank, and a Roman Catholic (there is the horrid part of the affair,) by which he would have been guilty of a sin against the state, and evinces great anxiety to prove that the crime was one of a much lighter dye—merely an adulterous connexion, by which he transgressed one of the Divine Commandments. This Mr. Fox also attempted to do in Parliament, when it was hinted by a member that the *liaison* was not of the character which usually subsists between individuals in the relative rank of the Prince and the lady, and the attempt was disgraceful enough even in a statesman—but in a minister of religion!—we leave it however to speak for itself.

In 1811, George the III. was a second time a lunatic, and the Prince ascended his throne, though only with the title of Regent, which he did not change for that of King until 1820, when the nominal monarch died, having survived his reason for nearly ten years. Ten years longer did the Fourth George sway the sceptre of the noblest empire in the world; and then he too mingled with the same dust as the meanest of his subjects. "C'est ainsi," in the words of Bossuet, "que la puissance divine, justement irritée centre notre orgueil, le pousse jusqu' au néant, et que, pour égaler á jamais les conditions, elle ne fait de nous tous qu' une même cendre."

During the last years of his life, George the IVth was the prey of various maladies, with which a remarkably strong constitution enabled him to struggle until the spring of 1830. His corporeal sufferings may have been one cause of his almost entire seclusion at Windsor Castle, where he was like the Grand Lama of Thibet, unseeing and unseen, except by a chosen few, but it cannot be doubted that the knowledge of the unpopularity under which he certainly laboured, had some effect in producing the slight communication which took place between him and his subjects. So notorious was his aversion to making an appearance in London, that when he was first announced, last April, to be seriously indisposed, it was rumoured for a time that the sickness was fictitious—a mere pretence to avoid holding a levee which had been fixed for a certain day in that month, and which was in consequence deferred. But before the period had arrived to which it was postponed, there was no longer a doubt that the angel of death was brandishing his dart, and that there was little chance of averting the threatened stroke. The bulletins which the royal physicians daily promulgated, though couched in equivocal and unsatisfactory terms, shadowed out impending dissolution. The reason of their ambiguity was currently believed to be the circumstance, that the King insisted upon reading the newspapers in which they were published; whilst the medical attendants were anxious to withhold from him a knowledge of his true situation.

Besides being in the public prints, these bulletins appeared, in manuscript copies, in the windows of almost every shop, and were likewise shown every day at the Palace of St. James, by a lord and groom in waiting, richly dressed, to all of the loving subjects who preferred repairing thither for the satisfaction of their affectionate solicitude. It was rather amusing to watch the manner in which this satisfaction was obtained. The bulletins were thrust into the faces of all as they entered into the great hall where the exhibitors were stationed, with laudable earnestness and zeal, and most of the visiters looked with great interest—upon the paintings with which the apartment was adorned. The multitudes of persons, however, of both sexes, and often of high distinction, who filled the rooms that were thrown open, during the fashionable hours of the day, rendered it an entertaining scene. The most anxious faces were those of the owners of dry-good shops, by whom the recovery of the monarch was indeed an object devoutly desired, as they had already laid in their varieties of spring fashions, which the universal mourning that was to follow the demise of the crown, would convert almost into positive lumber.

At length, on the 26th of June, intelligence was received that the monarch of Great Britain had been conquered by a still more powerful king. What mourning without grief! what weeping without a tear! The papers immediately commenced a chorus of lamentation and eulogy, in which but one discordant voice was heard. This was the voice of the "Times"—the only leading journal which had independence and spirit enough to vindicate its character as a guardian of the public morals, by disdaining to prostitute its columns to the purposes of falsehood. One paper affirmed, among other fulsome and mendacious remarks, that the royal defunct must have taken his departure from this world with a clear conscience, as he had never injured an individual! After such an assertion

> "Quis neget arduis
> Pronos relabi posse rivos
> Montibus, Tiberimque riverti?"

Did the shades of an injured wife and an injured father never rise before the imagination of the dying man? did the injury inflicted by a life of evil example never appal the recollection of the dying King? Yes, a life of evil example; we repeat the phrase. Look at his whole career, from the moment when it first became free from control, to its close. Does it not afford an almost uninterrupted series of the most scandalous violations of the rules which a king especially should hold sacred—the rules of religion, of morals? When young, he countenanced by his deportment the extravagance and profligacy of all the youth of the kingdom—when old, contemplate the avowed, the flagrant concubinage he sanctioned—see one adulteress openly succeeding another in his favour, and say whether his declining years furnished a more exemplary model for imitation than those of his boyhood. Worse than all, behold by whom, amongst others, his very death-bed, we may say, is surrounded—the mistress who had last sacrificed her virtue and honour, and the husband and the children of that woman, who were occupying places in the royal household, as the price of the wife and the mother's shame. It is well known that it was not until after the accession of the present sovereign, that Lady Conyngham, and the man from whom she derives the right of being so entitled, together with their offspring, received an intimation that their presence was no longer desirable at Windsor Castle, from which they departed, in consequence, amid the ridicule and scorn of the empire.

It was an interesting period for an American to be in London, that of the death of one king, and the accession of another; and, as such events are not of every-day occurrence, we esteemed ourselves particularly fortunate in being on the spot at the time. The various ceremonies consequent upon them,—the lying in state,—the obsequies,—the proclamation,—the prorogation of Parliament, and so forth, were well worth witnessing; but, by far the most interesting result they produced, was the general election which followed the dissolution of the legislature. We were enabled, through the kindness of a gentleman who was a candidate, to study the whole process of an election in a free borough, having accompanied him, at his invitation, to the scene of political strife, and remained there until the contest was brought to a close. By occupying a few pages with an account of it, we may, perhaps, communicate some degree of information and pleasure to a portion of our readers, without being guilty of too wide a digression.

The two first days subsequently to our arrival in the town, were spent in visiting those persons whose suffrages were not ascertained at the time when the candidates made their canvass, two or three weeks before, that is to say,—called personally upon every one who possessed a vote, and requested his support. In this, there is no mincing of the matter in the least,—the suffrage is openly asked, and as openly promised or refused; but it is only among the more respectable class, that this ceremonial is sufficient,—the others "thank their God they have a vote to sell." On the third day, the election commenced. Two temporary covered buildings had been erected near each other in the principal part of the town, in one of which were the hustings and the polls, and the other was employed for the sittings of a species of court, where the qualifications of suspected voters were tried. About nine in the morning, the candidates, three in number, proceeded to the former booth, if we may so term it, and, after the settlement of the necessary preliminaries, were proposed and seconded as representatives of the borough, in the order in which they stood on the hustings. These were partitioned into three divisions,—one belonging to each of the opposing gentlemen,—which were crowded with their respective friends. Directly below the hustings, which were considerably elevated, was a table, round which were seated the poll clerks, and others officially connected with the election. This was separated by a board running across the building, from the polls, which were also divided into three parts, or boxes, corresponding with the divisions of the hustings. All the proposers and seconders made speeches, as well as the candidates,—and nothing could surpass the amusing nature of the scene during the discourses of two of the haranguers, who were particularly obnoxious to a large portion of the assembled crowd. They were saluted with a vast variety of *gentle* epithets, and almost every method of annoyance and interruption was put in practice. After the *speechification* was concluded, the polling commenced. It was done by tallies. The committee of each candidate, marshalled in succession ten of their friends at a time, who appeared in the box belonging to their party, and, on being asked, one after another, for whom they voted, gave, vivâ voce, either a plumper for one, or split their vote amongst two of the candidates. This system was regularly prosecuted, until the diminished numbers of one of the parties, rendered it difficult to collect ten men in time, when as many as could be brought together, were sent in. On the last day of the election, not more than one vote was polled in an hour in one of the boxes.

The candidates were obliged to remain in their places on the hustings, day after day, from the opening until the closing of the polls, and thank aloud every one who gave them a vote. At the end of every day's polling, the three gentlemen made speeches, all pretty much of the same purport, expressing their thanks for the support they had received, and their perfect confidence of ultimate success. There were not more than six or seven hundred voters in the town; and yet, for eight days, was the contest carried on. On the ninth, one of the parties retired from the field, and the other two were declared duly elected; after which they were chaired. The reason of this protraction, was owing in part to the unavoidable slowness of vivâ voce voting, but chiefly to the number of votes objected to, by persons whose occupation it was to point out every flaw they could discover in the qualifications of those who appeared at the polls. One of those persons was in the employ of each candidate, and, as the struggle was close and somewhat acrimonious, objections were made on the slightest possible grounds, which were furnished in abundance, by the variety of circumstances that disqualified a man for voting in that borough. Whenever an objection was made, the objector stated the cause of it; and, having written it down on a piece of paper, handed it to the voter objected to, who repaired with it to the other booth. Here, having shown it to the assessor, or judge, who was invested with unlimited power to decide upon every question of qualification, he was tried in his turn. This was by far the more interesting and amusing of the two booths. The trial was conducted in regular form. The accused, so to call him, was placed at the bar of the court, where he was cross-questioned, and confronted with friendly and adverse witnesses; and then the lawyers in attendance, who had been respectively largely feed by the several candidates, pleaded for, or against his qualifications, according as he was a friend, or not, of their employer. When the arguments were finished, the assessor either rejected his vote, or sent him back to the polls with a certificate of qualification, which he exhibited, and had his suffrage recorded. In some instances, the trials were speedily despatched; but, generally, they occupied a considerable space of time, so that when the polls were finally closed, there were at least a hundred names on the books of the court, of persons who were yet to be arraigned.

It would require more space than is at our disposal, to enter into any detail of the odd speeches which were made, and the various scenes, laughable and serious, that occurred during the course of the election. For the same reason, we cannot dwell upon the observations which are naturally excited by the whole matter; but, we may remark, that we became fully satisfied, that frequent Parliaments, with the present election system, would be one of the greatest evils which could be inflicted on England. The seldomer, certainly, that such sluices of varied corruption are opened, the better. Here was a whole town for weeks in a state of the worst kind of commotion, — almost all the usual labours of the lower classes were suspended; unrestricted freedom of access to taverns and alehouses, at the expense of those who were courting their sweet voices, was afforded them; and some idea may be formed of the use that was made of it, from the fact that the bill brought to one of the candidates, by the keeper of an inn, for a single night's debauch, amounted to nearly a hundred pounds sterling. At the bar of the court where the qualifications were examined, abundant evidence was given, that this indirect species of bribery was not the only kind which was in operation. The intense eagerness manifested by the greater part of those to whose votes objections had been made, to obtain a decision of the assessor in their favour,—the quantity and grossness of the false-hoods they uttered, in order to effect that object, rendered palpable the existence of some very potent motive for desiring the possession of a suffrage. That these evils are to be attributed mainly to the vivâ voce mode of voting, we have little doubt, and, assuredly, the tree which produces such fruit, cannot be sound. But, we feel no desire to involve ourselves in a discussion concerning the best system of election, which has been debated *usque ad nauseam*, and we shall therefore return to our proper subject.

There are various pictures afforded by the different portions of the career of his late Majesty, which it may be of the highest benefit for republican Americans to contemplate. It was beautifully said by Sheridan, in one of the most brilliant of his speeches, that Bonaparte was an instrument in the hands of Providence to make the English love their constitution better; cling to it with more fondness; hang round it with more tenderness: and in the same way we may affirm that such kings as George IV. are eminently calculated to strengthen our attachment to the republican institutions of this country. The history of their lives furnishes that gross evidence of the absurdities involved in the doctrine of hereditary right, which cannot fail to disgust and revolt. It presents the spectacle of a ruler the least fitted to rule. It proves that princes, from the very circumstance of being princes, are the least likely to be able to execute those duties which devolve upon them, with efficiency or conscientiousness—that the situation in which they are placed by their birth, nullifies the very reason for which their order was first established, and renders them a curse instead of a blessing. What was the source from which royal privileges and authority first flowed? Was it not the superiority in various ways of the persons who were invested with them, and which caused them to be considered as pre-eminently qualified to discharge the functions incumbent on a king? And is not the name of king at present, a by-word for inferiority in every respect in which inferiority is degrading? Every deficiency indeed of talent, knowledge, virtue, is regarded so much as a matter of course in a personage of royal station, that the slightest proof of the possession of either, which in an humbler individual would just be sufficient to screen him from remark, is cried up as something wonderful. Think of a king being able to quote a Latin line, or make a speech of ten minutes in length!—the boast of Mr. Croly with regard to George IV. Such an unusual occurrence is deemed almost incredible, and many persons, even among his own subjects, will firmly believe that neither feat was performed in consequence of original information and faculties, but resulted from the suggestions of another.

But by far the most important light in which we republicans can contemplate the career of George IV. in connexion with the object of increasing our love for the institutions under which we live, is that of morality and religion. The point may be conceded, which is always advanced as the main argument in support of hereditary monarchical government—that it is better adapted to preserve the peace of a country by keeping the succession free from difficulty and doubt, though a reference to history may perhaps warrant the denial even of this position, by exhibiting the various usurpations, murders, unnatural rebellions of children against parents, and other heart-sickening crimes, the consequences of the right invested in one family of exercising sovereign rule, which have so often plunged whole nations into misery and blood;—but this point may be acknowledged; we may admit that elections of chief magistrates are more likely to be the source of frequent troubles. If it can nevertheless be shown, that there is that in the very essence of monarchical institutions which is in any way hostile to virtue, the question ought to be considered as settled in favour of the system that is free from this insuperable objection; for it cannot be denied, that any principle at all tending to aid the propagation of immorality, is the worst which can be admitted into the social and political compacts by which men are united together, and should most be deprecated and eschewed. No matter what apparent or real beneficial results may flow from it, they cannot counterbalance the detriment it may inflict upon the surest guarantee of permanent good to man, both in his individual and aggregate capacity—both with regard to his temporal and eternal interests. National happiness and prosperity of a durable character, are inseparable from national virtue. The evils produced by dissensions concerning the chief power in a state, are in a degree contingent and temporary; those engendered by immorality are certain and lasting. Let then the pages, not merely of the book which tells the story of George IVth of England, but of all history be consulted, and who will deny that they furnish overwhelming evidence that the moral atmosphere of courts has been at all times tainted and baleful; that they have been ever the centres of corruption and vice, and that they must ever be so? They must ever be so, we assert, because the natural and unavoidable result of raising any collection of persons above the opinion, as it were, of the rest of the world, and of surrounding them with a species of *prestige* which prevents their vices and follies from being viewed in their real hideousness, is to ensure amongst them the sway of immorality. They thus form a sanctuary for corruption, which can never be established in a country where no factitious distinctions exist; there profligacy can have no refuge when hard pressed by public opinion, no ramparts behind which to protect itself from the assaults of that potent enemy; and it will never in consequence be able to obtain there any other than individual dominion.

If we turn our eyes upon the condition of the English court as it now exists, although it may be less exceptionable than when George was at its head, we shall find sufficient justification of the foregoing remarks. The present sovereign, it is well known, is unfortunate in possessing a mind of that nervous description, which renders any considerable excitement a thing to be avoided; it was the effect produced upon it by his appointment to the Lord High Admiraltyship during his brother's life, which occasioned his removal from that post. His moral character is certainly less disreputable than that of his predecessor; but who can witness, without feelings akin to disgust, the spectacle of a family of illegitimate offspring exalted in the palace, and following him in all his perambulations? It is far from our wish to cast any reflection upon those unfortunate persons, who are in no way accountable for the ignominy and guilt connected with their birth. The shame and the reproach are for the author of the stain, who exposes himself to double reprehension, by the countenance he virtually lends to the cause of immorality. William IV., however, is a paragon in comparison to his next brother, the Duke of

Cumberland, a person, who, if he has given any warrant for the tenth part of the imputations which rest upon him, can only have escaped the penalties inflicted by the law on the greatest offences, because he is the brother of the king. We cannot convey a better idea of the estimation in which he is held in London, than by stating, that in all the caricatures where an attempt is made to embody the evil spirit, his person is used for that purpose.

> "What poor things are kings!
> What poorer things are nations to obey
> Him, whom a petty passion does command!"

These considerations, we repeat, are well adapted to promote the important object to which we have alluded, of causing our institutions to be properly appreciated and loved by ourselves. This is the great desideratum with respect to them—the chief thing necessary for their preservation. Our situation now is more enviable than that of any country of the earth; and all which is requisite is, that we should be aware of our own happiness, and rightly understand the source from which it springs—the republican form of government. Let us be thoroughly impressed with the conviction of the superior efficacy of this system over every other, in promoting the end for which political societies were instituted, and we are safe. We will then be furnished with the best defence against the principal enemy from which danger need be dreaded,—we mean that propensity to change, which is one of the common infirmities of the human breast,—that restlessness which renders the life of man a scene of constant struggle, tends to prevent him from estimating and enjoying the blessings he possesses, and often causes him to dash away with his own rash hand, the cup of happiness from his lips. "Our complexion," says Burke, "is such, that we are palled with enjoyment, and stimulated with hope,—that we become less sensible to a long-possessed benefit, from the very circumstance that it is become habitual. Specious, untried, ambiguous prospects of new advantage, recommend themselves to the spirit of adventure, which more or less prevails in every mind. From this temper, men and factions, and nations too, have sacrificed the good of which they had been in assured possession, in favour of wild and irrational expectations." To be satisfied, is, indeed, we fear, difficult for human nature, even where there is no good to be reached beyond what we already have obtained. A great object, in such case, is to be convinced that there is no such good to be acquired—to suppose that we have arrived at the utmost boundaries of mortal felicity.

Nothing, however, that we have advanced as fitted to aid that object, inasmuch as it respects our political condition, is of such influence for its accomplishment, as the contemplation of the actual state of the European world. When the tempest howls without, the domestic hearth is invested with a doubly inviting aspect; we gather round it with eagerness, in proportion to the dismal appearance of external nature, and bless it for the security which it affords from the rage of the heavens. Should we not, in like manner, embrace with redoubled fondness, the institutions which maintain us in prosperity and peace, now, especially, whilst we are enabled to behold the fearful operation of the consequences of monarchical rule—the horrors in which they are involving the fairest and most civilized portions of the globe; and when we know, too, that the motive which inspired the inhabitants of those countries with courage to encounter the storm, by which they are tossed about on the sea of revolution, was the hope of being driven by it into some haven like that which shelters us from the fury of winds and waves? When, if ever, they will attain to the possession of the blessings which we enjoy,—how all the troubles by which they are agitated will end, is what no human ken is competent to discern; but the philanthropist and the Christian need never despair. Out of chaos came this beautiful world; and the same Being who called it into existence, still watches over its concerns,—is still as potent to convert obscurity into brightness, as when He first said, "Let there be light," and there was light!

ART. III.

HIEROGLYPHIC SYSTEM,

Essay on the Hieroglyphic System of M. Champollion, Jr. and the advantages which it offers to sacred criticism. By J. G. H. Greppo, Vicar-General of Belley. Translated from the French by Isaac Stuart, with notes and illustrations. Boston: pp. 276.

In former numbers of this journal, there are several articles devoted to the subject of Egyptian hieroglyphics, particularly as connected with the labours of Mons. Champollion. Every day seems to give opportunity of additional observation, by furnishing new and interesting facts. How much further the investigations may be carried, it would be unsafe even to conjecture; but, in the present state of things, we are fully authorized to consider the problem of hieroglyphics as at last solved, and such general principles established, as must render subsequent investigations comparatively easy. Every age seems to be productive of some great genius peculiarly adapted to the accomplishment of some great design, connected either with the advancement of learning, or the melioration of the moral condition of mankind. The present appears fruitful of great men, and France, particularly favoured, whether we regard the great political events which have called out the most gigantic exhibitions of practical wisdom, or look at the onward march of science, which seems in no wise impeded, by convulsions which scatter every thing but science, like the yellow leaves of autumn. Let us not, however, be diverted from our object, — the sober investigation of a sober subject, alike deeply interesting to the philologer, the student of history, and the inquirer into the sacred truths connected with divine revelation.

The work which stands at the head of this article, purports to be an investigation of the hieroglyphic system developed in the published works of Mons. Champollion, Jr. and the advantage which it offers to sacred criticism. It is the performance of a clergyman of the Roman Catholic Church, J. G. H. Greppo, Vicar-General of Belley. The original work, however, is not before us. We examine it through the medium of a translation made by Mr. Isaac Stuart, son of the Rev. Moses Stuart, one of the most eminent scholars of our country, who vouches for the accuracy of the translation, having inspected the whole, and compared it with the original. Dr. Stuart has added some notes, where he has seen occasion to differ from Mr. Greppo, on some points of Hebrew philology and criticism. The reasons for his difference of opinion are given with that candour for which the writer is distinguished, and the intelligent reader is left to judge as to the merits of the question.

It is well known to the learned, that Mons. Champollion, the younger, has been spending several years in the uninterrupted study of the Egyptian hieroglyphics. In his capacity of Professor of History at Grenoble, he found his labours embarrassed by the immense hiatus which occurs in Egyptian history, and, to the filling up of this, he set himself to work with all the zeal and energy which genius could inspire. In this work, he had the advantage of youth, and a very superior education in the Coptic and other oriental languages, connected with a patience of investigation, which appears almost miraculous. He had the advantage of knowing, moreover, that, if ever any just conclusion was to be gained, he must seek it by getting some starting point, different from that whence all his predecessors had set out. There had been a variety of learned men whose investigations were directed to this point, such as Father Kircher the Jesuit, whose different works on Egyptian antiquities had been successively published in Rome, from 1636 to 1652—Warburton, the highly gifted author of the Divine Legation of Moses, the learned Count de Gebelin, and others of equal and less name. But these had all confessedly failed, and the learned almost gave up the subject in despair, so much so, that Champollion himself, states it as the only opinion which appeared to be well established among them, viz. "that it was impossible ever to acquire that knowledge which had hitherto been sought with great labour, and in vain."

In the midst of these discouragements, a circumstance occurred, familiar probably to our readers, but to which we allude merely to observe, that it seemed at once to open a new era of investigation, and is among the many evidences of the fact, that events of apparently the most inconsiderable description, are connected with results whose magnitude cannot be estimated. At the close of the last century, while the French troops were engaged in the prosecution of the war in Egypt, it is well known, that a number of learned men were associated with the expedition, for the prosecution of purposes far more honourable than those of human conquest,—we mean the exploration of a hitherto sealed country, with the express design of advancing the arts and sciences. One division of the army occupied the village of *Raschid*, otherwise called *Rosetta*; and, while they were employed in digging the foundation for a fort, they found a block of black basalt, in a mutilated condition, bearing a portion of three inscriptions, one of which was in the Egyptian hieroglyphics. The fate of the military expedition, lost to the French the possession of this stone, as it fell into the hands of the British, by the capitulation of Alexandria; it was afterward conveyed to London, and placed in the British museum. Previously to the termination of the war, however, the stone and its characters had been correctly delineated by the artists connected with the commission, and then, through the medium of an engraving, placed in possession of the learned. This is a brief history of the Rosetta stone, as it is called, but still it baffled the investigations of the learned. They had gone upon the supposition, that the hieroglyphic method of writing must, of necessity, be *ideographic*, i. e. figurative or symbolical, and that each of these signs was the expression of an idea. Here appears to have been the great root of all their mistakes on the subject, mistakes naturally fallen into by the moderns, inasmuch as the few incidental passages left on the subject in the writings of the ancients, all recognized this as a fact. Except Clement of Alexandria, one of the fathers of the church, not a solitary writer had left on record any other opinion; and the passage of Clement has itself never been understood, until since the discoveries of Champollion. It seems to be one of those curious facts connected with the history of the human mind, that it requires a great intellect to seize on the simplest element of truth. It is easy to speculate on data, which are assumed without a rigorous examination, and then to make an exhibition of learning which may astonish the world; but, it is the province of the greatest genius to lay hold of simple truth, and establish a foundation utterly immoveable, before there is any attempt at a superstructure. This was the business, and this the achievement of Champollion. Now that the discovery is made, we are amazed at the want of previous penetration. It struck the mind of Champollion, that, if the Egyptian hieroglyphics were *ideographic*, there must be *exceptions*, for two substantial reasons: first, because *proper names*, or names of persons, do not always admit of being expressed by any sign, that is, proper names have not in all cases a meaning; and, second, because *foreign names*, or those which have no relation to any particular spoken language, could not be represented by conventional signs. These principles appear now to be self-evident, and this is the basis of Champollion's discovery. On this he built the idea, that there must exist among the Egyptians *alphabetic characters*, which should express the *sounds* of the spoken language; and, in order to test this principle, he set about the investigation of the celebrated Rosetta stone. This stone, let it be remembered, had on it *three inscriptions in different characters*. One of these inscriptions was written in Greek, and of course easily decyphered; of the other two, one was written in hieroglyphics, and the other in the common character of the country. The course pursued by Champollion, was exceedingly simple, and, on that account, may be considered masterly. In the Greek text, the name of Ptolemy occurred, together with some names which were foreign to the Egyptian language. In the hieroglyphic inscription, there were certain signs grouped together and frequently repeated; and, what rendered them remarkable was, that they were enclosed in a kind of oval or ring, called a cartouche, and maintained a relative position which seemed to correspond with the Greek word Ptolemy. Champollion conjectured, that there must be some connection between the signs clustered in these rings, and the name of Ptolemy expressed by signs, which would *sound* like that word; and this led him to expect, that he would get at what he was persuaded was the truth, viz. that the hieroglyphic writing was *alphabetic*, rather than exclusively *ideographic*. With the view of testing this, he went into a close analysis of the group of signs which he supposed designated the name of Ptolemy; and, as the result of this analysis, obtained what he considered the equivalents to the letters in the name of this prince.

In order to give our readers an idea of his process of investigation, we will state the signs which he found in the group surrounded by a ring on the Rosetta stone. These are the following: a square—half circle—a flower with the stem bent—a lion in repose—the three sides of a parallelogram—two feathers, and a crooked line. The square, Champollion considered the equivalent of the Greek letter Π—the half circle, T—the flower with the stem bent, O—the lion in repose, Λ—the three sides of the parallelogram, M—the feathers, H,—and the crooked line, Σ. This gave the name Ptolmês. At this stage of his investigations, Champollion supposed that he had obtained seven signs of an alphabet; but, could he have gone no further, he would have established nothing, and his researches would have passed off with the labours of the learned who had preceded him. To test his principle further, it was necessary, therefore, that he should be able to get at some other monument, on which there should be recognized some name also known by some Greek or other connected inscription. Such a monument was found in an obelisk discovered in the island of Philæ, and transported to London. On this was discovered a group of characters also enclosed in a ring, and containing more signs than the former, some of them similar. On a part of the base which originally supported the obelisk, there was an inscription in Greek, addressed to *Ptolemy* and *Cleopatra*. Now, if the basis of Champollion was correct, there ought to be found in the name Cleopatra, such signs as were common to both, and they must perform the same functions which had been previously assigned them; and this was precisely the result. We have this strikingly set forth in a note of the translator, which is here presented.

"To prove that the conjectures of Champollion were true, the first sign in the name of Cleopatra should not be found in the name of Ptolemy, because the letter *K* does not occur in ΠΤΟΛΜΕΣ. This was found to be the fact. The letter *K* represented by *a quadrant*.

"The second sign (*a lion in repose* which represents the Λ), is exactly similar to the fourth sign in the name of Ptolemy, which, as we have already seen, represents a Λ.

"The third sign in the name of Cleopatra is *a feather*; which should represent the *single* vowel *E*, because the *two feathers* in the name of Ptolemy represent *double Epsilon*, which is equivalent to the Greek *H*. Such is its import. As Greppo remarks in a note, and as has been fully proved by subsequent investigations of Champollion, the sign which resembles two feathers, corresponds also with the vowels *E, I*, and with the diphthongs *AI, EI*.

"The fourth character in the hieroglyphic cartouche of Cleopatra, representing *a flower with a stalk bent back* (or a knop), corresponds to the *O* in the Greek name of this queen. This sign is the very same with the third character in the hieroglyphic name of Ptolemy, which there represents *O*.

"The fifth sign is in the form of *a square*. It here represents the *Π*, and is the same with the first sign in the hieroglyphic name of Ptolemy.

"The sixth sign, corresponding to the Greek vowel *A* in Cleopatra, is *a hawk*; which of course ought not to be found in the name of Ptolemy (as it has no letter *A*), and it is not.

"The seventh character is an *open hand*, representing the *T*; but this hand is not found in the hieroglyphic name of Ptolemy, where *T*, the second letter in that name, is represented by a half circle. The reader will see in Note G, why these two signs stand for the same letter and sound.

"The eighth character in the name of Cleopatra, which is *a mouth,* and which here represents the Greek *P,* should not be found in the name of Ptolemy, and it is not.

"The ninth and last sign in the name of the queen, which represents the vowel *A,* is *the hawk,* the very same sign which represents this vowel in the third syllable of the same name.

"The name of Cleopatra is terminated by two hieroglyphic symbolical signs, *the egg and the half circle,* which, according to Champollion, are always used to *denote the feminine gender.*"

These were great advances, and our readers will now easily understand the process by which the distinguished discoverer arrived at his results. Step by step, he has thus been able to form his *phonetic alphabet.* In September, 1822, he gave an account of his discovery, and of the principles of his system, in a letter to Mons. Dacier, perpetual Secretary of the Academy of Inscriptions, and of Belles Lettres. In 1824, Champollion published the first edition of his work, "Précis du système hièroglyphique des anciens Egyptiens, ou recherches sur les elémens premiers de cette ecriture sacrée, &c." This is the work which is reviewed in the number of this journal for June, 1827, p. 438. In the year 1828, a second edition of this work was called for, and this second edition is rendered more valuable, by having appended to it the letter to Mons. Dacier.

It is not the purpose of the present article, to go into an account of the results of Champollion's labours;—this has been amply done in preceding pages of this journal. The essay of Mons. Greppo, gave us a favourable opportunity, following the course of the author, of stating in brief, the process by which Champollion arrived at his most valuable and interesting conclusions. The object of the essay is to show the advantages which this discovery gives to the study of sacred criticism. This is the special aim of the work; and, in relation to this, the author has observed:;—

"Some of the numerous facts, which the study of Egyptian monuments with the aid of the hieroglyphic system has developed, will be applied to the Holy Scriptures in some of those portions which relate to Egypt, and they will shed much light upon these passages of the sacred annals. We shall endeavour to accomplish this work with all the precision and simplicity possible in researches which are necessarily scientific, but which are of high interest on account of their tendency; and it is on this account only, that we present them with such confidence.

"A religion whose origin is from above, is without doubt safe from the vain attacks of a few blinded men; and, while it has been defended for so many centuries by the most powerful minds that have shed a lustre upon the sciences and upon literature, it scarcely needs our weak defence. Yet it is consoling to a Christian, to witness the amazing progress of human knowledge. The mind is ever attaining to new truths, and is confirming the remark so often quoted from a celebrated English Chancellor, (Bacon) a remark which applies as well to revealed as to natural religion, of which Christianity is but the development; *Leves gustus in philosophia movere fortasse ad atheismum, sed pleniores haustus ad religionem reducere*: i. e. *superficial knowledge in philosophy may perhaps lead to atheism, but a fundamental knowledge will lead to religion.*"

The Essay of Mons. Greppo is composed of two parts, the first of which is an explanation of the hieroglyphic system of Champollion; and the second, the application of the hieroglyphic system to the elucidation of the sacred writings. The relations of the Hebrews with the Egyptians were such, that the history of the latter cannot be otherwise than most intimately connected with the religion of the Bible. In fact, there was no country in the world, foreign to Judea, whose name is so conspicuous in the Bible, as that of Egypt; beginning at the time of Abraham, and going down to the very Apostolic age; and it hence follows, that he who would study in detail, the historic annals of the Hebrews, ought to be as fully acquainted with those of ancient Egypt, as the largest means will allow. In carrying out his intention, M. Greppo has gone deeply into philological, historical, chronological, and geographical considerations. By making the "précis" of Champollion the basis of his argument, and bringing in to his assistance the labours of the elder Champollion, called by way of distinction Champollion Figeac, from the place of his residence; he has investigated the history of the Pharaohs, as connected with the accounts given in the books of Genesis and Exodus, and the later historical writings.

In the fourth chapter of the second part, there is an interesting discussion relative to the difficulty of reconciling the position taken in Exodus, as to the perishing of Pharaoh, with the conclusions drawn from the investigations of Champollion. The last Pharaoh of the Exodus, is ascertained to be the King *Amenophis Ramses.* According to Manetho, he reigned twenty years; viz. from 1493 B. C., to 1473 B. C., so calculated also by Champollion Figeac. But the departure of the children of Israel took place about the year 1491 B. C., consequently in the second or third year of this Prince. If this Prince perished in the Red Sea, how can this be reconciled with the fact, that Manetho states him to have reigned twenty years, and this is confirmed by the calculations of the elder Champollion. M. Greppo goes into an interesting discussion, to prove that the text of the Book of Exodus does not state that Pharaoh perished in the Red Sea. His examination of the sacred text will be interesting to many of our readers:

"Scripture does not compel us to believe that the Pharaoh with whom we now are concerned, participated in the fatal calamity of his army. And first, Moses says not a word to this effect, when he relates the miracle performed by the Lord in favour of his people. He informs us, it is true, that Pharaoh marched in pursuit of the children of Israel; *And he made ready his chariot and took his people with him. And he took six hundred chosen chariots, and all the chariots of Egypt, and captains over every one of them. And the Lord hardened the heart of Pharaoh king of Egypt, and he pursued after the children of Israel* (Exod. xiv. 6-8.). A little further on he says; *And the Egyptians pursued, and went in after them, into the midst of the sea, even all Pharaoh's horses, his chariots and his horsemen* (v. 23.). Finally he adds; *And the waters returned, and covered the chariots, and the horsemen, and all the host of Pharaoh that came into the sea after them; there remained not so much as one of them* (v. 28). Such are the principal features of the narrative which Moses gives of this Egyptian expedition, and of the terrible event in which it resulted. But in the circumstantial account of this disaster, he does not name Pharaoh personally except when he speaks of his departure. Now if the persecutor of Israel entered the Red Sea with his army, and was swallowed up with it, is it probable that the chief and legislator of the Hebrews would have been silent about such a circumstance as the tragical death of this prince? an event more important, perhaps, than even the destruction of his army, and surely very proper as a striking illustration both of the protection which God extended to his people, and of the chastisements his justice inflicted upon the impious. And further; to strengthen the faith of this people when in a state of distrust and murmuring, Moses often recounts to them their deliverance from Egyptian bondage, their passage through the Red Sea, and the other miracles which God had wrought for them; and on all these occasions, when the allusion to the death of an oppressive prince would have been so natural, he conveys no such idea.

"The circumstance related by Moses, that no one escaped, *there remained not so much as one of them*, proves nothing relative to the supposed disaster of Pharaoh. It refers to those who followed the Hebrews into the sea, among whom Moses does not enumerate this prince. We remark also, that the sacred historian seems designedly to leave room for making exceptions to the general disaster, by the precise manner in which he announces, *that the waters covered the chariots and the horsemen, and all the host of Pharaoh that came into the sea after them*; this literally signifies that the waters covered only the chariots and horsemen which entered into the sea, and leaves us to infer that all did not enter. The incidental expression in verse 28, *that came into the sea after them*, seems then to modify the more general expression in verse 23, *even all*, and authorizes us to understand it with some latitude, rather than to restrain it to its rigorous sense. All these circumstances of the narrative accord with the presumption, not only that Pharaoh did not enter into the Red Sea, but perhaps even that some of his infantry, if he possessed any, did not enter; and at least, that this is true of some principal chiefs who surrounded him, and who formed what we now call a body of *staff-officers*.

"In relating the miraculous passage of the Red Sea, the book of *Wisdom*, which describes so often and in such an admirable manner, the wonders of the Lord in conducting his people, and which celebrates the illustrious men whom he made his instruments, makes no mention either of Pharaoh or of his tragical death. It is limited to the remark, that in his wisdom he precipitated the enemies of Israel into the sea (*Wisdom of Solomon*, x. 19)."

Mons. Greppo appears to be aware, that there are difficulties attending his interpretation, arising out of the apparent positive declarations contained in other parts of the sacred volume: for instance, in Ex. ch. xv. 19th v., as also Ps. cxxxvi. 15th v. His answer to these objections, and some collateral arguments by which he endeavours to support his theory, are too long to be here introduced. Professor Stuart, in a learned note, part of which we feel compelled to quote, dissents from the reasoning of Mons. Greppo, and takes the safer course of leaving to further discoveries, what, in the present state of the researches, may not yet be considered as definitely settled.

"The modesty and ingenuity which M. Greppo has exhibited, in the discussion which gives occasion to the present note, certainly entitle him to much credit and approbation. Still it seems to me very doubtful, whether the exegesis in question can be supported. When God says, in Exod. xiv. 17, 'I will get me honour upon Pharaoh, and upon all his host, upon his chariots, and upon his horsemen;" and when he repeats the same sentiment in Exod. xiv. 18; the natural inference seems to be, that the fate of Pharaoh would be the same as that of his host, his chariots and his horsemen. Accordingly, in Exod. xiv. 23, it is said, 'The Egyptians pursued, and went in after them [the Hebrews] into the midst of the sea, *every horse of Pharaoh and his chariot*, and his horsemen, into the midst of the sea.' It is true, indeed, that וכל סוס פרעה רכבו may mean, *all the horses of Pharaoh and all his chariots*, viz. all those which belonged to his army. But is it not the natural implication here, that Pharaoh was at the head of his army, and led them on? And when in Exod. xiv. 28 it is said, that of all the host of Pharaoh that came into the sea after the Israelites, *there remained not so much as one of them*, is not the natural implication here, that Pharaoh at the head of his army went into the sea, and perished along with them?

"In the triumphal song of Moses and the Hebrews, recorded in Exod. xv., the implication in verses 4, 19, seems most naturally to be, that Pharaoh was joined with his army in the destruction to which they were subjected.

"But still more does this appear, in Ps. cvi. 11, where it is said, 'The waters covered their enemies [the Egyptians]; *there was not one of them left*.' How could this well be said, if Pharaoh himself, the most powerful, unrelenting, and bitter enemy which they had, was still preserved alive, and permitted afterwards to make new conquests over his southern neighbours? This passage M. Greppo has entirely overlooked.

"In regard to Ps. cxxxvi. 15, the exegesis of our author is ingenious; but it will not bear the test of criticism. For example; in Exod. xiv. 27, it is said, 'And the Lord *overthrew* the Egyptians, in the midst of the sea; where the Hebrew word answering to *overthrew* is רעניו from רענ. But in Ps. cxxxvi. 15, the very same word is applied to Pharaoh and his host; '*And he overthrew* (רענו) *Pharaoh and his host*. In both cases (which are exactly the same), the word רענ properly means, *he drave into* (*hineintreiben, Gesenius.*) Now if the Lord *drave* the Egyptians *into* the midst of the sea, and also *drave* Pharaoh and his host *into* the midst of the sea, we cannot well see how Pharaoh escaped drowning. Accordingly, we find that such an occurrence is plainly recognized by Nehemiah ix. 10, 11, when, after mentioning Pharaoh, his servants, and his people, this distinguished man speaks of the 'persecutors of the Hebrews as thrown into the deep, as a stone in the mighty waters.'

"As to any difficulties respecting *chronology* in this case, about which M. Greppo seems to be principally solicitous, it may be remarked, that the subject of ancient Egyptian chronology is yet very far from being so much cleared up, as to throw any real embarrassments in the way of Scripture facts. More light will give more satisfaction—as in the famous case of the zodiacs, so finely described in the last chapter of M. Greppo's book."

The fifth and sixth chapters of the work of Mons. Greppo, are devoted to the examination of the history of the Pharaohs mentioned in the sacred writings, down to the time of Solomon, and of the other kings of Egypt, who are distinguished by proper names.

The seventh chapter is devoted to the chronology of Manetho, the official historiographer of Egypt; and several questions are discussed, which relate to the difference between him, and the scripture chronologers. In the close of the chapter, the author draws two conclusions, which we are disposed to think entirely justified by the present state of the investigations—these conclusions will be better stated in the author's own words:—

"From the remarks which we have communicated to our readers, we infer that there is no foundation for that fear about the advance of Egyptian studies, which the religious zeal of some estimable men has led them to cherish; neither is there any occasion to distrust the *data* transmitted by the historian of the Pharaohs. Nothing can authorize such a distrust. On the other hand, every thing conspires to prove, at the present time, that the new discoveries and their application to chronology, will disclose more and more the truth and exactness of the historic facts in Scripture. We believe that men are too apt to form a judgment of systems when they hardly understand them; and perhaps they are too prone to forget that if true faith is timorous, it is not distrustful, like the pride which is connected with the vain theories of men; because it views the basis, upon which the august edifice of divine revelation reposes, as immoveable. Inspired with this thought, we have adopted, from entire conviction, all the satisfactory results elicited by the labours of the Champollions; and we wait, with impatience and with confidence, the new developments which they promise, persuaded beforehand that revealed religion cannot but gain from them."

In the eighth chapter of his essay, Mons. Greppo applies the discoveries of Champollion to the Egyptian geography, so far as the scriptures are concerned. If it be true, as he conceives, that the city of Rameses occupied the site of the Arabian city, now called Ramsis, there seems to be an irreconcilable difference with some of the scripture relations; for this city, *Ramsis,* is on the western side of the river Nile, and not less than one hundred and fifty miles from that position on the Red Sea, where it is believed that the passage of the Israelites was made. However the question may eventually be settled, it appears to us, that this location can in no sense consist with the text of the sacred writings; for, in the first place, it would have required that the Israelites should have crossed the Nile, on their journey towards Palestine. Of this there is no account; neither had they any means; and it would have required a miraculous interposition to enable them so to do. But, second, the sacred text informs us, that, at the close of the second day after the departure of the Israelites from Rameses, they reached the borders of the Red Sea. It is utterly impossible that they could have crossed the Nile, and travelled one hundred and fifty miles in two days. It is beyond all rational calculation to suppose that they could have travelled at the rate of more than twenty miles per day, and, consequently, we must look for the situation of Rameses at a distance not greater certainly than forty miles from the Red Sea, and on the eastern side of the Nile. If the integrity of the sacred writings is to be preserved, the idea that the Rameses of the Bible, and the Ramsis of the Arabians are identical, must be abandoned, or, at any rate, not adopted until something far more conclusive shall be found, than has yet been given. Professor Stuart, in a note which we have above condensed, refers to a previous work of his, where this subject is more largely discussed, and which, as it may not be familiar to the mass of our readers, being a work distinctly connected with theological studies, will be referred to for a moment. In this work, the Professor enters largely into the examination of the location of Rameses, which stands also for Goshen. He considers, and with vast power of argument and illustration, that the royal residence of the Pharaohs at the time of Joseph and Moses, was at Zoan, and not Memphis, as has been generally supposed. There can be no question, that Zoan was one of the oldest cities of Lower Egypt, and situated on the eastern shore of the second or Tanitic mouth of the Nile, and this was but a little distance from the Pelusiac or eastern branch, on which the residence of the Israelites has generally been supposed to have been. It was an extensive city, and its ruins in the time of the French expedition, occupied an extensive country. Champollion has remarked that the word signifies, "mollis, delicatus, jucundus," which would make Zoan to mean Pleasant town. The reader will be interested to observe, that, in Ps. lxxviii, the writer alludes to Zoan, as the scenes of the miracles of Moses: also Ps. v. verse 12, and also lxxii. verse 43. In the time of Isaiah, it is quite clear, that Zoan was the place where the Egyptian court resided, at least for a time. See ch. xix. verse 11. There are objections to this view of Professor Stuart, but not stronger, than to others; and the most probable is, that the kings of Egypt had different places of royal residence, as is still customary. We know that Cyrus, after conquering Babylon, spent part of his time there, and part at the capital of his native country.

Contrary, therefore, to the opinion of Mons. Greppo, Professor Stuart considers Rameses or Goshen, to be decidedly on the eastern side of the Nile, and this is rendered more certain, if, as the Professor has attempted to prove, *Zoan* was frequently a royal residence of the Pharaohs. The opinion taken by Mons. Greppo, that Rameses was on the western side of the Nile, in what may be called Lower Eastern Egypt, without the delta, is refuted in Michaelis *Supp. ad Lex.* Hebraica, p. 397. We make no pretentions to the ability of settling these disputed points, and consider it perfectly safe to abide by the present general idea, as to the location of Rameses, especially as there is nothing yet in the shape of positive testimony against it. The reader who is particularly interested in Biblical Archæology, will be highly gratified by consulting the work of Dr. Stuart, entitled—"Course of Hebrew Study." In the ninth chapter of his Essay, the author has made use of the discoveries of Champollion, to defeat certain objections to the genuineness and authenticity of the Books of Moses, which were started by Voltaire and others of his time. The high antiquity of the Pentateuch was doubted, on the ground that writing in the common language could not then have been known. Champollion has decyphered a manuscript, which contains an act of the fifth year of the reign of Thouthmosis III. This prince governed Egypt at a time when Joseph was carried there as a slave, and this was at least two hundred years previous to the time in which Moses wrote the Pentateuch.

An objection to the truth of the history of the Pentateuch, also, arose out of the circumstance, that the magnificence and excellence of the work said there to have been put upon the ark and its furniture in the wilderness, was utterly beyond the state of the arts at the time challenged in the relation. The discoveries of Champollion have overthrown a supposition which had been held almost indisputable, viz:—that the arts of Egypt had been indebted for their progress, to the influence of those from Greece under the domination of the Lagidæ kings. He has established the contrary, beyond doubt, and has proved that the most brilliant epoch of the arts in Egypt, was under a dynasty contemporary with the sojourn of the Israelites in Egypt.

The only remaining objection which is noticed by the author, is one which he considers as capable of receiving the same satisfactory solution.

It is objected that the name of *Sesostris* is not mentioned in Scripture, nor any feature of his history recognised. To this, the investigations made by Champollion and the calculations of Champollion Figeac are made to answer. The commencement of the reign of Sesostris is fixed by these, in the year 1473, B. C.; consequently, this was seventeen or eighteen years after the departure of the Israelites from Egypt. While they were wandering in the wilderness, Sesostris overran Palestine, which was then in possession of its primitive inhabitants, and before the Israelites reached that land, the expedition of Sesostris had long passed, for Diodorus tells us, that it terminated in the ninth year of his reign. The silence of Scripture, therefore, as to Sesostris, is in no wise remarkable, as the people of Israel had no connexion with him, either as friend or foe.

The tenth chapter of the Essay, relates to the Egyptian Zodiacs. To our readers who have examined the subject at all, the history of these is now familiar,—the curious may turn to the Number of this Journal for December, 1827, p. 520, where will be found an ample description.

We have thus given a detailed description of the Essay of Mons. Greppo, and we cannot resist the pleasure before we close, of presenting the few remarks with which he concludes his discussion.

"We come now to the conclusion of our undertaking. With the aid of the new discoveries in Egypt, we think that we have shed some light upon various passages of the sacred annals, and that we have resolved, in a more satisfactory manner, certain difficulties which were opposed to their veracity. We have attentively examined the resources which the writings and monuments of Egypt afford, in the interpretation and defence of a religion, whose lot has been, in all ages, to meet with enemies, when it should have found only admirers and disciples. But the researches to which we have been attending very naturally, as we think, give rise to a thought consoling to the Christian.

"Providence, whose operations are so sensibly exhibited in the whole physical constitution of the world, has not abandoned to chance the government of the moral or intellectual world. By means often imperceptible even to the eye of the man of observation, and which seem reserved for his own secret counsel, God directs second causes, gives them efficiency according to his will, and makes them serve, sometimes even contrary to their natural tendency, to accomplish his own immutable decrees, and to propagate and support that religion which he has revealed to us. It is in this way that, consistently with his own will, he delays or accelerates the march of human intellect; that he gives it a direction such as he pleases; that he causes discoveries to spring up in their time, as fruits ripen in their season; and that the revolutions which renew the sciences, like those which change the face of empires, enter into the plan which he traced out for himself from all eternity.

"Does not this sublime truth, which affords an inexhaustible subject of meditation to the well instructed and reflecting man, but which needs for its development the pen of a Bossuet,—does it not apply with great force to the subject that we have been considering?

"Since the studies of our age have been principally directed to the natural sciences, which the irreligious levity of the last age had so strangely abused to the prejudice of religion, we have seen the most admirable discoveries confirming the physical history of the primitive world, as it is given by Moses. It is sufficient to cite in proof of this fact, the geological labours of our celebrated Cuvier. Now that historic researches are pursued with a greater activity than ever before, and the monuments of antiquity illustrated by a judicious and promising criticism, Providence has also ordered, that the writings of ancient Egypt should in turn confirm the historic facts of the holy books: facts against which a *systematic* erudition had furnished infidelity with so many objections that were unceasingly repeated, though they had been a thousand times refuted. We cannot doubt that human knowledge, as it becomes more and more disengaged from the spirit of system, and pursues truth as its only aim, will still attain, as it advances, to other analogous results.

"Thus, as has been often said, revealed religion has no greater foe than ignorance. Far from making it *her ally*, as men who deny the testimony of all ages have not blushed to assert, she cannot but glory in the advance of the sciences. She has always favoured them, and it is chiefly owing to her influence, that they have been preserved in the midst of the barbarism from which she has rescued us. Thus the progress of true science, *the progress of light* (to use a legitimate though often abused expression,) far from being at variance with revealed religion, as its enemies have represented,—far from being dangerous to it, as some of its disciples have appeared to fear, tends, on the contrary, each day to strengthen its claims upon all enlightened minds, and to prove, in opposition to the pride of false science, that this divine religion, confirmed as it is by all the truths to which the human mind attains, *is the truth of the Lord which endureth forever.*"

We have ventured upon this protracted notice of the Essay of Mons. Greppo, because the subject itself is one of gratifying pursuit even to the mere scholar, but still more because it is vitally connected with the evidences of revealed religion in which we hope that none of our readers are altogether uninterested. There is in the Essay, no question as to any of the minor points of the Christian faith,—there is here nothing but what all may peruse with satisfaction. The question is one entirely connected with evidence; and science and literature are pressed fairly into the service of truth. The work is peculiarly valuable, because it is the only work connected with the labours of Champollion which has been made to wear an English dress. The works of both the Champollions are locked up in a foreign language from most of our readers; and we fear that the time will not soon come when there will be sufficient encouragement either to translate or publish in this country the splendid volumes of these brothers, who are, by their discoveries, raising up for France the gratitude of the world. Until there shall be liberality enough in our republic of letters, to enable us to possess these works, with all their riches of illustration, and thus have ancient Egypt brought to the inspection of American eyes, we would recommend the work of Mons. Greppo, as the best, and indeed only substitute at present known, always excepting the pages of our own journal.

It is needless to say, that the merits of the translation cannot be questioned, after the testimonials furnished by the learned Dr. Stuart; without the advantage of comparing it with the original, we can speak of its excellence relatively, for the style is clear, concise, and classical.

ART. IV.

IRON,

1. — *Memorial of the workers in iron of Philadelphia, praying that the present duty on imported iron may be repealed, &c.*

2. — *Report of the Select Committee (of the Senate of the United States,) to whom was referred "the petition of upwards of three hundred mechanics, Citizens of the City and County of Philadelphia, employed in the various branches of the manufacture of iron," and also, the petition of the "Journeymen blacksmiths of the City and County of Philadelphia, employed in manufacturing anchors and chain cables."*

3. — *Report of the minority of the Select Committee on certain memorials to reduce the duty on imported iron.*

4. — *Remarks of the majority of the Select Committee on the blacksmiths' petition in reply to the arguments of the minority.*

5. — *Manuel de la Metallurgie de fer par C. I. B. Karsten, traduit de l'Allemand, par F. I. Culman, seconde edition, entierement refondue, &c. 3 vols. 8vo. pp. 504, 496, & 488. Mme. Thirl: 1830: Metz.*

6. — *Voyage Metallurgique en Angleterre, par MM. Dufrenoy et Elie de Beaumont. 1 vol. 8vo. pp. 572. Bachelier: Paris: 1827.*

The discussion contained in the petitions and legislative reports which we have prefixed to this article, is one of the most powerful interest, not merely to those concerned in the manufacture of iron, and the articles of commerce of which it is the material, but to the whole community. Iron, if the cheapest and most abundant, is intrinsically the most valuable of the metals. It may supersede, and gradually has, in its applications, superseded the greater part of the rest, and has taken the place of wood and stone in a great variety of mechanical structures; it is indispensable in the modern arts of the attack and defence of nations; and its possession is the distinctive difference between civilized man and the savage. Well was it said to Crœsus exhibiting his golden treasures, that he who possessed more iron, would speedily make himself master of them, and the truth of the maxim was even more powerfully verified, when the accumulated riches of the Aztecs and Incas were acquired at the cost of a few pounds of Toledo steel.

When we compare the state of manners and arts of the Mexicans and Peruvians with that of their Spanish conquerors, we are almost compelled to admit, that the possession of iron was perhaps the only real superiority in civilization which the latter possessed. Gunpowder played but a small part in the contests where handfuls of men routed myriads; the courage of the Indian warrior is not less firm than that of the descendant of the Goths.

The sciences and arts which are now the boast of European civilization, were then but awakening from a slumber of ages; in the latter, the workmanship of Europe was in many instances inferior to that of the new world, and in the former, to take as an instance that which occupies the highest place, astronomy, the civil year of the Mexicans was intercalated and restored to the solar, by a process more perfect than that we even now employ; and the latter was not introduced into Europe until half a century after the throne of Montezuma fell. The bloody human sacrifices which excited to such a degree the abhorrence of the conquerors, were not greater marks of savage cruelty, than were their own *auto da fes*, and the tortures inflicted on Guatemozin. Yet if not superior in bravery, in the arts, the sciences, and the more distinctive attribute of civilization, humanity, the possession of iron was sufficient to ensure the triumph of the Spaniards.

Of all the metallurgic arts, that by which iron is prepared from its ores, demands the greatest degree of practical skill, and is the most difficult to bring to perfection. Although ages have elapsed since it first became an object of human industry, its manipulation and preparation are yet receiving improvements, while those of the other ancient metals appear hardly susceptible of modification or advancement. Copper and its alloys, tin, lead, and mercury, were as well and as cheaply prepared by the ancients as by the moderns; and the reduction of the precious metals has received no important change, since the process of amalgamation was first applied to them,—while the preparation of iron is daily improving under our eyes, and its cost diminishing. It may even be doubted whether the iron we first find mentioned in history, was an artificial product, and not obtained from the rare masses in which it is found existing in the native state, and which are supposed to be of meteoric origin.

The original use of iron is ascribed in the sacred writings to Tubal Cain, who lived before the flood;—but we have no proof that he did not employ a native iron of this description. Be this as it may, the united testimony of antiquity exhibits to us an alloy of copper used for the purposes to which we apply iron, and the latter metal as comparatively scarce, and of high value. The qualities of iron were known and appreciated, but the art of preparing it was not understood. The reason is obvious; those ores of iron which have an external metallic aspect, are difficult of fusion and reduction, those which are more readily converted, are dull, earthy in their appearance, and unlikely to attract attention,—while gold and silver manifest in their native state their brilliant characters, and the ores of copper and lead exhibit a higher degree of lustre than the metals themselves.

If, then, history does not show us the ancient nations employing iron for their arms and instruments, it is because they were unable to prepare it. Even in the middle ages, we find copper in use for arms, because the nations that employed it, could not conquer the difficulties that attend the preparation of iron.

The books of Moses, however, show that iron was known at that era to the

Egyptians, and the distinction he draws between it and brass, seems in favour of our view of the origin of that which was then employed. The stones of the promised land were to be iron, but brass was to be dug from the hills. Twelve hundred years before Christ, if we receive the testimony of Homer, who, if he be rejected as an historian, must still be admitted as a faithful painter of manners. The Greeks used an alloy of copper for their arms, but were unacquainted with iron, which they estimated of much higher value.

> Αυταρ Πηλειδης θηχεν σολον αυτοχοωνον,
> Ον πριν μεν ριεπτασε μεγα σφενος Ηεβιωνος.
> Αλλα ητοι τον επεφνε ποδαρχος διος Αχιλλευς,
> Τον δ αγετ εννηεσσι συν αλλοισιν χτεατεσσιν.
> Στη δ ορθος χαι μυθον εν Αργειοισιν εειπεν.
> Ορνυσθ, οι χαι τουτου α εθλου πειρησησθε!

&c.   Iliad, Book XXIII, 1. 826.

From this passage and the following lines, we learn the two-fold fact: 1. That a mass of iron of no greater weight than could be used as a quoit, by a man of great strength, was esteemed of sufficient value to be cited as an important article in the spoil of a prince: 2. That its use was confined to agricultural purposes, and not applied in war. Hence the more valuable form steel, and its tempering, were unknown.

Five hundred years later, Lycurgus attempted to introduce the use of iron, as money, into Sparta. The reasons usually cited for this act, do not seem to apply; and we ought not to accuse that lawgiver of the want of knowledge in political economy that is usually ascribed to him, in endeavouring to give a base material a conventional value to which it was not entitled. The iron was still, probably, more costly than brass, and the error of Lycurgus did not lie in ascribing to it a value beyond its actual cost, but in depriving it of the property of convertibility to useful purposes, which was necessary to maintain its price.

In the construction of the temple by Solomon, 130 years before the æra of Lycurgus, iron was employed in great abundance; and, from the cost lavished upon that building, we are almost warranted in considering it as still bearing a high value, even in that country, so far in the advance of Greece in the arts of civilized life.

Herodotus ascribes the discovery of the art of welding iron to Glaucus of Chio, 430 years before the Christian æra. But, before this period, the Greeks had carried the art of working it into Italy, Spain, and Africa; and the famous mines of Elba, that are still worked, were probably opened 700 years before Christ.

It is from the working of these mines that we are to date the introduction of iron in such abundance as to reduce its price, bring it into general use, and finally cause it to supersede wholly the alloys of copper. This ore is of extremely easy reduction, by processes of great simplicity, which furnish iron of excellent quality, and are, as we shall hereafter see, still in use. We cannot, indeed, infer with certainty, that these were the processes used by the ancients; but their simplicity is a strong argument in favour of their remote invention.

Steel seems to have been known as different in qualities from iron, at a very remote period; that is to say, it was understood that there were varieties of iron, which when tempered, became hard, whilst others remained soft. The intentional preparation of it, as a different species, seems to have taken its rise among the Chalybes, a people of Asia Minor, and it was afterwards obtained from Noricum. We still find in the latter country, (Styria,) an ore that furnishes steel, by processes as simple as those by which the iron is obtained from the ore of Elba, and hence can form some tolerable guess at the mode in which the steel of the ancients was obtained.

The third form in which we find iron as an article of commerce, namely, cast iron, is of far more recent origin. It has been traced to the banks of the Rhine, and it is certain that stove-plates were cast in Alsace in A. D. 1494. From this epoch, then, dates the great improvement in the preparation of iron, by which its price has been so far lessened, as to render it available for innumerable purposes, from which a small addition to its present cost would exclude it.

Iron, as may be inferred from what has been stated, is known in commerce in three distinct forms—wrought or bar iron, cast or pig iron, and steel. The received chemical theory on this subject is, that the former is metallic iron nearly in a pure state, and that the two latter are chemical compounds of iron and carbon. How far this is true will be examined in the sequel.

When wrought iron is nearly pure, it has, when in bars of not less than an inch square, or plates not less than half an inch in thickness, a granular structure. From the appearance of these grains, an estimate may be had of its quality; grains without any determinate form, neither presenting, when broken, crystalline faces, nor arranging themselves in plates; and which, in the fracture of the bar, exhibit points, and even filaments, manifesting the resistance they have opposed, are marks of the best quality. If, when broken, a crystalline character is exhibited, the quality is bad, and will, according to a disposition difficult to describe in words, either break under the hammer when heated, or be subject to rupture when cold. These two opposite defects are, in the language of our manufacturers, called red and cold short, or shear. The former fault unfits it for being easily worked; the latter destroys its most important usefulness. When the manufacture has been badly conducted, crystals will appear mingled with tenacious grains, and a want of uniform consistence will render it unfit for being cut and worked by the file. Iron of the latter character may, notwithstanding, possess great tenacity.

In still smaller bars, good iron, in breaking, exhibits filaments like those shown by a piece of green wood when broken across; this is technically called nerve; and as it does not show itself in larger bars, it has been supposed that it is the result of the process of drawing out the bars. This is partially true, although the iron that presents a crystalline structure will not acquire nerve, however frequently hammered. To obtain nerve in larger masses, it is necessary to form them of bundles of smaller bars, a process known under the name of faggoting.

Iron contains in its ores many impurities of different natures, according to circumstances, and is in its preparation exposed to several others; by these its quality is frequently much affected. Its valuable ores all contain the iron in the state of oxide. The oxygen, it is generally believed, is not wholly separated even in the best malleable iron, but enough still remains to impair in some degree its good qualities. In its manufacture it is exposed to the action of carbon, with which it is capable of combining. Much iron appears to contain some of the combinations of this sort, existing in the form of hard particles, technically known by the name of *pins*.

Of inflammable bodies, sulphur and phosphorus are frequently contained in the ores of iron; and when pit coal is used in the manufacture, the former substance is present, and may influence the product. The union of sulphur, in very small quantities, with the iron, creates the defect called red short, although it is probably not the only substance that produces the same fault; but when it is caused by sulphur, all the good properties of the iron are impaired, which is not always the case when it arises from other impurities. The defect of breaking when cold, has been attributed to the presence of phosphorus by high authority. There are, however, ores in this country, containing a phosphate of lime, which yield iron of excellent quality.

A mixture of sulphur and carbon deprives iron of its property of welding, and in the highest proportion gives the opposite defects of being both red and cold short.

Ores of iron contain the earths, silex, alumina, lime, and magnesia. With the bases of these earths the metal is capable of forming alloys; those of the three first are often thus combined. Silicium has been discovered combined with iron to the extent of 3-1/2 per cent. It has been found to render this metal harder, more brittle, and more similar in structure to steel; so small a quantity as 1/2 per cent. has been sufficient to render it liable to break when cold; and it appears probable, that by far the greater part of the cold short irons owe this fault to the presence of silex, rather than to that of phosphorus. Iron obtained from the ores by means of coal, is, under circumstances of equality in other respects, more likely to be combined with silicium than when made with charcoal. Karsten infers that a combination with aluminum produces similar defects, and denies the assertion of Faraday, that the good qualities of a steel brought from India are due to an alloy with this earthy base. A combination with the metallic base of lime, lessens the property that iron possesses of being welded, but does not render it more liable to fracture, either under the hammer or when cold.

Of the metals proper:—

Copper renders iron red short.

Lead combines with iron with great difficulty, so that its presence in the ores can hardly be considered dangerous, but when the combination is formed, the iron is both liable to break when red-hot and when cold.

A very small quantity of tin destroys the strength of iron in a great degree when cold, but still leaves it fit to be forged.

Wrought iron does not appear to unite with zinc, but its presence in the ores is injurious to the manufacture, for a reason that will be hereafter stated.

Antimony renders iron cold short, the alloy is harder and more fusible, and approaches in character to cast iron.

Arsenic produces a great waste in the manufacture of iron, and when alloyed with it, injures or destroys its capability of being welded.

Ores which contain titanium, according to universal experience in this country, give an iron inclining to the defect of red short, but possessing the highest degree of tenacity. Such are several of the ores of the northern part of New-Jersey, and of Orange County, New-York.

Manganese in small quantities renders iron harder, but injures none of its good qualities. Many of our ores contain manganese, but when carefully manufactured the iron appears to contain but an insensible trace of this *metal*.

Nickel unites with iron in all proportions, and gives a soft and tenacious alloy; no good property of the iron appears to be injured by it. United with steel it gives an alloy of excellent quality. Nickel is rare among the ores of iron that are not of meteoric origin. But native malleable iron is occasionally found in large masses alloyed with this metal, and its extrinsic source has been fully ascertained. The masses are sometimes of very great size; we have already expressed our opinion that the iron that first came into use was derived from this source, and had been employed for ages before the processes for preparing it from its more abundant ores were discovered.

Cast iron is distinguished into two varieties, which are obviously distinct in character, the grey and the white; a mixture of the two forms that which is called mottled. It is generally believed, and usually stated in the books, that both of these are combinations of iron with carbon, and that their difference in appearance and quality grows out of the difference in the proportions in which the two substances exist; that the grey iron contains the greatest dose of carbon, and the white the least. There is, as will be seen, good reason to question the latter part of this statement.

The grey iron requires the greatest degree of heat for its fusion, is more fluid when melted, is softest, best fitted for castings which require to be turned or filed, and for those that must be thin; the white iron is very hard and brittle; the greatest degree of strength and tenacity is due to the mixture, or mottled iron, and to that variety of mottled in which the grey rather predominates.

The different varieties are readily convertible, for the grey iron when melted and suddenly cooled becomes white, when cooled more slowly is mottled, and when carefully preserved from rapid loss of heat, retains its colour. On the other hand, experiments on a small scale have shown, that white cast iron, subjected to a heat equal to that at which the grey melts, and allowed to cool slowly, becomes grey. Hence their difference can hardly be ascribed to chemical constitution. Neither can the presence of a greater or less quantity of oxygen, as is sometimes supposed, produce the difference, for under circumstances in all other respects similar, except the rate at which they are cooled, iron of the three different varieties may be produced, We therefore feel warranted in rejecting the usual theory, particularly as the reception of it has rather impeded than advanced the manufacture of iron.

The theory of Karsten is far more consistent with the facts, and is directly applicable to the practical purposes of the iron master. We shall endeavour to give a succinct exposition of this theory, introducing all that is necessary for its full explanation.

The ores of iron, which are all oxides, are reduced by exposing them to the action of carbonaceous matter, at a high temperature. The carbon first separates the oxygen from the ore, which becomes metallic, but as it has for the carbon a high affinity, that substance tends to combine with it. The iron combined with carbon is rendered far more fusible than it is when pure, and thus readily melts; when the heat of the furnace is little more than is sufficient for effecting this fusion, the two substances are uniformly mixed, and probably form a compound analogous to a metallic alloy; this is the white cast iron. When the compound is exposed to a heat higher than is sufficient to melt it, a separation appears again to take place, the carbon tending to assume in part the form of plumbago, the iron to retain no more of carbon than is sufficient to keep it liquid at the new temperature, and thus passes from the state of cast iron to that of steel, and finally approaches to that of malleable iron. If the cooling take place slowly, the carbon, obeying its own law of crystallization, arranges itself in thin plates, and the iron, consolidating afterwards, fills up all the interstices with grains or imperfect crystals; and thus the mass assumes a dark grey colour, partly owing to the natural colour of the iron, but in a greater degree to the plumbago. When the cooling is rapid, the carbon still disseminated throughout the mass, does not crystallize separately, but the two substances again form an uniform compound.

Thus, according to the theory, there is no essential difference in the proportion of carbon between grey and white cast iron, but the former is a mechanical mixture of crystals of carbon, nearly pure, with iron containing a less proportion of carbon than the white, while the white iron is a homogeneous alloy of carbon and iron.

Upon this theory may be explained all the facts which have been found wholly irreconcilable with the other.

1. The more intense the heat of the furnace, the deeper the colour, and consequently the higher quality of the cast iron.

2. The changes that take place from grey to white cast iron, merely by difference in the rate of cooling.

3. The reconversion of the white variety into grey, by simply heating it above its melting temperature, and allowing it to cool gradually.

4. The formation of imperfect crystals of plumbago (*kish*) on the surface of grey iron.

5. The approach to malleability of the grey iron, which is utterly irreconcilable with its being a homogeneous compound, more charged with carbon than the white.

The basis of white cast iron, appears to be a definite chemical compound, of two atoms of iron to one of carbon, and is therefore analogous in its chemical constitution to carburet of hydrogen and carburet of sulphur, but like all metallic alloys it is capable of containing an excess of one of the substances in a state of mixture during fusion, and which does not separate on rapid cooling. The iron alone is found in excess in this substance.

Steel appears to contain but half the quantity of carbon in its chemical proportions that white cast iron does, but, like it, is susceptible of a variety of mixtures; if the proportion of carbon amount to three per cent., it loses the property of malleability, if the proportion fall as low as one per cent. it can no longer be tempered, and is identical with the harder varieties of bar-iron. As the carburets of iron, whether in the form of pig or of steel, may be considered as alloys, if they be presented to other metals, the results must necessarily be different from what occurs when pure iron is exposed to the same substance. The union that may take place in the one instance may not occur in the other. It may often happen, that when the iron is pure, a true chemical combination will occur, while in the other case, no more than a mechanical mixture can be effected. For the same reason, the consequence may be totally different when the third substance is presented to the iron when first deoxidated, in the presence merely of an excess of carbon, and when the combination with that substance has actually occurred.

If reduced at the same time with the iron, the other metals will unite with it more readily than with the carburet, and they may afterwards prevent its union with carbon, for there are few, if any metals, besides iron, which have any affinity for carbon.

Cast iron may contain the bases of the earths that form a part of its ores. Of these, silicium is the most usual, and there is probably no cast iron that does not contain a portion of it. It appears to render this form of the metal harder and less suitable for the purposes of the moulder, but is separated almost wholly when it is converted into wrought iron.

We have seen a parcel of pig iron that was marked with a species of white efflorescence, ascertained on examination to be silica; this was rejected for its hardness by the founder, but on being manufactured by the process of puddling, gave bar iron of good quality.

From what has just been stated, it appears that the other metals more generally exist in cast iron, in a state of alloy with pure iron, which is intimately mixed with the carburet. Thus as a general rule, the pig which contains them, will be more likely to be grey in colour than that which does not, but it may, notwithstanding, be injured in quality. The exact effect of such alloys upon cast iron, does not appear to have been fully examined.

The ores whence iron is obtained, are all oxides, with the exception of a carbonate whence steel is in a few places obtained directly. They contain, in combination with the iron, or forming parts of a heterogeneous aggregate, a variety of earthy substances. In the reduction of these ores, two objects are to be accomplished, the separation of the oxygen, and the fusion of the earthy mass. Carbon, in some one of its native or artificial forms, is used to effect the former purpose, upon the same principle that it is applied to the other metallic oxides. Thus a furnace in which a fire of carbonaceous matter is kept up and urged to the highest possible degree of intensity by blowing machines, is necessary. When the earths are pure, even the highest heat of furnaces is incapable of fusing them, and although the oxides of the ancient metals, and among the rest, the oxide of iron, increase the fusibility of one of the earths; still, if but one earth be present, it is only in a few cases that the simple ore will furnish the means of its own fusion. We are therefore compelled to make use of the property possessed by the earths, of rendering each other more fusible.

Silica is the earth to which we have referred, as being susceptible of fusion when mixed with the oxide of iron. Silica, also, when mixed with the other earths, renders them more fusible than is its own mixture with oxide of iron. Hence it may be stated as a general rule, that ores which do not contain silica, cannot be decomposed without the addition of that earth. The most of our American ores contain silex in sufficient abundance; hence it is usual to add to them, in the process of reduction, carbonate of lime, which is called *flux*. Did not the ore contain silica, this would not produce its effect, and a due admixture of the three earths, silica, alumina, and lime, appears to be necessary to cause the most advantageous results.

The remarks of Karsten on this head are new and worthy of attention.

> "It is upon the choice and the just proportion of the flux, that the profit of the manufacturer in a great degree depends. Employed in too great quantities they fail in the important purpose of giving to the scoriæ a proper consistence. It is very difficult to fix their proportions exactly, and, in truth, these ought to vary with the manner in which the furnace works; but a proportion determined for a state of the furnace when the temperature is neither too high nor too low, is usually adopted.

> "Chemists and metallurgists, have endeavoured to determine the degree of fusibility of the earths when mixed with each other; but their researches have shed but little light upon the management of blast furnaces. We are, in spite of them, still compelled to have recourse to experience. Far, however, be it from me to depreciate the attempts of Achurd, Bergman, Chaptal, Cramer, &c.; they are valuable at least, in pointing out the road that is to be pursued in the experiments.

> "It follows, in general terms, from these experiments, that lime, silica, alumina, and magnesia, are infusible when not mixed with each other; that no mixture of earths is fusible without the presence of silica; that the fusion of the oxides of iron cannot take place by the addition of any simple earth other than silica; that ternary mixtures are more fusible than binary; that quaternary mixtures vitrify even more readily, and that the oxide of manganese promptly determines the liquefaction of all the earths.

> "The theory of the vitrification of oxides, aided by trials on a small scale, points out the kind of earthy mixture which ought to be employed, but it cannot fix the exact proportion of the different

earths that ought to be adopted; nor does it teach the means of replacing an earth by its chemical equivalent, as, for instance lime, by magnesia. The solution of the question will depend rather upon the properties of the silicates of lime and magnesia at high temperatures, than upon the action of these silicates upon iron. It is hardly probable that the iron obtained from all ores, could be equally good, even if the most proper fluxes could be added to these ores. Those who have maintained this opinion, have erroneously imagined that the reduction of the ore could always be effected under the same circumstances, which would not be the case, even if these fluxes were ascertained and made use of."

Most of the ores of iron require, before they are subjected to the process of reduction, a preparatory operation called roasting. This consists in exposing them to a comparatively low heat. The more important use of this process is to render the mass more susceptible of mechanical division, but it also serves in many cases to separate the sulphur and arsenic that may exist in the ore. There are some ores, as, for instance, those of a number of mines in Morris and Sussex counties, New-Jersey, which are so free from impurities, and which yield so readily to the mechanical means employed for separating them, that this process is wholly unnecessary; but such ores are rare, and the process of roasting must, generally speaking, be performed.

The mechanical division, which exposes a larger surface to the action of heat and of the chemical agents, is called stumping; this is usually performed by appropriate machinery, but was in the infancy of the art effected by hand.

The reduction of rich ores of iron, such as are almost wholly made up of its oxides, and contain but little earthy matter, may be performed in a common smith's forge. The reduction in this case takes place immediately in the blast of the bellows, where the intensely heated ore is in contact with the burning charcoal; and if a carburet be formed, it is immediately decomposed, and pure iron is the result. Such is probably the more ancient of all the processes for obtaining malleable iron, and it is still used to a certain extent even at the present day. The hearth in which the operation is at present performed, differs from the forge of a common smith only in its greater size, and in the increased power of its bellows. A cavity is prepared, in which a charcoal lire is lighted, and to which the nozzle or *tuyere* of the bellows is directed; ore in minute fragments is thrown upon the ignited fuel, fresh coal and ore are added from time to time, and the latter being reduced to the malleable state descends, as the charcoal burns away, to the bottom of the cavity. Here the successive portions, still kept hot by the fuel above them, agglutinate, and form a porous mass, containing in its cavities a black vitreous substance, which is composed of the earthy matter rendered fusible by the metallic oxide. This porous mass is called the *Loup*.

It would be unsafe to subject the loup immediately to the action of heavy hammers of iron. It is, therefore, after being withdrawn from the fire, beaten with wooden mallets, to bring its parts into closer contact, and press out the vitreous matter. While this is performed, it cools so much as to require to be again heated, which is done in the same fire. Indeed, the same forge is used in all the successive heats that the iron in this process requires.

After the loup has been again heated, it may be subjected to the hammer. This unquestionably was anciently one moved by hand; but now, in all manufactories of this character, a heavy mass of case hardened iron is employed for the purpose; this is lifted by machinery impelled by a water wheel, and permitted to fall upon the loup. The loup is again heated, and again beaten into an irregular octangular prism, called the cingle; this, after a third heat, is formed into a rectangular block, called a bloom; and the whole, or a proper proportion of this is drawn into a bar, at three successive heats; the middle being beaten out first, and the two ends in succession. Thus, in addition to the heat employed in the original reduction, the iron must be at least six times reheated before it becomes a finished marketable bar.

In this manner the ore of Elba is still manufactured in Catalonia and Tuscany, and there can be little doubt that it is identical with the original rude process, by which the iron of that most ancient of known mines was prepared to be an object of commerce. The processes in these two districts differ from each other in some minute particulars, and are known on the continent of Europe as the processes *à la Catalane* and *à l'Italienne*. This method is known in the United States by the name of *blooming*.

Bloomeries are frequent in the United States, being found in many parts of the primitive country, where the magnetic ore of iron is abundant. The iron manufactured by blooming is, generally speaking, remarkable for its nerve, being strong and tenacious in the highest degree, unless the ore be in fault. It is not, however, homogeneous, being liable to contain what are called pins, or grains that have the hardness and consistence of steel.

Blooming is comparatively an expensive process. It requires, indeed, little original capital, but the product in proportion to the capital employed is but small. It is wholly impracticable with poor ores, and demands a great length of time and expenditure of fuel, unless the ore be very fusible. Another objection to it is common to a process we shall hereafter describe, that of refining, and lies in the numerous successive heats, which the small extent of fire, and the slow process of hammering render necessary, before the bar is finished. It has been attempted in New-Jersey to lessen the expense attending these heats, by performing them in reverberatory furnaces. A saving of fuel to a small amount would probably thus be effected, but the number of heats would still remain the same. A more important and useful improvement has superseded the last; the process of rolling, which will be hereafter described, has been introduced, and by means of it a bar may be drawn out at a single heat, and at far less expense of manual labour. Such establishments exist at Dover and Rockaway, New-Jersey, which receive the iron completely reduced from the neighbouring forges, and fashion it into bars.

A forge fire, and, consequently, the process of blooming, is insufficient to convert poor ores, or those that contain much earthy matter, into iron. Treated in this way, those ores, if fusible at all, would become a mass of slag, as the earth would require, at the temperature of a forge fire, the whole, or the greater part of the metallic oxide for its fusion.

Iron being introduced, and its valuable applications known, it became necessary, in those countries that do not afford rich ores, to discover a method by which the poorer might be reduced. This could only be effected by giving such a degree of heat, as would render the earthy matter capable of melting, at a less expense of metal. To increase the mass of fuel, by increasing the depth of the cavity, and actually forming it of walls, thus enabling it to contain a greater quantity, would be obvious means of attaining this end. The ore must be added in smaller proportions, and, being longer in contact with the heated charcoal, would become carbureted; the carbon must therefore be finally burned away, before malleable iron could be attained. A rude but efficient process of this sort, is described by Gmelin as in use among the Tartars; an analogous method, whose use has been superseded by iron imported from Europe, was found among the nations of Guinea; and Mungo Park saw a more perfect application of the same principle at Camalia, on the Gambia. Furnaces of similar character, but more skilfully constructed, are still used in some parts of Germany, and are called *stuckoffen*.

As a carburet, or actual cast-iron, must be formed in these processes, and, as the separation of carbon at the bottom of a deep cylinder, and where the metal would probably be covered by a vitreous liquid, is difficult, the iron might sometimes resist the efforts made to render it malleable, and run from the furnace in a liquid form. It might therefore have readily occurred, that it would be less costly to finish the process in a forge. The *stuckoffen* were therefore converted into *flossoffen*, or melting furnaces, whence the liquid carburet was withdrawn, and afterwards converted into bar iron. Such was probably the cause that led to the original discovery of cast iron, a discovery that cannot be traced further back than the end of the fifteenth century.

The uses of cast iron for purposes to which wrought iron is inapplicable, and the readiness with which it is fashioned, by pouring it into moulds, led to the increase of the size of the *flossoffen*, and in the power of the blowing apparatus, which has caused the introduction of the blast furnace. This forms the basis of the methods by which iron in all its forms is chiefly prepared at the present day, and is hence worthy of particular consideration.

The difference between the blast furnace proper, and the ancient fires from which it gradually took its rise, consists wholly in its superior height, and in the greater power of the blowing machines, by which its combustion is supplied with air.

This increase of height adds to the mass of the contained combustible,—additional air is therefore required for effecting its complete inflammation, and the joint effect is, that a much higher temperature is generated. By this, the earthy matters either contained in the ores, forming portions of the combustible, or added as *fluxes*, are rendered fusible at a less expense of oxide of iron; the carburet formed, becomes more fluid, and the product is more likely to assume the character of grey pig-iron.

Charcoal, as in the other processes, was the fuel originally employed, and is still principally used in most countries. But coal deprived of its volatile parts, and charred or converted into coke, has been substituted in some regions, as will hereafter be stated. Each of these combustibles requires a furnace of appropriate character, and demands a difference in the mode of management.

A blast-furnace is a hollow chamber enveloped, generally speaking, in a mass of masonry, of the form of a truncated pyramid. The chamber is composed essentially of three parts; the upper has the figure of a truncated cone, whose greatest base is lowest: this may be called the body of the furnace; the middle portion has also the figure of a truncated cone, whose greater base is uppermost, and is common to it and the upper portion: this contraction is called the *boshes* of the furnace; the lower position is called the hearth, and is usually enclosed on three sides by walls of refractory substances, on the fourth it is bounded by two stones, one serving as a lintel, which is called the tymp, the other resting on the foundation, and known by the name of the *dam*. Such at least is the shape of the blast furnaces in common use, and which will suffice for our present purpose.

The blast is introduced into the hearth, at a small distance above the level of the upper edge of the dam, and is now generally performed by means of two *tuyeres*; in the more ancient furnaces, there was but one. The furnace being completely dried, a fire is lighted in the hearth, and fuel gradually added, until the whole is filled to the *trundle head*, which is the open and lesser base of the truncated cone that forms the body of the furnace. The blast may then be applied, slowly and gently at first, and increasing gradually, until it reach its maximum of intensity. As the blast proceeds, the charcoal gradually burns, and descends; its place is supplied at top by fresh fuel, by ore, and by the earthy matter used as a flux. This is styled *charging* the furnaces. The earlier charges often contain no ore, but are wholly composed of charcoal and flux, and, in all cases, the proportion of ore and flux is at first small, and is gradually augmented. The charges are made as often as the mixed mass in the furnace descends sufficiently low to admit the quantity that is chosen as the proper amount. The charcoal is thrown in first, and the ore and flux are spread and mixed upon its surface. The principles which govern the amount of the charge, are as follows:—

> "The volume of the charges depends upon the capacity of the furnace. If they be too large, they cool the upper part of the furnace, which will cause great inconveniences, particularly if zinc exist in the ore. On the other hand, small charges of charcoal will be cut or displaced by the ore, which will occasion a descent by sudden falls, in an oblique direction, or in a confused manner. It follows that the volume of the charge, although proportioned to the volume of the furnace, must be augmented: when the charcoal is light and susceptible of being displaced; and with the friability, the weight, and the shape of the fragments of the ore."

> "The heat, considered in any given horizontal section of the furnace, will be intense in proportion to the thickness of the layer of charcoal that reaches it. It follows, that the fusible ore requires smaller charges of charcoal than one that is more refractory. If

the beds of charcoal and mineral are too thick, the upper part of the furnace will not be sufficiently heated. Hence it is obvious, that there must be a maximum and minimum charge for every different dimension of furnace, and for every different species of ore and fuel." *Karsten.*

The charge of charcoal being determined upon such principles, it is added by measure, and always in equal quantities, while the proportion of ore and flux is made to vary, not only by a gradual increase at the beginning of the operation, but according to the working of the furnace. The manner in which the furnace is working can be inferred, even before its products are ascertained, by the appearance of the flame at the trundle-head, and at the tymp, by the manner in which the charge descends, and more surely still, by the appearance of the scoriæ. By a strict attention to these circumstances the proportion of the charge of ore may be regulated. A fortnight usually elapses from the time of the first charge until it reaches a regular state of working, and variations will occur even after that period, in consequence of the greater or less moisture of the combustible and minerals, the continual wearing away of the sides of the furnace, the variations in the state of the atmosphere, and in the play of the blowing machines, the greater or less attention of the workmen, and numerous other accidental circumstances.

The mode of proceeding when coke is the fuel employed, rests upon the same principles, but the dimensions of furnace that are best suited to the different combustibles are different. As a general principle, the height of furnaces must depend upon the force of the blast and the density of the fuel. If the fuel be dense, and the blowing machine weak, the furnace must not have a great height; and even if the blast can be made strong, too high a furnace is disadvantageous for light charcoal. Coke, on the other hand, may be used in furnaces of greater height than any species of charcoal, provided the blast be of sufficient power. So long as the imperfect bellows were used in blowing, the height of the furnace was limited wholly by their action. More powerful apparatus in the form of cylinders, analogous in form and arrangement to those of steam-engines, and like them, either single or double acting, have now been introduced; the intensity of the blast is in them only limited by the moving power, which is applied to them, and when this is the steam engine, it may be said, that no limit can arise from the want of blast. We may, therefore, at the present day, regulate the height of furnaces by the nature of the fuel that is consumed in them.

The greater part of the furnaces in our country still retain the ancient and imperfect form of bellows, hence their height is restricted to the limits of from eighteen to twenty-four feet, and rarely or never reaches thirty. But when the apparatus is such as to supply a proper quantity of air, it has been found that even with light and porous charcoal, such as is given by white pine, the height ought not to be less than thirty feet, and when hard woods are used should be as great as thirty-six feet. Furnaces of even forty feet have been found to answer an excellent purpose, where the charcoal was prepared from oak. When coke is used, furnaces have been made as high as fifty, or even as seventy feet; but experience in England has shown, that from forty-five to forty-eight feet is the proper limit. This height is not at present exceeded in that country, even when the furnace has the greatest dimensions in other respects, and has been found efficacious, even when the vast quantity of eighteen tons has been furnished daily by a single furnace.

The force of the blast will depend upon the nature of the fuel, the volume of air, the quantity of mixed material the furnace holds; and thus furnaces in which coke is used, will require the most powerful blast, whether we have regard to the volume or the intensity. The latter may be measured by a column of mercury adapted in a syphon tube to the air pipes, exactly as the gauge is adapted to the pipes of the steam engine.

The reduction and liquefaction of the metal take place progressively, as the charges descend in the furnace. The separation of the oxygen is due to the presence of carbonaceous matter at high temperatures, begins at the surface of the pieces of ore, and proceeds gradually inwards; the earthy parts of the ore, of the fuel employed, and the flux, unite and melt; they are thus separated, and being sooner fused than the metal, make their way through the charcoal, and descend first to the hearth. The reduced metal, continuing in contact with the burning carbon, acquires a greater or less portion of that substance, becomes fusible, melts, and follows the liquified earths. Dropping into the hearth that already contains the liquid vitrified earths, it passes by its superior gravity to the bottom, and is protected by them from the blast. Even at the bottom of the hearth, the heat is sufficient to retain the carbureted metal in a liquid state, and this is permitted gradually to accumulate, until it rises nearly to the level of the dam.

It now becomes necessary to withdraw or *cast* the metal. This is done by forcing a way through a channel left beneath the dam in the masonry of the hearth, and closed with clay; the inner portion of this is baked hard, and requires to be broken through with a steel point. As soon as the passage is opened, the metal runs out, and is received in a long trench formed in the sand floor of the moulding house, to which are adapted a number of less trenches, at right angles, each containing about one hundred weight of metal. The metal in the longer trench is also broken into pieces of the same size, and the ingots thus formed are called *pigs*, whence the term for this variety, *pig iron*.

From one to three days will elapse from the time of the first charge until the furnace can be tapped, and pigs cast. From that time the casting succeeds with tolerable regularity, according to the working of the furnace, and at intervals depending upon the volume of the charge, and the capacity of the hearth.

It appears probable that the fusion of the iron is effected always by a direct chemical union of that metal with carbon, in the proportion of two atoms of the former to one of the latter. This constitutes, as we have seen, the white variety of pig iron. But as it continues, generally speaking, in the furnace, long after its fusion takes place, it acquires a temperature higher than its proper melting point, and a tendency to separation takes place, the iron retaining in combination no more of the carbon than is necessary to maintain it in a fluid state at the increased temperature. Thus the grey variety of pig iron is formed; and on casting it, the carbon, in a form similar to that of plumbago, is disseminated throughout the mass, or forms on its surface the efflorescence that is called kish, and which is always a sign of a high quality in the iron it accompanies.

In conformity with this theory, we find that a high temperature in the furnace always produces grey cast iron; and that a low temperature, from whatever cause it may arise, renders the iron more or less inclining to white. So also if the metal be not exposed to the heat for a sufficient length of time, it becomes white.

Karsten classes these several causes of whiteness in the product, in the following order:—

"In conformity with the observations that have hitherto been made, white cast iron is obtained:

"1. By the use of ores that are too easily fusible, or which is the same thing, by an excess of flux, by a want of density in the charcoal, and by too strong a blast, even when the working of the furnace is regular.

"2. By a surcharge of ore, which deranges the action of the furnace, and produces impure cinder, containing uncombined iron.

"3. By boshes of too rapid a slope, and a blast of too great a velocity; and this may occur even where the cinder is pure.

"4. By too low a temperature, even when the cinder is pure, and the furnace works regularly.

"5. By a derangement in the action of the furnace, arising not from a surcharge of ore, but from an irregularity in the descent of the charge.

"6. By the substances contained in the body of the furnace exercising too great a pressure upon those beneath; the heat in this case, concentrated in the hearth, cannot reach the boshes, and the upper part of the furnace; the working may be regular, the cinder and flame may in this case give no sign of derangement.

"7. By too great a breadth in the furnace.

"8. When coke is used, it may arise from too great a quantity of ashes, or of fossil charcoal, (anthracite,) being contained in it. The presence of these will keep down the heat of the furnace. An excess of ashes may be remedied, by using the ore and flux in proper proportions to fuse them, but a diminution in the charge must be made; the cinder becomes viscid, and likely to obstruct the descent of the charges.

"9. By an accidental cooling, arising from humidity, and other similar causes."

Among the last may be reckoned the presence of zinc in the ore. This metal, although volatile, is not separated at the temperature given in the process of roasting, nor does it sublime in the upper and cooler parts of the furnace. But, as the ore descends, it passes into the state of vapour, and requires for its conversion, great quantities of heat that becomes latent. It hence cools the lower part of the furnace far more rapidly than even wet coal, or moist ores. The cooling thus caused, may not be effected until the melted metal reach the hearth, and may there cause it to become solid. Thus the solid mass called a salamander, may, in some cases, be formed; and thus may be explained the fact, that ores of iron that contain the more easily fusible metal zinc, are more liable to interrupt the action of the furnace in this manner, than others. The volatilized zinc rises to the upper part of the furnace, where the heat is often insufficient to retain it in the state of vapour, and is then deposited on the sides. In this position, it will also disturb the action of the furnace.

Coke being more dense than charcoal, will, in its combustion, furnish a more intense heat;—hence it is hardly possible to obtain by a charcoal fire, iron of as deep a colour as may be procured by the use of the former fuel. It will also resist the pressure of far greater weights than charcoal, and hence the proportion of ore may be much greater when it is used; containing more and less fusible earthy matters than charcoal, it requires a greater quantity of flux.

In the manufacture of cast iron then, coke gives iron better suited for small castings, for those which require turning or filing, and yields a far greater quantity from a furnace. Hence arises the very great superiority which Great Britain has, until recently, possessed over most other countries, in those fabrics in which these qualities are valuable; and hence it has been found until lately, in this country, hardly possible to manufacture fine machinery that requires workmanship after it is cast, without the aid of the higher qualities of Scotch iron, which, in these qualities, exceeds even the English. Recently, however, iron fully equal to the best Scotch, but like it wanting in tenacity, has been manufactured at the Bennington furnace in Vermont:—so also at the Greenwood furnace in Orange county, N. Y., and at West Point, iron approaching to the Scotch in softness, but very superior in strength, has been produced. In these cases, the height of the furnace has been carried up to the limits we have before laid down, and powerful blowing cylinders substituted for the ancient bellows.

When the pig iron is to be used for re-casting, every effort ought to be used to obtain it of the deepest possible colour. This, as may be seen from what has been already stated, will be effected by keeping the furnace at the highest possible temperature, and exposing the metal to it a sufficient length of time. In effecting this, however, certain defects may arise:—thus a longer exposure to a high heat, will cause the reduction of other oxides that may be present, as of manganese and the metallic bases of the earths; and the iron in becoming more soft, and approaching in fact more nearly to the form of the pure metal, will combine and form alloys with these bases. In this way, it will, as has been stated, become cold short; and to this may be attributed the want of strength in the greater part, if not all, of the British iron. The use of coke as a fuel, tends to increase this defect, in consequence of the great quantity of earthy matter it contains.

When the ores are pure, cast iron manufactured by charcoal, is not liable to such a fault. Hence the cast iron of Sweden and the United States, manufactured from the magnetic iron, or, in some cases in this country, from rich hæmatites, has very superior tenacity, insomuch that these two nations have alone been able to use this material in the construction of field pieces. When white iron is obtained from a furnace, it may have two different qualities. The first arises from a mere defect of heat, where all other circumstances are favourable, and the ore is completely reduced. The second arises when the reduction is not complete, and the separation of the earths and other oxides has not been fully effected. Of all the varieties of cast iron, this latter is by far the worst. It is indeed more easily converted into wrought iron than the other species, but the product is always of very inferior quality; it is rarely or never produced by furnaces fed with charcoal, but may be obtained by accident or design in those where coke is used, by a surcharge of ore, or by too great a proportion of flux, and sometimes cannot be avoided in warm and moist weather, where the air is rarefied and charged with vapour.

The grey iron obtained by the use of each of the different kinds of fuel, has its own peculiar advantages; that made with coke possessing, as a general rule, when melted, a higher degree of fluidity which adapts it for more delicate castings; being softer and better suited for fitting; while that manufactured with charcoal, possesses a greater degree of strength. One solitary instance has been quoted, in which a manufacturer of great intelligence has obtained by the use of charcoal, from a very pure ore, a union of both these valuable properties, and another, in which iron as soft as that made with coke, has been produced by means of charcoal.

In spite of this apparent balance in the properties of the two fuels, the introduction of coke into the art of reducing iron has been attended with the most important advantages. These lie in the superior economy of the process, and in the enormous quantity of the product. The manufacture of iron by charcoal is limited, by the growth of the forests, which replace themselves only at distant periods, by the large space they occupy, and the consequent labour of transportation; by the cost of cutting the wood and preparing the coal; and finally, even when the fuel can be obtained in abundance, and at small cost, the burden of the furnace, and the heat obtained in a given space are less than when coke is used, and the quantity of metal yielded is in consequence comparatively small. The coke furnaces of Great Britain, have therefore supplied cast iron in such abundance and at such diminished prices as to have brought it into use for a great variety of purposes, to which, until recently, it was hardly considered applicable.

In England, as in other countries, charcoal was the only fuel at first used; and after bloomeries had been in vogue for centuries, the blast furnace was introduced from the shores of the Rhine. For many years the growth of the forests proved sufficient to supply the demand, but at length the increase of population caused them to be encroached upon by cultivation; the growth of the manufacture was first prevented, and finally, almost extinguished.

The method by charcoal appears to have reached its acme of prosperity, at the close of the reign of the First James, when the furnaces of the kingdom yielded 180,000 tons of pig iron. About this period, Dudley first proposed the use of pit coal; but the time had not yet arrived in which it was absolutely necessary to seek for a new process, in consequence of the failure of the old one.

In 1745, or in the course of one hundred and thirty years, the forests had been so far encroached upon, that the product of the furnaces had fallen to 17,000 tons per annum, and in 1788, the quantity made with charcoal had dwindled as low as 13,000 tons. At this epoch, coke was introduced into blast furnaces, and in eight years the whole quantity produced by both methods had mounted up to 150,000 tons, or increased more than tenfold.

At nearly the lowest ebb of the British manufacture, the art of preparing iron was introduced into her then provinces, the present United States; and in 1737 it was attempted to obtain permission to introduce the product into England. The attempt failed, and in 1750 an act was passed to protect the exportation of English iron to America, and to prevent the establishment of forges. Had the other policy prevailed, England would probably have seen her manufacture of iron transferred to the United States, and with great immediate advantage both to herself and her then most valuable colony; but she would probably have seen herself at the present day degraded from her high stand in the scale of nations, to the secondary place in which the extent of her territory would keep her, were it not for the superiority of her manufacturing industry, of which iron is the basis. The quantity of iron now produced in England, exceeds that furnished by the rest of the world united, and does not fall short of 800,000 tons. It has a value even in its raw state of near four millions sterling, and is of far greater intrinsic worth, in consequence of the spur which its abundance gives to every other branch of industry.

Bar iron is at the present day principally manufactured from the pig. The process originally used for this purpose is called refining. The fire in which it is performed is a forge, similar in form and character to that employed in blooming. In blooming, the iron must be reduced, combines with carbon, and is subsequently decarbureted; while in the refining, the latter part of the operation alone remains. In this last process, while the carbon is burning away, the metallic bases of the earths are then oxidated, combine with oxide of iron, and form a vitreous substance. Hence, when it is carefully conducted, by far the greater part of the impurities contained in the cast iron may be removed. Refined iron, if made from ore of equal purity, is not inferior in tenacity to bloomed, and is superior in other respects, being more homogeneous, free from pins, and more easily treated by the smith. As a general rule, it is also less costly, that is to say, the same quantity of charcoal and workmanship will furnish a greater quantity of refined iron. It requires, however, a much greater capital, and the labour of transporting the coal from the greater distances which the increased consumption of a single blast furnace and several refineries will demand, may swell the cost of that article. A bloomery fire does not require more than 2000 acres of woodland, while a blast furnace will use the charcoal of 5000. Thus it happens, that it may be more advantageous to spread a number of bloomeries over a given district of country, than to unite a blast furnace and an equal number of refineries in a single place. The celebrated iron of Sweden and Russia is refined, and our country furnishes iron prepared in the same manner not inferior in quality. The principle objection to the process is the great expense of the fuel employed, in the successive heats to which the iron must be exposed in drawing it into bars, after the processes of conversion and the separation of impurities have been effected.

As charcoal became scarce in England, it was attempted to employ coke in lieu of it, in the refineries. This, however, constantly failed, in consequence of the great intensity of the heat, by which the pig was melted suddenly instead of being exposed to the blast, long enough to burn away the carbon. Reverberatory furnaces were next tried, and with partial success, but a combined process has finally been introduced which has been successful and which is called, from a part of the operation, the method of *puddling.*

The manufacture of wrought iron, by means of bituminous coal, is executed at three successive processes, and is facilitated by very great improvements in the machinery. Where hammers are still used, they are much increased in weight, and driven with greater velocity; but by far the greater part of the operation of drawing the bars is effected by means of rollers. The plan of these is in some measure borrowed from the slitting mill, in which bar iron is reduced into rods and thin rolls for various uses. These rollers are in sets, composed each of two of equal diameter, lying in a horizontal position, and placed one vertically above the other. Grooves corresponding to each other are cut in the two rollers, between which the heated iron is drawn by their revolution, and forced to assume a section that just fills up the two grooves. By passing in succession through grooves gradually decreasing in size, any form or magnitude may be given to the bars; and the operation is so rapid, that the bar may be drawn from the loup at a single heat.

The first operation to which the pig iron is subjected, consists in melting it in a fire called a finery, similar in form and character to the bloomeries and refineries of which we have spoken, but in which the fuel is coke. The melted metal is drawn off by tapping the furnace from beneath, and is cast into thin plates. In this way it assumes the characters of the white cast iron, which has been described as formed, when the reduction of the metal is complete, a form that cannot be given when the blast furnace in which it is made is supplied with coke. The rapidity of the cooling is increased, by throwing water on the surface of the plates. It thus appears, that this operation is adopted in order to bring the cast iron into a slate that it may often assume when manufactured by charcoal, and which cannot be given to it by coke. In conformity with this view of the subject, it has been found, that when wrought iron is manufactured by puddling, from American pig prepared by charcoal, this preliminary operation is unnecessary.

The fine metal, obtained in the manner we have described, is next broken into pieces, and subjected to heat in a reverberatory furnace. A rapid heat is given at first to liquefy the iron, and is then diminished by means of dampers; the melted mass is violently stirred to expose it to the action of air and heat, by which the carbon is burnt away, and a part of the oxides of iron and the earthy bases combined and vitrified; as the carbon is separated, the metal gradually loses its liquidity, and finally dries, or assumes the consistence of sand: this shows that the carbon is separated, and the iron has assumed its malleable nature. The addition of water aids the oxidation of the several substances, and facilitates the process. The heat is again increased, and the metal collected under it, and rolled together into parcels suited to the action of the drawing machinery, and to the size of the bar that is to be made; these are pressed together, and a partial union takes place among their particles. When they have attained a white heat, they are withdrawn in succession. In some cases, where the number of puddling furnaces is great, they are immediately carried to the rollers and drawn down. But where quality is more regarded than quantity, they are first subjected to the action of the hammer, and finally rolled. The latter process has the advantage of separating more completely the vitrefied oxides, than can be done by rolling alone, but it will often require a second heat, which is given in a forge fire called the *chaffery*. When rollers are used alone, a minute and half is sufficient to form the bar; and a power of thirty houses will roll two hundred tons per week.

The iron in this state is still of very inferior quality, although its external appearance may be good. It is, notwithstanding, sometimes thrown into the market, and this has given rise to the impression that prevails in this country of the bad quality of English rolled iron. It may, however, be used in some cases, where it need not be fashioned by forging; thus, where it requires no more than to be cut into lengths, or where the original bars will answer the purpose, its cheapness may recommend it. Iron for rail-roads is of this quality; and the punching of holes, by which it may be fastened down, is effected by a simple addition of steel teeth, at proper distances, to the last groove through which it is passed. In this form, ready to lay down, rail-road iron may be shipped from England at the low price of 7*l.* 10*s.* sterling per ton; and a similar quality in the simple bar may probably be afforded at about 7*l.* We have never heard of its being sold so low as is stated in the evidence before the Committee of Congress, say 5*l.* 5*s.* There was, however, a period, when an excess of production, caused by a competition between the manufacturers of Wales and Staffordshire, entailed ruin on many of them, and their articles were sold far below the price of production. The price which we have stated is lower than that which has recently been paid in England for rail-road iron, and is that of some shipped from Liverpool, 1st March, 1831, when a considerable fall had taken place.

In order to render the iron which has undergone this process merchantable, it is subjected to the third of the operations which we have enumerated. For this purpose, the bars are made from three to four inches in breadth, and half an inch in thickness. These are cut into lengths, proportioned to the weight of the bar of finished iron that is to be made, and piled together by fours, in a reverberatory furnace, similar in character to the puddling furnace. Here they are exposed to a white heat, by which the four pieces of each pile are made to adhere; they are then withdrawn, and subjected to rollers similar to those used after the puddling process, but of more careful workmanship. The cost of finishing bar iron in this way, when the pig is made by the manufacturer himself, as ascertained upon the spot by Dufrênoy and de Beaumont, is, in Wales, 8*l.* 15*s.*, in Staffordshire, 9*l.* 12*s.* The cost of making pig iron in Wales is 4*l.* 7*s.*, or about half that of the finished bar iron, and in Staffordshire 5*l* 2*s.*

The iron prepared by the three processes of which we have spoken, although merchantable, and suited for various common purposes, is still far from good. We give the characters by which it is distinguished, from the work of Karsten:—

"The iron prepared in the English manner, appears dense and exempt from cracks and flaws. But this goodness is only apparent; the uniform pressure to which the bars are subjected at every point, masks their defects. If a piece of this kind be taken, that in its fracture appears dense and homogeneous, and it be heated in order to be drawn out under a common forge hammer, it dilates and exhibits numerous flaws, that sometimes increase to such a degree, that the bar will fall to pieces under the hammer. It is probable that the cause of this phenomenon is due to the scoriæ, which, in this mode of working, remain mixed in the mass."

The translator adds:—

"It is not however true, that the English method of itself, injures the quality of iron,—experience has proved the contrary: it appears that soft irons lose their harshness in this operation, and become better for many uses."

It may therefore be inferred, that, when the English method is applied to pig iron, that would produce a good wrought metal by the process with charcoal, it will produce one that is equally good by means of coal, but that the latter is capable of hiding the apparent defects of even the worst iron.

The inferiority of the puddled iron is well understood in England, and therefore when it is to be used for chain cables and anchors, it is again heated, and rolled a third time, its price will be then raised to 10*l.* 10*s.* Another quality still superior, is made by uniting scraps of the better qualities that we have mentioned, into loups in the puddling furnace, drawing it in the puddle rolls, balling or piling, and again rolling. Its cost will thus be raised to 12*l.* Even this is yet inferior to Swedes and Russia iron, which sell in the English market from 13*l.* to 15*l.* sterling per ton. For particular purposes in the fabrication of machinery, charcoal is still used in England, in manufacturing a very small quantity of iron, but of very superior quality; this, we have recently understood from good authority, is sold as high as 22*l.* per ton.

Thus it appears that the manufactories of England produce five different descriptions of wrought iron, four of which bear a lower price, and are therefore inferior in quality to those of Sweden and Russia, and, consequently, to the best American iron. No more than one of these, and that the lowest in quality, is usually shipped to this country, and it was the influx of this cheap and almost worthless material, which in 1816 and '17, completely prostrated the American manufacture. Under a protecting duty, it has again revived, but has not reached its former level. New capital has been invested in it under this protection, and it would be a breach of faith suddenly to withdraw it. Still sound policy would dictate that this protection should not be perpetual, provided it can be incontestably proved that it bears so hard upon other branches of industry, as to injure the country through them to a greater extent, than the benefit it derives from the manufacture of iron. But this is far from being the case. The manifest and habitual policy of our government, is to derive its revenue indirectly through the custom house, instead of seeking it in direct taxation. When these duties descend to a level with the minimum expenditure, they cannot be considered burthensome, because they in fact replace revenues that must be drawn from other sources. If, for instance, the iron employed in a specific object, appear to cost more than in some other country, that object may yet be afforded cheaper with us, in consequence of its maker being free from other burthens, which the repeal of the duty on iron, would throw upon him as a necessary substitute. If then our furnaces and forges, when a sufficient capital shall be invested in them under a protecting duty, can afford iron as cheap as it can be imported from other countries, under a minimum of duty, it cannot in truth be said, that this raw material will enhance the price of the articles manufactured from it. Let us see whether there be any reasonable prospect that we shall have iron produced in our own country, which will compete with foreign iron of equal quality, paying a duty of 25 per centum. If this be the case, the profits arising from the present protection, must, in a few years, call forth such production as will reduce the price to a proper level.

The best grey pig iron of American manufacture, superior in strength, and equal in all other respects to the Scotch, is now sold in the New York market at $45 per ton. Good grey iron of the usual character, is worth $35 per ton, and there is no question that forge pig could be obtained by the manufacturer of bar iron, for $25. If it were even to cost $30, it is still cheaper than Staffordshire iron, far less fit for the purpose, can be imported. The Muirkirk iron, so valuable for the casting of machinery, used to cost to import it, at the present rate of duty, $55 and $56. The Bennington furnace commenced the competition with it at this rate, but has been compelled, after driving the Scotch iron from the market, to sell at $45, which is as low as the foreign could be imported at a minimum duty.

Taking the cost of forge pig at $25, the price of converting into bars by charcoal, would be, according to the Philadelphia memorial, $18, and the ton of wrought iron ought to cost no more than $43. We however believe that this cost is far underrated, and that even by the aid of rollers in a part of the process, iron of the best quality could not be produced under $50. This is as cheap as merchantable English puddled iron can be imported, paying 25 per cent. duty. But, even if the pig cost $35, and the wrought iron, $60, it is still cheaper than the English iron, worth in that market 10*l.* 10*s.* can be imported; and the latter is the cheapest which can be obtained in that country, suitable for the manufacture of anchors and chain-cables. At the present moment, however, iron cannot be produced so cheaply, for the forges and furnaces may be considered as in a great measure new, and undergoing all the difficulties of new establishments. Capital above all is wanting, from a want of confidence in the success of the enterprize, growing out of a fear of the repeal of the duty, and the recollection of the former catastrophe; and even credit, so essential where capital is deficient, is at a low ebb. Hence, if profit be made, it rather centers in the capitalist who makes the advances, than in the maker. Thus we have known iron in the bloom, sold at $45 per ton; and, when finished for the market by rolling, bring $100. The latter price, however, could not long be maintained, and has descended to $75 and $80, which still leaves the greater part of the profit to the capitalist.

But we are of opinion, that the manufacture of iron by charcoal is not that to which our country should look for its final supply. It is at best a precarious resource, and its production must diminish with the advance of agriculture, and the consequent demand, while every increase in the price of land must raise the cost. It is then to a total change in the seat and mode of manufacture, that we are to be hereafter beholden for the supply of this first necessary of civilized life. A change will first take place in the sites of the two branches; pig iron will continue to be manufactured by charcoal, and the bar converted by coal. For this the great coal field of Pennsylvania will afford the earliest facilities. No doubt can be entertained that the more freely burning varieties of anthracite will work well in the puddling furnace, as they have been successfully employed in the rolling and slitting of bar iron. When the same species of coal is mixed with charcoal in the blast furnace, it produces excellent forge pig, and thus the two species of fuel may be advantageously united, although the coal alone will not answer the purpose. The value of this coal in the mine and the cost of raising it, is as yet less than that of bituminous coal in any part of Europe, and thus we cannot avoid concluding that when it shall be brought into use, our manufacturers might compete with the English even if unprotected by duty. Our fields of bituminous coal are yet too distant from dense population, and too far removed from easy communication, to be looked to at present, but unless modes be invented by which the anthracite coal can be used without mixture in the blast furnace, these will become the ultimate seats of the manufacturing industry of the United States.

But for reducing the price of iron, by competition within our country, to a level with that of other countries, capital is required, and to divert it to this purpose, the capitalist must feel assured that he shall derive a certain profit from its investment, and that he shall be subjected to no fluctuations in price and still more in demand, from a vacillating course in the government. The establishment of works so perfect as to compete in their manipulations with the English, is a serious business, and till they be established in numbers, we must be dependent on foreign countries for no small proportion of the important article of iron that we consume. A forge for manufacturing puddled iron cannot be profitable unless its machinery be kept in regular employ, for the cost of that will be the same in all cases. This constant employment cannot be given by fewer than eighteen reverberatory furnaces, and the first cost of the works will not be less than $100,000, of which the machinery alone costs $50,000. To supply an establishment of this magnitude with pig, would employ three blast furnaces working with coke, or six with charcoal, the cost of which would reach at least $120,000. The value of the manufactured article would not fall short of a million of dollars, and would require to carry it on a floating capital of not less than $250,000. Thus it appears that a system of works for the manufacture of iron, which should compete to advantage with those of England, would find employment for a capital of half a million of dollars, even with the advantage of credit, and the ready conversion of its securities into cash through the banks. So long, then, as the policy of our government is unsettled, we can hardly expect that so vast an operation can be undertaken either by individual or by corporate funds. A division of the business has been indeed attempted; there is more than one puddling forge in the United States that relies upon the purchase of pig for its supply. These unquestionably do a fair and profitable business, but do not act to the same advantage as they would were the two branches of the manufacture united. The chief difficulty under which they labour is, that they must consult, in their location, convenience in the supply of the raw material, and must therefore neglect what would in the abstract be the most important consideration, the supply of fuel. Thus, at least one of the puddling forges of which we have spoken, is compelled to use imported fuel, and none are situated where alone the nation could derive essential benefit from them, immediately over a rich bed of coal.

It is not pretended to maintain that the present duties on iron are not too high in general for a permanent rate, and that the distribution of their rates is not injudicious. All that we would contend for is, that there shall be no sudden change in the principle, by which a valuable branch of industry would be at once destroyed beyond the possibility of re-establishment. We have been able to discover no argument in the blacksmith's petition, or in the report of the majority of the committee of the Senate, in favour of an entire repeal of duty on raw iron, that does not apply equally to the articles manufactured from it; and we presume that those useful and respectable mechanics would think their principles carried a step too far, should they be made to bear upon the fabrics of their own industry. We are willing, in addition, at once to admit that where the scale has been founded upon improper principles, it ought to be instantly changed.

To attain the first object, as we presume it will not be contended that iron shall ever be imported free of duty, while the nation needs a revenue to meet its current expenditure, let a minimum be fixed beyond which it shall not descend, and which will, evidently, when correctly viewed, place our consumers of iron on an equal footing with those who pay direct taxes in other countries; to this minimum, after a certain definite period, let the duty be gradually and almost insensibly reduced. Less than twenty-five years would probably be insufficient to effect this without incurring a wanton waste of property. We are aware, indeed that our national legislature can perform no act which its successors may not annul, but a hearty concurrence on the part of Mr. Dickerson and Mr. Hayne, representing, as they do, the two great opposing interests in this question, would be a pledge that might be acted upon by capitalists. The expediency of investment would then become a subject of strict calculation, and we do not fear the result.

As to the injudicious adjustment of the scale, the higher rates of duties fall upon articles, which under present circumstances are not capable of being protected, except by actual prohibition. These are the small forms of rod and round iron, hoops and sheets. The introduction of the joint operations of puddling and rolling, has altogether changed the manner of manufacturing these in Europe; they are now, with the exception of sheets, made directly from the pig, by as few operations as common bars; our own puddling forges are adopting the same method, and so soon as they are capable of supplying the market, must drive out the articles of these descriptions, made by those who use merchantable bar iron, and roll it down or slit it. The slitting and rolling mills which are conducted on this last principle, are therefore beyond the reach of support. The inequality in the duty too, is more than the cost of performing the additional operation upon the bar, and is hence rather injurious than otherwise, to the interest of the producers of the raw iron, while it bears with great severity upon those consumers who are themselves manufacturers of hardware. The duty upon these articles should then be adjusted so as to bear the proportion to that upon bar iron, which their values do in the foreign market whence they are derived.

On the other hand, there are certain articles, of which the price of the raw material, whether cast or bar iron, forms the chief value, and which are actually convertible to the same purposes with their base. On these, there can be no question, that every consideration of policy and justice requires that the duty should be raised. Several articles of this description are enumerated by the Philadelphia memorialists, where the fabric is of wrought iron; and it is obvious that there are others, made at a blast furnace from the metal at its first reduction, which might be used as a substance for pig. Such articles, however, cannot be numerous; for iron is, after all, a material of such low price, that it can be hardly wrought into any important species of goods, in which the value of the workmanship will not exceed the cost of the raw article. The *ad valorem* duty must, therefore, in most cases, be an efficient protection, both to the maker of iron and the manufacturer of hardware. Where however it is not, an easy principle will restore the irregularity; for it is only necessary to collect the duties by weight, and affix to them the same rates which the raw iron pays.

The plan we have proposed, of continuing the present duty for a limited time, is consistent with the policy of all civilized nations, who do not hesitate to grant monopolies for definite periods to the inventers of new processes in the arts, and most of whom give equal encouragement to those who merely introduce them. Our government, indeed, has never adopted the latter principle, but it may well be questioned whether it have not in this way prevented the introduction of many important branches of manufacture. The former has been adopted in its full extent, and its utility is unquestioned. If, then, it be sound and highly profitable policy, to grant a monopoly to individuals for limited periods, thereby excluding our own citizens from advantages which in most cases lie open to foreign countries, much more will it be politic and profitable, to protect a whole class of our own artificers from external competition for a similar period, leaving the price to be lessened by the competition that security, from a change of system, will infallibly create. The usual limit of a patent right having been found efficient in drawing forth inventive talent, an equal duration of protecting duty might be depended upon as sufficient to induce the investment of capital in a business whose processes are understood, and in relation to which strict calculations can be made. But these protecting duties must not suddenly cease; for if they do, a spirit of speculation, both on our part and on that of foreign merchants, would infallibly throw into the market an excess of the article from abroad; and although the importer might not be exempted wholly from the ruinous consequence of the over trade, infallible destruction would visit our own establishments. Such was the case in 1816 and 1817. The losses on the iron trade were not confined to our own manufacturers, but visited the importers, whether British or American, and reached in their remote consequences, but with diminished effect, the forges and furnaces of England. The latter were, however, protected by the whole capital of the merchant, which was annihilated before the ruin could reach them, while the American establishments were directly exposed to it. The adventurous spirit of British commerce, in fact, produced on this occasion an effect similar to that which the people of the continent have erroneously ascribed to the government of that country. New markets are no sooner opened, than loads of British fabrics are thrown in, and necessarily sacrificed; those who see no more than their own domestic misfortunes, naturally ascribe to the policy of the nation, what is in fact the misjudged enterprise of rash individuals. The effect has, however, been in many cases the same, as if the act had been the result of a deliberate national system; for the foreign industry has been often prostrated, while the capital of the British has enabled it to bear the momentary shock, and then to replace its losses by the undivided enjoyment of the disputed market.

Having proposed that the duty on imported iron, after remaining for a limited period at its present rate, should thereafter be gradually reduced to a minimum, it remains that we should examine at what rate this minimum should be fixed. This we conceive may be adjusted merely as a question of revenue. Raw iron being a material of great weight, in proportion to its value, cannot be smuggled; it will therefore bear, among all articles, nearly the highest rate of impost, in proportion to its cost. This rate of duty should be calculated upon the higher qualities of wrought and bar iron, and be applied equally to all the different shades of each article. For a wise policy would dictate that the import of the inferior sorts should be more impeded than that of the best descriptions. This is analogous to the system at present sanctioned by law, and is dictated by sound views. Fixing then the minimum duty at about twenty-five per cent, on the value of the better qualities of the two varieties of raw iron, it will amount to about seven and a half dollars on the pig, and fifteen dollars on the bar. To this limit we believe that the duty may be finally reduced, without causing injury to our own trade, provided the present duties remain in force for fourteen years, and be then gradually lessened to this assumed minimum.

It will be seen, that our views neither go the whole length of those of the sticklers for either system, the *tariff* or the *anti-tariff*, — and we fear, that, at the moment, they will be equally objectionable to the advocates of both. We however cannot but believe, that they are founded upon sound and just principles. We give the fullest meed of praise to that policy which has recalled into existence by a protecting duty, the most important of manufactures, because the basis of all the rest. But, we cannot see that it would be judicious to continue this duty, after it shall have produced its whole vivifying effect. While, therefore, on the one hand, it appears to be no more than a fulfilment of a solemn contract, that the manufacture of iron shall be protected, we cannot urge that that protection should continue forever; and, in relation to the diminution of duty, we conceive that it ought to be gradual, and not sudden. Modified in conformity with such principles, we conceive that a "judicious tariff" might be rendered popular in all parts of the Union.

In the northern and eastern states, the tariff policy has no opponents, except in the merchants engaged in foreign commerce; in the western States, the opinion in favour of the present system, is almost unanimous. The southern states, and a portion of the mercantile interest of the north, are alone in direct opposition to protecting duties. The agricultural interest of the north and west, seeing and feeling directly the benefits which the establishment of manufactures confers upon it, has given what is called the American system, — which is in principle, if it err occasionally in detail, the sound and true policy of the nation — its full and undivided support. We cannot but hope to see the day arrive, when the mist raised by designing politicians, and *soi disant* economists, shall be dissipated, and when the southern states will see that they are not merely indirectly, but as directly benefited by the creation of manufacturing industry in the northern districts of the Union, as they have been by that part of the system which has secured them a complete monopoly of the home market for their own products. Of all the states of the Union, Louisiana has derived the most immediate and important advantages from protecting duties, but they have also been shared by her neighbours; and we cannot hesitate to conclude, that, next to Louisiana, South Carolina has been most benefited. The cotton of India, which would have been preferred, from its low price, for the manufacture of the coarse articles with which our factories have in all cases commenced their business, is in fact prohibited; the creation of the growth of sugar has occupied land and capital, which, if applied to the culture of cotton, must have driven the whole upland staple from the markets of the world; and, more than all, a growing domestic demand has arisen, which foreign interference cannot controul or diminish. In return for such advantages, it might fairly have been expected that some burthen would fall upon the southern states, and no doubt it might appear to be capable of plausible proof, that a portion of the increased duties amounted to an actual tax. But this appearance on which so much stress has been laid, is only upon paper, and does not exist in reality, for we believe that they may be challenged, and must fail if they attempt, to prove that the cost of the production of any one staple has been in the slightest degree increased. We believe that it has, on the contrary, diminished. It would lead us too far to show how this has been the natural result: we appeal therefore to the fact alone.

And so in respect to the clamour which it has been attempted to excite among importing merchants, we might appeal to the growing prosperity of that interest, as a proof that the clamour has no foundation. We however believe that the obvious cause lies, in the latter instance, upon the surface, and exists in the plan of credit duties, the wise conception of the illustrious Hamilton, by which, so long as the limit at which smuggling would be profitable, or consumption diminished, is not reached, every addition of duty increases the effective capital, and adds to the net profits of the importer. In illustration of this view of the subject, we may cite the well-established fact, that most of the great mercantile fortunes of our commercial cities, have owed their more important increase to the judicious employment of the capital, thus in effect loaned by the government without interest.

To use the words of the majority of the Committee of the Senate of the United States, quoted at the head of this article:

> "Of all the metals, iron contributes most to the wealth, the comfort, and the improvement of society. It enters most largely into the consumption of all ranks and constitutions of men. It

furnishes the mechanic with his tools, the farmer with the implements of his husbandry, the merchant with the means of fitting
out his ship, and the manufacturer with the very instruments of
his wealth and prosperity."

The wisdom of Europe draws very different conclusions, from a similar view of the importance of iron, from those which are deduced by the majority of the Committee of the Senate.

"The preparation of iron has become the most essential branch of industry, in consequence of the immediate profit it produces to the masters of forges, of the general good that society draws from it, and of the advantages it offers to governments. No other occupies so many arms, produces so active or so constant a circulation of money, or exercises so direct an influence on the riches of the state and the ease of the people. It is therefore the particular interest of every government to favour it, to sustain it by the most efficacious measures, and to carry it to the highest degree of prosperity." *Karsten* — (*Introduction.*)

The measures proposed for this purpose, include bounties, the advance of capital, and the prohibition of foreign iron. Such is the uniform practice of by far the greater part of the nations of Europe. The governments receive the most advantageous returns for such protection.

"In the imposts of all kinds, that it derives directly or indirectly from the establishments themselves, the workmen employed, and the numerous *personnel* whose existence is linked to that of the manufacture of iron. But that which ought most particularly to fix the attention of government, consists in the precious advantages which are derived from it by rural economy, by other branches of industry, and which it affords for internal security and external defence." *Karsten*.

It has been seen, that we cannot consider that measures of such extent are required in our own country. Still, were we, as all European nations are, in direct contact with rival or hostile powers, their necessity would be imperative.

ART. V.

THE SIAMESE TWINS,

The Siamese Twins. A Satirical Tale of the Times, with other Poems, by the Author of Pelham, &c. J. & J. Harper: New-York: pp. 308.

This production furnishes one of the most remarkable instances to be found in the history of literature, of the wide difference between notoriety and merit. No work ever came from the press whose anticipated excellence was more loudly proclaimed, and none, we are persuaded, ever more disappointed high-wrought expectation. That the author of Pelham was about to favour the world with a great poetical production of a satirical character, was announced in the different periodical works, with all that elation and pomposity which indicated the assurance that some important addition to the poetical literature of England, was about to take place. Prophetic eulogy was strained to the uttermost. Public anxiety for the appearance of the mighty work, became all that the booksellers could wish. Every one was not only eager to read, but prepared to admire, and impatient to praise — for the fashion of praising this author, whether he wrote well or ill, had set in; and who in this age of polite pretensions, would dare to be unfashionable?

Nor has the attentive author himself been deficient on this occasion, in the fatherly duty of bespeaking public opinion in favour of his offspring. In a preface remarkable for that startling species of modesty by which a man becomes the trumpeter of his own greatness, he predicts that, if not immediately, at least in eight or ten years hence, his works will make such an impression, as to occasion a revolution in the poetical taste of mankind, and become the model of a new school in the "Divine Art." The confidential puffers to whom the idea was imparted, in despite of whatever doubts they might entertain on the subject, scrupled not to give publicity to the prediction. A work destined to such an illustrious career, could not fail to be endowed with an exalted and overpowering excellence of some kind, and also of a kind different altogether from any that had hitherto given satisfaction to the readers of poetry. The poetical tastes and habits of our nature were, in fact, to be entirely changed by the influence of this mighty satire. No wonder, therefore, that curiosity respecting the work was sufficiently awakened to occasion for it a large demand on its first appearance.

Many of the conductors of the periodical press, who gave publicity to this exaggerated strain of praise, were, no doubt, sceptical as to its being altogether merited, and must have acted from motives either of interest or of courtesy. Yet there may have been some who believed in the possibility of the wonders which were predicted. Indeed, in this strange age, when miracles are scarcely to be accounted wonders—when ships are propelled without wind, and carriages without horses—when schoolboys and journeymen printers overturn governments and make and unmake kings with almost as much facility as the manager of a play-house casts the character of a drama; what extraordinary things may not with propriety be credited? Even philosophy may now, without reproach, believe in absurdity; and thoughtless paragraphists, without being laughed at, may be permitted to suppose that an adventurous rhymester may speak truth, when he asserts that he is about to revolutionize the principles of poetical taste and composition!

When mutation is the order of the day, why may not human nature itself be changed? When all physical obstructions to locomotion, and all impediments to the march of mind, are yielding to the ingenuity and activity of man, why may not his own natural feelings and dispositions also yield, and become changed? But hold—the author of this Siamese satire has discovered that they have already changed! Not merely have the opinions and pursuits of society taken a new direction, and the habits and views of the present, become different from those of the past generation—this would be readily admitted—but a much more important alteration in the constitution of man, he affirms, has taken place. It is not only the *condition*, but the *nature* of the species that he asserts to be changed. With the last generation, all the old impulses of the heart—all susceptibility of love or hatred, friendship or enmity, pity or revenge—all feelings of pride, avarice, ambition, or love of fame—all emotions of joy, grief, anger, remorse—all generosity, charity, desire of happiness, and self-preservation—all, all are passed away!

"Has not a new generation," our author asks, in his odd and hardly intelligible preface, "arisen? Has not a new impetus been given to the age? Do not *new feelings* require to be expressed? and are there not new readers to be propitiated, who sharing *but in a feeble degree the former enthusiasm*, will turn, not with languid attention, to the claims of fresh aspirants."

These are some of the changes which have brought about, as he imagines—the circumstances that call for the new and "*less* enthusiastic" school of poetry, which, founded by him, is to secure the admiration of at least part of the present, and the whole of the ensuing generation. "A poet," he says, "who aspires to reputation, must be adapted to the coming age, not rooted to that which is already gliding away." He admits that "the worn out sentiments, the affectations and the weaknesses of our departed bards, may, by the elder part of the community, be still considered components of a deep philosophy, or the signs of a superior mind." But, for this unfortunate circumstance, which militates so much against the immediate success of his new school, he consoles himself with the persuasion that "the *young* have formed a nobler estimate of life, and a habit of reasoning, at once founded upon a homelier sense, and yet aspiring to more elevated conclusions."

What this, as well as many other equally awkward sentences in this presumptuous preface, exactly means, it is not easy to say. Our sons, on whose admiration of his poetry, Mr. Bulwer depends for the success of his new system, are, in order to qualify themselves for relishing its beauties, to form a *nobler* estimate than we entertain of life, while their habits of reasoning are to be founded on a *homelier* sense; and yet, homely as they are to be in their reasoning, they are to aspire to *more elevated* conclusions! If, indeed, such inconsistencies are to characterize our sons; if their intellects are to be so utterly confused and perplexed as is here predicted, they may possibly become admirers of the new school, of which the redoubtable satire before us is to be the origin. But we hope better things of our posterity. We cannot think that their natural feelings will vary so very far from our own, as to induce them to prefer insipid verbosity and unintelligible doggerel, to the animating strains of genuine poetry, or the sprightly wit and stinging ridicule of true satire.

Since the work which was to perform such miracles has appeared, and has been found so egregiously to disappoint expectation, why do those who puffed it on trust, still continue to extol it? The expression of their favourable anticipations might be excused; for they may have believed all that they asserted. But their eyes must now be open. The most prejudiced, on perusing the work, must be convinced of its imbecility as a satire, and its insipidity as a poem. Why, then, persist in error? Complaisance to the prevailing fashion, and a desire to swim with the current, may be the feelings which generally prompt to such conduct. But they are poor apologies for wilfully deceiving the public in a matter so essential to the interests of poetical literature. The critic who knowingly recommends an undeserving poem, ought to be aware that he is contributing to destroy the public confidence in all new poetry; for when men find that tame and uninteresting works are so freely recommended, they very naturally conclude that the times produce none others worthy of recommendation.

We should think, indeed, that experience had, by this time, taught the world the little reliance which ought to be placed generally on contemporary criticism, particularly that description of it usually found in newspapers. But the wide diffusion of this species of periodical work, gives them an influence which no experience, however palpable, of their erroneous judgments in literary matters, has yet been able to counteract. The public, in truth, has hitherto had its attention but little drawn towards this subject. The fate of a new book seems to be a matter so uninteresting to any but the author and the publisher, that whether editors speak of it favourably or unfavourably, or pass over it with entire neglect, is considered of no importance. It is forgotten that *good* literature forms the chief and most permanent glory of a country; that its prosperity is, therefore, of much national value, and ought, for the public benefit, to be assiduously promoted. But the chance of good literature being properly encouraged, will be ever extremely small, so long as worthless productions are forced into even temporary eclat, by those ready and often glowing commendations of careless editors, which must always, more or less, give direction to public patronage.

There is an erroneous opinion, unfortunately too prevalent among all classes, that no book can become generally noticed and much praised in the periodical works, but in consequence of its merit. To those who hold this opinion, the system of reverberating praise from one journal to another, must be unknown. In this country this system is, at present, carried to a great extent. It is chiefly produced by indolence or want of leisure, preventing our editors from carefully reading and judging for themselves, aided by a desire which actuates many of them to be thought fashionable in their opinions. The literary idol of the day is generally set up in the English metropolis. Of course, the fashion of worshipping him commences there. We soon hear of him on this side of the ocean. We wait not to examine whether he be entitled to homage. We take that for granted, since we are told that he is considered so in London. With slavish obsequiousness, we hasten to follow the capricious example of the great metropolis, and shout pæans for the fashionable idol, with as much zeal as if we really discerned in his works merit sufficiently exalted to entitle him to such applause, although the probability is, that, while we are bestowing it, we have scarcely glanced over his productions.

Now all this is, on our parts, exceedingly ridiculous and irrational. It not only exposes our servility, but it betrays our ignorance of many of the temporary excitements in favour of certain authors and their works, which take place in London. It shows that we are not aware of the fact, that, in the majority of cases, the rage for a new book, is owing to circumstances not at all connected with its merit. An influential and enterprising publisher,—a striking or a popular subject,—a sounding title,—a bold,—a wealthy or an eccentric author,—and, above all, a continued series of well-managed puffs, invariably do much more towards making a new book fashionable, than any excellence it may possess; and the inducement to purchase it is more frequently the knowledge that it is fashionable, than the conviction that it is good. Hence, it is to their title-pages, rather than to their nature or quality, that new books are mostly indebted for their immediate success. Their permanent success—that is, their enduring fame—is another matter. Merit, and merit only, can secure that; for it is the result of the cool and deliberate approbation which is awarded by the judgment of mankind, when the adventitious circumstances which first excited attention towards the book, have passed away, and can operate no longer on curiosity. The history of literature amply proves this. Books have often had, for a time, great mercantile value, and been highly profitable to the booksellers, that have been utterly worthless in a literary point of view. Of this fact the book-dealers are so well aware, that, rather than risk the expense of publishing the most beautiful composition of an unknown author, they will pay largely for manuscripts of the merest trash, from the pen of one to whom some lucky accident has already drawn public attention. Many of our well-meaning echoers of the London puffs of new books, are certainly ignorant of this circumstance, or they would not lend their aid to give circulation and temporary repute to much of the vile literature, which, under the names of novels, poems, travels, &c. the press of London has so largely poured forth, during the last eight or ten years, to the great deterioration not only of the literary taste, but of the manners and morals of the age.

It is indeed a sad mistake to suppose, that nothing but the literary excellence of a new book, renders it saleable. Yet it is a mistake so very general, that the booksellers find that the most effectual mode of recommending a new work, is, to allege that it *sells* rapidly. Who does not know, when a book with the reputation of being in great demand, comes amongst us, the eagerness with which it is sought after? No matter how dull it may be, while it is considered saleable, it is perused with delight. A thousand beauties are discovered in it, which cool and unprepossessed judgment could never discern; and, as to faults, although they should stare the deluded reader in the face, as thickly and visibly as trees in a forest, he will doubt the accuracy of his own sensations, rather than admit that he perceives them. Such, over weak minds, is the magic influence of a fashionable name,—nay, such is the influence, when the name is only *supposed* to be fashionable.

That the work before us would sell well, at least for a season, let its poetry be ever so bad, was to be expected, from the circumstances under which it appeared. Its publishers, Colburn and Bentley, are now the most fashionable in London, and are considered to possess more influence over the periodical works, than even the magnificent Murray; its author is a man of bustle, boldness, and notoriety, who has acquired considerable repute as the writer of three or four novels, which got into extensive circulation by professing, however untruly, to give genuine and unsparing delineations of fashionable life. To speak technically, *his name was up*; and, by the aid of this lucky elevation, his active publishers could not fail to dispose of an edition or two of his satire, in despite of its worthlessness as a literary performance.

We have thus, we imagine, satisfactorily shown that it is possible for a work to be, for a time, noted, saleable and fashionable, without possessing any great share of literary merit. We may, therefore, be allowed to deny, that the present demand for this poem, which, we believe, will be of but brief continuance, is any evidence of its deserving that unlimited homage which its author claims for it. That it will ever effect the great poetical revolution which he so modestly anticipates, we imagine that, by this time, few are more inclined to believe, than ourselves. From its appearance, therefore, we feel no alarm for the stability of that reputation which our favourite bards have gained by those immortal works, to whose noble and animating strains, the hearts of millions have so often responded!

But, it is time that we should enter into some examination of the character of this work, and show our reasons for the disapprobation of it as a poem and a satire, which we have so freely expressed.

It will be admitted, we presume, that, when an author does not succeed in accomplishing his design, his work is a failure. The design of the author of this poem was, as we are informed by the title-page, to write a satire, has he done so? Those who are loudest in commendation of the poem, have acknowledged its satirical portions to be feeble, and without point. But they contend that it contains a sufficiency of good poetry of another description, to atone for this defect. We confess that we have not been fortunate enough, after a careful perusal, to discover this redeeming poetry. Whether it be of the sentimental, descriptive, or ethical species, we therefore cannot tell. Perhaps it is an ingenious mingling of them in one mass, in which the beauties of each, conceal those of the others from view? If so, how many disinterested readers will submit to the trouble of extricating them from the confusion in which they lie, so as to see them distinctly, and become fully aware of their *latent* splendour? We attempted, as in duty bound, to hunt for these gems. We discovered a few that sparkled a little,—but they were indeed so few, and their lustre so faint, that we could not consider them worth the labour of exploring one moiety of the abundance of rubbish in which they are buried. We believe that the generality of readers will be equally disappointed; and that the book will be almost invariably laid down with a feeling that it is tedious, awkward, and dull,—in short, in respect to its *poetical* as well as its satirical character, a failure without redemption.

But the author calls it a satire. It is therefore as a satire, that it ought to be judged. In our opinion, it is no more a satire than a sermon; nay, we have read sermons in which the satiric thong is wielded with much more effect against wickedness and folly, than in this production. We need not enter into a philological explanation of the term satire,—the word is common enough, and we presume that every reader who understands plain English, knows its meaning. To render vice disgusting, and folly ridiculous, is the legitimate office of the satirist. Sarcasm and wit are his most usual and effectual weapons. Ridicule and reprobation are also used; the former when the intention is to excite derision, and the latter when the arousing of indignation is the object. The great aim of the satirist ought always to be the reformation of depraved morals, corrupt institutions, absurd customs, or offensive manners. The contemporary prevalence of such, is what excites his indignation, or provokes his ridicule; and, if he possesses power and dexterity to apply the lash, he performs a real service to society, and acquires a deserved and enviable name among the useful and agreeable writers of the day.

Has Mr. Bulwer applied the lash in this manner? Against what vice does he awaken the indignation of his readers, or what folly does he expose to their contempt? We ask for information, for we have not, with our best efforts, been able ourselves to make the discovery. It is true, that, in the perusal of his work, we met with some awkward attempts to be witty at the expense of Basil Hall, the Duke of Wellington, Thomas Moore, Joseph Hume, and two or three others of the conspicuous characters of the times. But, if satire never launches keener arrows against these men, than are to be found in this book, we fear that, whatever may be their faults or foibles, no dread of her power will induce them to reform. The only feelings they can experience from the harmless missiles of Mr. Bulwer, are pity for his vanity, and contempt for his weakness.

There is but one passage in this long poem which contains upwards of eight thousand lines, that deserves to be called satirical. It is in relation to the missionary Hodges. In this some tolerable *hits* are made at the union of selfishness and prejudice which too frequently characterize the religious missionaries of all sects, who are employed by the zeal of the wealthy and pious at home, to convert to Christianity the heathen inhabitants of foreign countries. The missionary in question, who is the only character in the work drawn with any power of dramatic conception, is represented as haranguing the people of Siam on the inferiority of their institutions to those of England, (in which, by the by, neither Americans nor Englishmen will be apt to discover much satire,) and threatening, in language as coarse as that of the canting Maworm, to reform them, whether they will or not, from the evil ways of their ancestors. We shall quote part of the passage, and as it is unquestionably the cleverest satirical portion of the whole poem, the friends of Mr. Bulwer cannot accuse us of doing him injustice by the selection.—

> "Accordingly our saint one day,
> Into the market took his way,

Climbed on an empty tub, that o'er
Their heads he might declaim at ease,
And to the rout began to roar
In wretched Siamese.
'Brethren! (for every one's my fellow,
Tho' I am white, and you are yellow,)
Brethren! I came from lands afar
To tell you all—what fools you are!
Is slavery, pray, so soft, and glib a tie,
That you prefer the chain to liberty?
Is Christian faith a melancholy tree,
That you will only sow idolatry?
Just see to what good laws can bring lands,
And hear an outline of old England's.
Now, say if *here* a lord should hurt you,
Are you made whole by legal virtue?
For ills by battery or detraction,
Say, can you bring at once your action?
And are the rich not much more sure
To gain a verdict than the poor?
With us alike the poor or rich,
Peasant or prince, no matter which—
Justice to all the law dispenses,
And all it costs—are the expenses!
Here if an elephant you slay,
Your very lives the forfeit pay:
Now that's a *quid pro quo*—too seri-
Ous much for beasts *naturæ feræ*.

* * * * *

* * * * *

These are the thing's that best distinguish men—
These make the glorious boast of Englishmen!
More could I tell you were there leisure,
But I have said enough to please, sure:
Now then if you the resolution
Take for a British constitution,
A British king, church, commons, peers—
I'll be your guide! dismiss your fears.
With Hampden's name and memory warm you!
And, d—n you all—but I'll reform you!
As for the dogs that wont be free,
We'll give it them most handsomely;
To church with scourge and halter lead 'em,
And thrash the rascals into freedom."

This fine speech, it appears, had much the same effect on its auditors, that we believe Mr. Bulwer's poem will have on nine-tenths of his readers;—it produced a sensation of disdain for the understanding as well as the principles of its author. Under the influence of this feeling, the men of Siam could not forbear executing a practical joke on the orator. They elevated him in a palanquin, raised by means of tall poles, to a great height above their heads; from which altitude, after parading him in mock triumph through the streets of their chief city, they, with little regard to consequences, tossed him into the air. The poem says—

> "So high he went, with such celerity,
> It seemed as for some god-like merit he
> Carried from earth, like great Alcides,
> To Jupiter's ambrosial side is.
> But, oh! as maiden speakers break
> Down when their highest flight they take;
> Ev'n so, (while fearing to be crushed
> Each idler from beneath him dodges),
> Swift, heavy—like an avalanche—rushed
> To earth the astonished form of Hodges.
> He lay so flat, he lay so still,
> He seemed beyond all farther ill.
> They pinched his side, they shook his head,
> And then they cried, 'The man is dead!'
> On this, each felt no pleasing chill;
> For ev'n among the Bancockeans,
> A gentleman for fun to kill,
> Is mostly punished—in plebeians.
> They stare—look serious—mutter—cough—
> And then, without delay, sneak off;
> Nor at a house for succour knocked, or
> Thought once of sending for the doctor."

The twins, Chang and Ching, remain behind, and taking pity on the maltreated missionary, convey him to their father's house, which was convenient. Here he is treated with kindness, and soon recovers of the contusions and a broken leg, occasioned by his fall.

A notable scheme now seized the fertile brain of the money loving missionary. The *lusus naturæ* which connected the bodies of the twins, he conceived would render their exhibition profitable in England. He obtained the consent of their father to carry them to Europe, by stipulating to allow them one-half of the earnings of their exhibition. The acquiescence of the youths themselves he easily procured by inflaming their curiosity to witness the glory and happiness of England, which he described in the most glowing terms of national panegyric.

The twins, however, resolved to consult one of the magicians of the country relative to the result of their intended enterprise, before they should commit themselves to the care of an absolute stranger who was to convey them so far from home. The account of this consultation—the temple of the magician—his manner of consulting the fates, and the mystical style of his addressing the twins, form by much the most fanciful and readable portion of the book, and would certainly entitle the author to some credit for wild and weird conceptions, were it not for the unfortunate circumstance, that the whole is a palpable imitation of the celebrated incantation scene in Der Freischutz. It is also infested with the besetting sin of the whole poem, prolixity. Mr. Bulwer too plainly shows in this work, that he is a bookmaker by profession, and if the faculty of hammering a given number of ideas into as many words as possible, be a useful branch of the craft, it is one in which he has assuredly few competitors.

The arrival of Hodges and the twins in London, is at length announced in the newspapers, and then begins what the author unquestionably intended should be the principal business of the poem—namely, the quizzing of London life and manners—or to use his own phrase, satirizing the times. The idea of bringing Oriental strangers to Europe in order to exhibit their surprise at witnessing customs and manners totally different from those of their own country, is rather stale, and the humour of it, if there be any humour in it, has been exhausted by much finer writers than Mr. Bulwer has as yet shown himself to be. Various essayists, both of France and England, have had recourse to this method of exposing the vices and absurdities of their respective countries. Turkish spies, Persian envoys, and Chinese philosophers, have all been brought into requisition for this purpose. No novelty, therefore, can be claimed for the employment of our Siamese adventurers on such trodden ground. It is, indeed, sufficiently apparent, that the idea of making them a vehicle for satire upon the English, was suggested by Goldsmith's Citizen of the World. To try his strength with such a writer as Goldsmith, especially in the walks of satire, was at least courageous on the part of Bulwer; and if any circumstance could, in our estimation, atone for his woful failure, it would be the hardihood which induced him to make the attempt. We believe no reader ever became wearied of perusing Goldsmith's Citizen of the World. But how any reader can toil through this Siamese production, without becoming exhausted, we own is beyond our comprehension.

In London, the twins meet with various adventures, which, no doubt, the author intended should be extremely amusing to the reader. To us they appear extremely jejune and silly. For instance, Lady Jersey sends one of them a ticket of admission to Almacks, without recollecting to pay the same compliment to the other. On appearing for entrance, the door-keeper refuses to admit him who had been neglected. This obstacle, of course, prevents the other from availing himself of his right to enter. Lady Cowper, however, very soon sets all right by furnishing them with another ticket. Now what there is either facetious or satirical in this, we confess we cannot conceive. Equally silly is the incident of the one brother being seized by a recruiting sergeant who had enlisted him, while the other is arrested by a bailiff for debt. But as the brothers cannot be separated, they get clear, the recruiting officer not daring to carry off Ching who had not enlisted, and the bailiff being equally afraid of the consequence of imprisoning Chang against whom he had no writ—an old joke.

Now such bungling inventions appear to us insufferable. In the first place, there is no emotion whatever, either of surprise, merriment, or pity, awakened by the narrative, and in the next, the occurrences are so contrary to all probability, that even poetical license, in its fullest range, will not sanction their introduction. The deformity of the twins would render either of them ineligible to be enlisted. The bailiff's writ might, it is true, authorize the arrest of one only; but even that is inconsistent with the statement previously made that their earnings and expenses were all in common. We should suppose, therefore, that no creditor would make such an invidious distinction between partners so closely connected. These inconsistencies, however, might be pardoned, if the stories were told with sufficient sprightliness and vigour to make them interesting. But when an ill-contrived tale is drowsily told, the reader must possess an immense fund of good nature not to scold the author in his heart.

We shall pass over the rest of these dull adventures, which rebuke no vice, and satirize no folly, and shall give a very brief outline of the remainder of the poem. The brothers, unlike the real twins from whom the title of the poem is borrowed, are represented as of entirely different characters. Chang's disposition is grave, contemplative, and sentimental, while Ching is light-hearted, gay, and volatile. Their protector, Hodges, has a handsome daughter, with whom the meditative Chang falls in love; but, without any apparent cause, he imagines that she has given her heart to Ching. He becomes exceedingly jealous, and absurdly enough, considering the nature of their connexion, meditates the murder of his brother. He however discovers his mistake in time to prevent the deed, and feels a reasonable share of remorse. In the meantime, Mary, the lady in question, who commiserates their condition, contrives, while they are asleep, to introduce a surgeon and his assistant, who successfully cut through the connecting bond of flesh, and, to the great joy of Chang, who had long felt much mortification at the unnatural union, they are separated. Chang now cherishes strong hopes of becoming acceptable to Mary, which are destined soon to be blasted for ever. By an incident which detracts much from the sentimental dignity with which he has been hitherto invested, for it represents him as an eavesdropper, he discovers that she is irrevocably engaged to her cousin, who is called Julian Laneham. This discovery arouses him to a certain fit of magnanimity. He understands that Mary's father objects to her union with Laneham, on account of the young man's poverty. He suddenly disappears; and four days afterwards, two letters are received, one by Hodges, and one by Ching, which, as the author says, "shows the last *dénouement* of the story." The public curiosity had rendered the brothers rich; and in his letter to Hodges, Chang generously bestows on him his share of their property, on condition that he will give his daughter to Laneham.

The old gentlemen agrees to the compact; and if the reader should have patience enough to carry him so far through the book, he will, towards its conclusion, be rewarded with a marriage, according to the old established laws of romance writing. Why did Mr. Bulwer so far forget the "originality of matter and of manner," in other words, the new school of poetry, which he promised us in the preface, as to put us off with so trite a conclusion?

In a passage towards the close of the poem, the indomitable egotism of our author appears, in a curious allusion which he makes to the failure of his efforts to become a member of parliament at the last general election. His hero Laneham, for he is the true hero of the work, had been a more successful candidate for the people's favour. The poet says, without jealousy, we presume,—

"Moreover in the late election
He won a certain Burgh's affection.
Dined—drank—made love to wife and daughter,
Poured ale and money forth like water,
And won St. Stephen's Hall to hear
This parliament *may* last a year!
The sire's delight you'll fancy fully—
He thinks he sees a second Tully;
And gravely says he will dispense
With Fox's force and Brinsley's wit,
So that our member boast the sense
Of that great statesmen—Pilot Pitt!
For me, my hope lies somewhat deeper;
We'll now, they say, be governed *cheaper!*
So Julian, pour your wrath on robbing,
And keep a careful eye on jobbing.
If you should waver in your choice
To whom to pledge your vote and voice,
You'll waver only, we presume,
Between an Althorpe and a Hume.
But mind—ONE vote—o'er all you hold,
And let the BALLOT conquer GOLD.
Don't utterly forget those asses,—
Ridden so long,—the lower classes;
But waking from sublimer *visions*,
Just see, poor things! to their *provisions*.
Let them for cheap bread be your debtor,
Cheap justice, too—that's almost better.
And though not bound to either College,
Don't clap a turnpike on their knowledge.

* * * * *

And ne'er forget this simple rule, boy,
Time is an everlasting schoolboy,
And as his trowsers he outgoes,
Be decent, nor begrudge him clothes.

* * * * *

In these advices towards your policy,
Many, dear Julian, will but folly see;
Yet what I preach to you to act is
But what *had been your author's practice*,
Had the mercurial star that beams

Upon elections blessed his dreams,
Had—but we ripen with delay,
And every dog shall have his day!"

From the last couplet, it appears, that our author has not yet relinquished his expectations of being gratified with a seat in St. Stephens.

In the following concluding lines, which succeed those we have just quoted, the Twins are finally disposed of. We insert them here as a notable instance of long efforts to kindle a blaze, at last dying away in the suffocation of their own smoke.—

"And Ching?—poor fellow!—Ching can never
His former spirits quite recover;
Yet he's agreeable as ever,
And plays the C——k as a lover.
In every place he's vastly *fêted*,
His name's in every lady's book;
And as a wit I hear he's rated
Between the Rogers's and Hook.

But Chang?—of him was known no more,
Since, Corsair like, he left the shore.
Wrapped round his fate the cloud unbroken,
Will yield our guess nor clew nor token.
He runs unseen his lonely race,
And if the mystery e'er unravels
The web around the wanderer's trace—
I fear we scarce could print his travels.
Since tourists every where have flocked,
The market's rather overstocked—
And so we leave the lands that need 'em
Throughout this 'dark terrestrial ball,'
To be well visited by freedom,—
And slightly nibbled at by Hall!"

ART. VI.

EUROPE AND AMERICA;

Europe and America; or, the relative state of the Civilized World at a future period. Translated from the German of Dr. C. F. Von Schmidt-Phiseldek, Doctor of Philosophy, one of his Danish Majesty's Counsellors of State, Knight of Dannebrog, &c. &c. By Joseph Owen. Copenhagen: 1820.

Although the translator of this book professes in his Preface to have been principally induced to undertake the task by "the desire of being the humble instrument of imparting to the American nation, that picture of future grandeur and happiness, which the author so prophetically holds out to them," we believe it is but little known among the readers of this country. Yet it is in every respect a very interesting and curious work. It will be seen by the title-page, that it was not only translated into, but printed in English, at Copenhagen, with the view of disseminating a knowledge of its contents among the people of the United States. Yet we do not recollect that it was noticed at the time of its publication in any of our critical journals, and the only copy that has ever fallen under our notice is that now before us, which has been in our possession many years. Nevertheless, it is the work of a man of very extensive views, and of deep sagacity. His speculations on the state of the different kingdoms of Europe, in relation to the past and the present, seem to us equally just and profound; and the predictions which ten years ago the author announced to the world, are every day, nay, almost every hour, becoming matters of history.

It has been said, and said reproachfully, that the people of the United States are somewhat boastful and presumptuous. One reason doubtless is, that they have had to bear up on one hand against much obloquy and injustice, and on the other against certain airs of affected superiority on the part of the nations of Europe, equally offensive. Those who are perpetually assailed, are perpetually called upon to defend themselves; and what in other cases would be an offensive pretension, is, in ours, simply self-defence. It is not boasting, but a manly assertion of what is due to ourselves, in reply to those who take from us what is our right. But even if the charge of national pride were true, we are among those who rather approve than lament it. National pride is a commendable and manly feeling; it is the parent of virtue and greatness—the foundation of a noble character; and if the nation which has led the way in the bright path of freedom—which, young as it is, has become already the beacon, the example, the patriarch of the struggling nations of the world—has not a fair right to be proud, we know not on what basis national pride ought to erect itself.

For these reasons, we feel no hesitation in calling the attention of the people of the United States, to a work eminently calculated to awaken the most lofty anticipations of the destiny which awaits them. Nothing but good can come of such contemplations of the future. They will serve to impress upon the nation the necessity of being prepared for such high destiny; of fitting herself to maintain it with honour and dignity; of attaching herself, heart and hand, body and soul, to that sacred union of opinions, interests, and reflections, which alone can lead us steadily onward in the path of prosperity, happiness, and glory.

> "The 4th of July in the year 1776," observes Dr. Von Schmidt, "points out the commencement of a new period in the history of the world. Not provoked to resistance by the intolerable oppression of tyrannical power, but merely roused by the arbitrary encroachments upon well earned, and hitherto publicly acknowledged principles, the people of the United States of North America declared themselves on that memorable day independent of the dominion of the British Islands, generally speaking mild and benevolent in itself, and under which they had hitherto stood as colonies, in a state, not of slavish servitude, but of partial guardianship, under the protection of the mother country."

The author has here marked the nice and peculiar feature which distinguishes the American Revolution from all others, and confers on it a degree of philosophical dignity. It was not a ferment arising from momentary impatience of existing and operating hardships; nor the result of extensive distresses pressing upon a large mass of the nation. When the people of the United Colonies rose in resistance to the mother country, they were in possession of a greater portion of all the useful means of happiness, than the mother country itself. It was not therefore a revolution originating in the belly, but the head; it was a revolution brought about by principles, not by distresses. The early emigrants to the new world, brought these principles with them from England;—every year added to their strength, and every accession of strength, brought the crisis nearer to maturity. The annals of each one of the colonies, exhibit every where evidence of the existence of this leaven of freedom, which was perpetually rising and agitating the surface; and, although like the eruption of a volcano, it broke forth at first in one particular spot, it was only from accidental causes. The whole interior was equally in a ferment, and the boiling mass must have forced a vent somewhere, and soon. It had long been evident, that, wherever the pressure should be greatest, there would be the point of resistance.

That the American revolution, though unquestionably precipitated, was not produced by a sudden excitement originating in any particular measure of the British government, we think must appear to all those who read with attention the early records of our colonial history. As long ago as the year 1635, representations were made to the government of England, touching the disloyalty of the people of Massachusetts.

"The Archbishop of Canterbury," says Hutchinson, "the famous High Churchman Laud, kept a jealous eye over New England. One Burdett of Piscataqua, was his correspondent. A copy of a letter to the Archbishop, wrote by Burdett, was found in his study, and to this effect: 'That he delayed going to England, that he might freely inform himself of the state of the place as to *allegiance*, for it was not new discipline which was aimed at, but *sovereignty*; and that it was accounted perjury and treason in their general court, to speak of appeals to the king.'"[4]

But to return to the immediate subject before us. Dr. Von Schmidt-Phiseldek, after stating the result of this declaration in the establishment of our independence, proceeds to notice the second war between the United States and England, in which the former successfully maintained the positions she had assumed, as the grounds of hostility:—

"By these occurrences," he says, "which we have only cursorily touched upon, the North American confederacy had tried her strength, preserved her dignity by the rejection of illegal pretensions, and vigorously proved and maintained her right as an active member in the scale of nations, to take part in the grand affairs of the civilized world. *From that moment, the impulse to a new change of events, ceased to proceed exclusively from the old continent, and it is possible that in a short time it will emanate from the new one.*"

The author then proceeds to deduce the attempts of the South American Provinces, which, however, at that period, had not been consummated, from the example of North America, which had inspired them with the desire of emancipation:—

"This word, as intimating the resistance of a people feeling themselves at maturity, to their wonted tutelage, and desirous of taking upon themselves the management of their own affairs, most suitably expresses the spirit of the times, *which, being called to light in 1776, has spread itself over the new and old world.*"

Having indicated his belief, that the South American States will acquire independence, Dr. Von Schmidt-Phiseldck gives it as his opinion, "that the similitude of their constitutional forms, and an equal interest in rejecting the European powers, will unite these new states in a close compact with the North American confederacy; and, if a quarter of a century only elapsed before North America began to act externally with vigour, it may be presumed that the younger states of the Southern Continent, endowed with more ample resources, and more ancient culture, will require a shorter period to arrive at a state of respectable force."

Having traced a rapid sketch of the situation and prospects of the new world, the author next turns his attention to the old governments of Europe, of which he gives a masterly analysis:—

"The new spirit which had been called to life on the other side of the Atlantic, and the universal fermentation it caused, hap-

[4] Hutchinson's History of Massachusetts, Vol. I, pages 84, 85.

pened at a period in which the most excessive laxity reigned predominant on the old continent. The political existence of the people was for the most part extinguished; their active industry had been directed abroad, and the governments finding no opposition or dangerous collisions internally, followed with the stream. Commerce, exportations, colonial systems, every means of acquiring money, were cherished and protected,—riches presenting the only possibility of investing the low with consideration and influence, and the high with power and inordinate dominion. The maxims by which the nations were governed, lay less in the ground pillars of an existing constitution, than in the changeable systems of the cabinets, and the character of their rulers; there remained, for the most part, nothing for the great body of the people, but to be spectators.

"Germany, the grand heart of Europe, presented now nothing more than the shadow of a political body united in one common confederacy; the imperial governments, as also the administration of the federal laws, were without energy, and united efforts to repel invasions from abroad, had not been witnessed since the fear of Turkish power had ceased to operate. The larger states had outgrown their obedience, and often ranged themselves in opposition to the head, which was scarcely able to protect either itself or the weaker states against injuries.

"The internal affairs of the individual vassal states, were exclusively conducted according to the will of their regents; the energy and importance of the representative popular states, were become dormant, and the standing armies which had been introduced by degrees even into the smallest principalities, since the peace of Westphalia, being perfectly foreign to the hearts and dispositions of the people, threw an astonishing weight into the scale of unlimited sovereignty. Being mercenary soldiers recruited from every nation, modelled upon a system of subordination, and raised by Frederick of Prussia to the highest pitch of perfection, they had been accomplices in diffusing this system of despotism over all the relations of the state, *and in leaving the people who were freed from military services, nothing but the acquisition of gain.*

"Agriculture, agreeably to the direction given it, had been improved, and with a population increased; industry supported by the progress of the mechanical arts, had also been considerably extended. But each separate state had its own little jealous feelings of aggrandisement, its own petty internal policy, viewing its neighbour with a jealous eye; and the whole of Germany never reaped any beneficial result from a system, which, had it been general, would have conduced highly to the wealth and power of the confederated states, of which it was composed. All these various institutions, at the same time that they conflicted with each other, were reared on loose foundations, and it was evident must fall together, on the first external shock,—circumstances like these were incapable of producing an universal national character. There, where no reciprocal tie binds the individuals of a state together, who, living under the equal laws of one community, ought to form one solid whole, the spirit of the nation loses itself in different directions; the attainment of individual welfare is possible in such a state of things, but never will a sense of what is universally good and great, be promoted.

"If in Germany," proceeds the author, "where the imperial crown represented a mere shadow, deprived of power and consequence, the mighty vassals were all; in France the crown was every thing, after it had subdued the powerful barons of the country. The people represented, indeed, one body, but were deprived, like the several German states, of all political weight, and were arbitrarily subjected to every impulse of the government. The same was the case with Spain and Portugal, where religious intolerance more powerfully suppressed every utterance of contrary opinions, and every doctrine which might lead to a deviation from the maxims of the state, so intimately connected with those of the priesthood. The latter, chained since Methuen's celebrated treaty, to the monopoly of England from which it had vainly attempted to free itself under Pombal's administration, was nearly sunk to the condition of a British colony working its gold mines in the Brazils for the benefit of the proud islanders.

"Italy, parcelled out amongst different powers, presented upon the whole, the same political aspect as Germany, only with this difference, that it was totally divested of the shadow of unity, which the latter at least appeared to present. Upper, and a great part of middle Italy, being dismembered, were entirely subservient to foreign impulse. The lower part, with the fertile island on the other side of the Pharos, presented, to be sure, since 1735, the outward appearance of one national whole, but was too weak to withstand the fate of the more powerful Bourbon families, from which, according to treaties, it had derived its sovereigns. There reigned in the papal state alone, which could not derive its weight from its worldly sovereignty, but from the spiritual supremacy of its ruler, the ancient maxims of the Romish pontificate, with the economical state faults of a clerical government. But the consideration and the power of the former were visibly sunk; the journeys of the pope of that period to Vienna, were like the contemporary ones of the Hierarch of Thibet to China, rather prejudicial, than favourable to spiritual dignity; and the faulty internal administration of the state seemed to invite every attempt at innovation.

The republics on the east and the west of the Adriatic Gulf, were, since the rise of the other great naval states, only the ruins of past glory, sinking daily into insignificance. But notwithstanding this, neither was the image of former greatness blotted from their memories, nor a proper feeling for it extinguished in the minds of the inhabitants of the luxuriant peninsula. The pride of the more noble, fed itself on the sublime remains of Iionian antiquity; and the monuments of the golden age of the family of Medicis indemnified a people given to the arts, and full of imagination for the loss of present grandeur, and kept up a lively anticipation of a better futurity, founded on the merits of its ancestors.

"Helvetia, hemmed in between Italy, Germany, and France, by its mountains, continued in the peaceable enjoyment of its liberties through the respect its venerable age had universally diffused. Nevertheless, the disturbances at Geneva, and the increased spirit of emigration, were sufficient to indicate that a people who become indifferent to the present order of things, would willingly have recourse to a system of innovation, and that the ancient ties which had held the Swiss nation so many centuries together, were gradually relaxing.

"The dissolution of the existing form of government, in the north-western Netherlands, which ought never to have been separated from the German corporation, was more visibly approaching. The unwieldiness of their disorganized union had no remedy to administer to the decline of their commerce, and naval power, which became more and more felt, being a natural consequence of the daily concentration of the larger states; and it was evident that the fate of the republic would be decided by a blow from abroad.

"The British islands, at that time the only country in Europe which united under a monarchical head, moderate, but on that account more solid principles of freedom, with an equal balance of the different powers of the state, were at the commencement of the American disturbances in a progressive state of the most flourishing prosperity. For this happy condition they were indebted to their freedom and eligible commercial situation, together with the inexhaustible treasures nature had deposited in their mines of coal and iron, on the existence of which the industry of their diligent inhabitants is principally founded. Political ebullition existed in no higher degree than was necessary to give proper life, and less, perhaps, than was necessary to preserve it in all its purity, a constitution which, long since acquired after the most bloody struggles, was more deeply rooted in the modes of thinking, and in the manners and customs of the nation, than it was imprinted on them by the letter of the law. The government had sufficient leisure to direct its attention abroad, and by means of hostile enterprises, and political treaties, which must sooner or later give a naval power a decided ascendency, held out a helping hand to the commercial spirit of the people who aimed at making (and with increasing hopes of success) the remainder of the world tributary to it, for the productions of its fabrics and manufactures.

"The plan of supporting commerce upon territorial acquisitions, and of forming an empire out of the conquered provinces of India, whose treasures should flow back to the queen of cities on the Thames, was already fully developed, and the exasperation against the western colonies was to be attributed as much to a mistaken commercial interest as to a spirit for dominion. The ingredients of the British national character, ever more coldly repulsive than amiable or attractive in its nature, had produced an almost universal antipathy not alone of the public mind, but also of the individual affections, against a people in so many points of view so highly respectable, and being unceasingly fed by that envy which every species of superiority involuntarily creates, produced the most conspicuous influence in the development of subsequent events."

The author then proceeds to notice the proceedings of Russia, Austria, and Prussia, in relation to Poland, until its final dismemberment in 1795:—

"It is unnecessary," he says in conclusion, "to give a further exposition of the leading principles of the three courts which began this work of annihilation, and still persevered in it, contrary to the solemn stipulations of treaties lately entered into, just at the moment when a new constitution, enthusiastically received, had offered every guaranty of security, the want of which had served to give an air of legitimacy to the first spoliations. External aggrandisement in the acquisition of territory and population, and internal considerations, so far as they afforded means of attaining the object in view, are, in short, the features of these unnatural principles. This economical digestion of an administration merely of things, not persons, may be termed excellent in its kind. Taken in this point of view, the Prussian government gave the most splendid proofs of the beneficial results which may be attained by military organization. Austria and Russia had followed this example; *and it required later events to prove, that the calculation is not always correct, that a standing army, forming a state within the state, is the only support and rallying point of a government, and that no system is safe, but that which is founded on the internal strength and unanimity of the people.*"

Having sketched the political situation of Europe, at the commencement of the American revolution, the author proceeds to notice the interference of France and Spain;—the situation in which the colonies of North America were left after the acknowledgment of their independence;—the adoption of the new constitution;—the extraordinary prosperity which followed;—the immense acquisitions of territory, and the accession of wealth and numbers. He then traces the effects produced in Europe, and most especially in France, by a participation in the struggle between England and her colonies, and the contemplation of their subsequent prosperity and happiness. The spirit of emancipation was caught from the new, and was fast spreading itself over the old world. This spirit first produced its practical effects in France, whence it reached England, and almost all the states on the continent of Europe, begetting a revolution of ideas at least, if not leading to the revolution of governments, as it did in France.

The spirit of conquest which was perhaps forced upon France, by the necessity of giving to the enemies of the new order of things, employment at home, in order to prevent their interference abroad, was fatal to the beneficial results of the revolution. The rapid conquests achieved by Napoleon, drew the eyes and hearts of a people fond of glory, and full of a military spirit, from their internal affairs, to foreign conquests; and, while they were subduing a world, they were themselves subdued by the same power. Then came the empire of Napoleon; the confederacy of nations,—not merely of kings and their armies, but of nations, instigated partly by their own wrongs, and partly by the promises of their rulers, to rise in mass, and do what neither their kings nor their armies had been able to perform. It was the people of Europe that at length overthrew Napoleon.

When, after this great event, it became necessary to reorganize Europe, which had been cast from its ancient moorings, by the gigantic power, and gigantic mind of the child of democracy, who had devoured his mother, there arose a schism between the people and their sovereigns. The former expected the fulfilment of those promises, which the latter had made in the hour of extreme peril, in order to rouse them to effectual resistance against the French. These promises in Germany, Prussia, the Netherlands, &c. consisted principally in the establishment of representative governments, which would leave the sovereign in possession of a hereditary power, checked by a body elected by the people. On the other hand, the sovereigns, unmindful of the preservation of their thrones, which they owed to *the people*, refused to fulfil their solemn stipulations. In the hour of success, they as usual forgot the hour of adversity, and insisted upon the unconditional re-establishment, if not of old boundaries, at least of the old political regime. Hence we may trace the origin of what is called seriously by some, in derision and scorn by others, *the Holy Alliance*, which originated in the fears and the weakness of kings, who, being unable to maintain singly their antiquated pretensions at home, sought in a close union of policy and interests, the means of doing that, which each one alone was inadequate to achieve. By this alliance, Europe was dismembered—millions of acres, and millions of people, were parcelled out among the different sovereigns, and the balance of Europe was either believed, or affected to be believed, restored by placing whole nations under a dominion which they abhorred. It is obvious that such an unnatural state of things could endure only while cemented by a mutual fear of the powers which had constituted it; which fear would subside immediately, or very soon after the dissolution of the great confederacy. A large portion of Europe had been fermenting for nearly fifteen years, under the oppressions of this union of despots, and the moment of its separation, would naturally be that of the downfall of the system they had attempted to impose on mankind. But we are anticipating our brief analysis of the work before us:—

> "After twenty-three years of blood and revolution," continues the author, "Louis was again seated on the throne of his forefathers, and the principles of monarchy seemed firmly established in Europe. But the principle of government was in reality no longer the old one, and the spirit of the relation in which the ruled stood to the rulers, although it had not yet been brought to light in visible forms, and specified limits, was materially changed. Mutual struggles of kings and their people against foreign aggression, and mutual sufferings in consequence of the division between the people and their rulers, the latter of whom owed esteem and acknowledgment for services rendered by the former, laid the foundation of a relation between them mutually more honourable. For centuries, indeed, the monarchs of Europe had not been identified and interwoven with their people; nor had they shared as now, the privations and humiliations, the domestic and public calamities, of the nations they governed; nor had they fought by their sides, and conquered by their efforts, as they had lately done in the late stormy period of the world."

Mutual suffering had taught them to feel a community of interests they had not before recognised. Calamity brings all ranks to a level, and the monarch exiled from his throne, can sympathise with the peasant driven from his hovel.

In this state of feelings, one would suppose Europe might have reposed in peace. But the elements of internal discord, lay buried deeply in her bosom, and the internal relations of the different powers had been so altered, as to present ample materials for dissension abroad. With the necessity of appealing to the patriotism of their people, by promises of privileges and immunities, expired the disposition to comply with them. This breach of faith, produced on one hand indignation and discontent, on the other, jealousy and apprehension. The discontents of the people, caused their rulers to depend more on the support of their standing armies, than on the attachment of their subjects, and these armies were accordingly augmented to such an extent, that the unfortunate people were at length impoverished by the very means used in enslaving them. At this moment, nearly the whole of Europe, including the British islands, constitutes a mass of military governments. Every where the civil power is inadequate to the preservation of order, the enforcement of obedience to the king and the laws, and every where a standing army under some form or other presides over the opinions and actions of the people. Hence results the curious and ominous, not to say awful spectacle of the rights of property at the mercy of a mob; and on the other hand, the rights of person, the liberties of the citizen, subject to the arbitrary domination of the bayonet. At this moment, such is the state of every monarchy in Europe.

Such a juxtaposition of kings and their people, must of necessity alienate them from each other every day; and thus by degrees, the feeling of loyalty towards the one, and of parental affection towards the other, will be finally extinguished in mutual fears and mutual injuries, that will for ever disturb their repose, until the people are either perfectly satisfied, or totally subdued.

Another fruitful source of the discontents now agitating all Europe, is the state of the labouring classes, not only manufacturing but agricultural. The means of producing the necessaries and luxuries of life have been multiplied by the increase of paper capital and artificial expedients, until the supply exceeds the demand, and the price of labour, even where labour can be procured, bears no proportion to the price of bread. During fifteen years of peace, America and Europe have augmented their powers of supplying their own wants and those of the rest of the world, by means of improvements in arts, sciences, machinery, &c., to an extent which cannot be estimated. The whole world is glutted with the products of machinery, and exactly in the proportion that these increase upon us, is the increase of the poverty of the labouring classes. Millions of people in Europe, the largest proportion of whom are inhabitants of the richest country in the world, and one producing the greatest quantity of the results of industry, want bread, because they either have no employment, or their wages will not obtain it for them. Let political economists reason as they will, this is the state of the labouring classes of Europe, and this state is aggravated precisely in the proportion that the facility of supplying the necessities and luxuries of life by artificial means is increased.

The cause of this singular state of things to us is sufficiently obvious. The powers of wealth, the force of example, opinion, authority, laws, of every concentrated influence that can be brought to bear upon human affairs, have, all combined, been directed to a reduction of the price of labour, and consequently to diminishing the consumption of the products of human industry; for the great mass of mankind have nothing but the fruits of their labour to offer in exchange for those products which are necessary to their subsistence and comfort. In vain may it be urged, as we have seen it done repeatedly, and most especially in an address of a clergyman of England to the labouring classes of that country—in vain may it be urged, that the decrease of the price of labour has been met by a corresponding decrease in the price of the necessaries of life, and that, therefore, the labouring classes are no worse off, nay better off, than before the vast increase of machinery either threw them out of employment, or forced them to labour for almost nothing. This comfortable gentleman, who, we understand, has a good fat living, and will probably be made a bishop if he can only stop the mouths of the sufferers with reasons instead of bread, asks these poor people if they don't get their hats, shoes, &c. one half cheaper in consequence of the perfection of machinery, the improvements of the arts, &c. But he takes care not to ask them if the difficulty of earning this half price is not increased in a much greater proportion, in consequence of the diminution of their wages, and whether bread, meat, beer, and all the essentials of human existence, are not enhanced rather than diminished in price. We could illustrate the theory of the reverend gentleman, by an honest matter of fact story, which we can vouch for, as it happened to a near relative of ours.

He had a gardener named Dennis, an honest fellow, full of simplicity, and a dear lover of Old Ireland, as all Irishmen are, at home or abroad. One day he was dilating with much satisfaction on the difference between the price of potatoes in this country and Ireland. "In Ireland, your honour, now I could git more nor a barrel of potatoes for a pishtareen, but here it costs as much as a dollar and a half." The gentleman asked him good naturedly why he did not remain where potatoes were so cheap. Dennis considered a moment, and answered with the characteristic frankness of his country—"why to tell your honour the honest truth, though the potatoes were so cheap, I never could get the pishtareen to buy them."

Here is the solution of the whole enigma. Every thing is cheap we will say; but labour, which is the only equivalent a large mass of mankind have to offer for every thing, is cheaper than all. Evident, as we think this will appear, still it seems to have no influence on those who govern mankind. And how should it? Their emoluments, their means of expenditure, are derived, not from their own physical labour, but the labours of others. The cheaper they can procure this, the deeper they can revel in luxuries. With them, the relative proportion between the remuneration of toil, and the means of living is nothing. Hence the rulers of nations, hence capitalists, and all the brood of monopolists, are stirring their energies abroad, to increase the supply of the products of labour, at the same time that they take from the labourer the due rewards of his labours, and thus prevent the consumption of the vast accession of manufactures, &c. occasioned by the increase and perfection of machinery. Inanimate powers are daily substituted for human hands, and productions continue to multiply in an equal ratio. This is a benefit to a single nation, while it possesses all the advantages of superiority, and is enabled to supply a portion of the rest of the world. But when other nations, as is the case now, adopt the same system, and avail themselves of the same means of supply, a glut takes place in the market, at home and abroad, and poverty and distress among the labourers are the inevitable consequence.

Such seem to us the principal elements of combustion now at work in Europe. Political disgust, and physical distresses are co-operating with each other, and in order to quiet these disturbances, it is not only necessary to give them more liberty, but more bread. But to return once more to the speculations of our author,—

"If we turn our view to the present state of agriculture," continues Dr. Von Schmidt, "in many countries of Europe, it will appear evident, that even the paternal soil in many districts, is becoming too confined to afford nourishment to those who have remained faithful to its bosom. If in the mountainous countries, as for example, in the west and south of France, on the Alps, and along the Rhine, every spot is occupied, and the very earth and manure have for centuries been carried aloft upon the naked rock attended with the most boundless labour, in order to furnish soil for the vine, the olive, and for the different species of cerelia, and at present no further room exists for a more extended cultivation; it is not possible for a more numerous growing generation to find nourishment in these districts, whose productions are not susceptible of increasing progression. The too frequent practice of parcelling out common lands, and large estates, originally beneficial in itself, has produced similar consequences in other states. It was undoubtedly a wise and humane plan to transform commons, and extensive pastures into fruitful fields, and by dividing large estates which their owners could not overlook, into smaller lots, thus ensure more abundant crops, and an increasing population, by a more careful cultivation. But if, as is the case at the present day, in many places, useful lands have been split into so many small independent possessions, as to render it hardly possible for families occupying them, to subsist in the most penurious manner, by cultivating them; whence, then, is sustenance to be obtained for their more numerous posterity, and from what source is the state to derive its taxes? It is evident, that this condition of things must lead to the most poignant distress, and that a breadless multitude, either driven by irretrievable debts from their paternal huts, or voluntarily forsaking them on account of an inadequate maintenance, will turn their backs upon their country; and it may be considered a fortunate resource if they, as has frequently occurred in later times, carry with them the vigour of their strength to the free states of America, which stand in need of no one thing but human hands, to raise them to the highest degree of prosperity. Those governments in which such an unnatural distension of the state of society prevails, ought not, most assuredly, for their own advantage, and for the sake of humanity, by any means to throw obstacles in the way, but rather favour such emigration, and render it easy and consolatory for all, since they have it not in their power to offer a better remedy for their present misery. By doing this, they will prevent dangerous ebullitions and unruly disaffections of a distressed and overgrown population; they will lighten the number of poor which is increasing to a most alarming extent, and put an end to that angry state of abjectness and misery which is felt by every honest heart, and under which thousands have sunk down, who, with numerous families in hovels of wretchedness, prolong their existence upon more scanty means than the most common domestic animals, and who appear only to be gifted with reason in order to be more sensible to their forlorn and pitiable fate."

From the foregoing premises, the author deduces the conclusion, that the free states of North America will increase in population more rapidly than any other country has ever done, partly from emigration, and partly from the unequalled facility of obtaining the comforts of life, by which the numbers of mankind are regulated. The people, equally free from political oppression, and the evils of abject poverty, such as scanty nourishment, and crowded habitations, will at first make a rapid progress in the useful, and subsequently, in the elegant arts, and more abstract sciences. The freedom of their institutions will continually offer every stimulus to the development of the features of independence, and animate that spirit of intelligence, which always increases in proportion to the freedom with which the human faculties are exercised. Thence he proceeds to the supposition, that the states of South America having attained to independence, will establish constitutional governments similar to those of the North, whose example first stimulated them to resistance to the mother country,—that this similarity will naturally produce a close union of interest and policy among all the states of the Western Continent, and that such a union will give a death blow to the colonial system of Europe, at no distant period.

The discovery and colonization of America, led to consequences which re-modelled all Europe; and her emancipation from European thraldom will, in like manner, force upon that portion of the world a new state of things. *Europe, in her present situation, cannot do without America,—while, on the other hand, America has no occasion for Europe.* America can, and will, therefore, become independent of Europe; but, in the present state of things, Europe cannot become independent of America. That almost universal empire which Europe attained by the superiority of her intelligence,—by the tribute she exacted from every other quarter of the globe, and by the superiority of her skill as well as of her industry, cannot be sustained for a much longer period.

Wrapped up in a sense of his superiority, the European reclines at home, shining in his borrowed plumes, derived from the product of every corner of the earth, and the industry of every portion of its inhabitants, with which his own natural resources would never have invested him, he continues, as the author observes, revelling in enjoyments which nature has denied him;—accustomed from his most tender years, to wants which all the blessings and donations of the land and the ocean, produced within the compass of his own quarter of the globe, are unable to satisfy. While, therefore, the rest of the world has become tributary to him, he, in return, has become dependent on it, by those wants,—the supply of which, custom and education have made indispensably necessary.

America alone furnishes in a sufficient quantity those precious metals, which constitute the basis on which the existing relations of all the different classes of society, and indeed the whole concatenation of the civil institutions of society in general, have been formed, and retained to the present time. All the elements of modern splendour were derived from her,—and it was her gifts to Europe, which changed almost all the constituents of social life. The costly woods of the new world, banished the native products of the old;—her cochineal and indigo furnish the choicest materials for the richest dyes;—her rice is become an article of cheap and general nourishment to the European world;—her cotton, tobacco, coffee, sugar, molasses, cocoa and rum;—her numerous and valuable drugs;—her diamonds and precious stones;—her furs, and, in time of scarcity, the rich redundant stores of grain she pours forth from her bosom, constitute so large a portion of the wants and luxuries of Europe, that it is not too much to say, the latter is in a great measure dependent upon America. A great portion of these cannot be domesticated in the former, or produced in such quantities, as to supply the demand which custom has made indispensable, nor upon such terms, as would enable the people of Europe to indulge in their consumption. On the contrary, experience has demonstrated, that all the natural productions of Europe, its olives, and even its boasted vines, can be naturalized in some one of the various regions of this quarter of the globe, which comprehends in itself every climate and every soil. There is not the least doubt, that, when the habits of the people, or the interests of the country point to such a course, all these will be produced in sufficient quantities, not only for domestic use, but foreign exportation.

America, thus standing in need of none of the natural productions of Europe, and possessing within herself much more numerous, as well as precious gifts of nature, than any other quarter of the globe, will soon be able to dispense with the products of foreign industry. Whenever she can command the necessary stock of knowledge, and a sufficient number of industrious hands, which emigration, aided by her own increasing population, will soon place at her disposal, this will inevitably take place. Where there exist materials, and understanding to use them, the freedom of using them at pleasure, and security in the enjoyment of the fruits of labour, the spirit of enterprise is inevitably awakened into life and activity, and with it must flourish every species of industry:—

> "North America," observes the author, "at the commencement of her revolution, found herself nearly destitute of all mechanical resources and means of resistance,—whereas now she possesses fortifications, and plenty of military supplies of all kinds, with the means of multiplying them, as occasion may require. She has already formed an efficient, spirited and increasing navy, which will before long dispute the empire of the seas; she is complete mistress of the several branches of knowledge, and contains within herself all the mechanical institutions requisite for the increase and maintenance of these things. She can equip an army or a navy, without a resort to Europe, for the most insignificant article."

The author then goes on to express an opinion that the complete emancipation of South America, which he anticipates as soon to happen, will lead to similar results, in that portion of the continent, and produce an entire and final independence, political as well as commercial. He does not pretend to designate the precise period in which this will take place, but confines himself to the assertion, that in the natural and inevitable course of things, it must and will happen, after a determined opposition from European jealousy.

An inquiry is then commenced, into the possibility that Europe will be enabled to supply the loss of America, by means of new connexions with the other quarters of the globe. If she cannot procure a new market for her surplus manufactures, how is she to acquire the means of purchasing those productions of the new world, which have become indispensable to her existence, in the sphere she has hitherto occupied? To do this she must not only retain in their fullest extent, all the remaining branches of her commerce, but obtain others, by entering into new connexions with Asia and Africa, and colonizing new regions. To do this, not only does the necessary energy seem wanting, but Europe will have to encounter the competition of America, with all our unequalled celerity of enterprise, and all our rapidly increasing powers of competition. She is much more likely to lose her remaining colonies than to acquire new ones; and it approaches to an extreme degree of probability, that she will be driven from many of her accustomed branches of commerce, by the superior energy and enterprise of America, rather than obtain new marts for her manufactures. Already the North American cottons are finding their way to India, and banishing the productions of the British looms from the markets of the southern portion of this continent. The trade to China is already assuming an entire new character, and will probably before long be carried on without the instrumentality of Spanish dollars.

We think the positions of our author are eminently entitled to consideration. The situation of a part of the continent of America, south of the Isthmus of Darien, is much more favourable to a commercial intercourse with Asia, western Africa, than that of Europe. The coast of Guinea can be much more easily visited from Caraccas, Cayenne, and Surinam, than from any portion of Europe; and the Cape of Good Hope, lying directly to the east of the great river La Plata, is much better adapted to an intercourse with Rio Janeiro, and Buenos Ayres, than any of the Dutch or English colonies. The Isles of France, Bourbon, and Madagascar, situated between the Cape of Good Hope, and the eastern coast of Africa, are much more suited to a communication with the new states of South America, than with the mother countries. Such is the case with the Philippine islands, New-Holland, the Marquesas, the Friendly and Society islands. The geographical relations between all these, and different portions of South America, sufficiently indicate that when the reins shall have fallen from the hands of Europe, the intercourse will in a great measure change its course, and centre in the new instead of the old world.

The principle, we are aware, has been assumed, that whatever state supports the most powerful navy for the protection of its commerce, will always take the lead. But it hardly now remains a question, whether the states of the new world will not be able ere long, to direct trade into the free channel which nature herself seems to point out for all nations, but which the exorbitant naval power of one has forced into artificial and circuitous directions.

Europe will not for ever be able to wield the trident of the seas, nor sway the sceptre of intellectual superiority. There is a time for all things. There was a time when she borrowed her arts, her literature, her refinements, and her civilization, from Asia. These are for ever passing from one nation, and from one continent to another. The descendents of Europeans in the new world, have not degenerated, and possessing as they do as many advantages of situation as were ever enjoyed by any people under the sun, with as great a field for their exercise as was ever presented for human action, it would be departing from the natural order of things, and the ordinary operations of the great scheme of Providence; it would be shutting our ears to the voice of experience, and our eyes to the inevitable connexion of causes and their effects, were we to reject the extreme probability, not to say moral certainty, that the old world is destined to receive its impulses in future, from the new. Already we see the bright dawnings of this new relation, in the universal diffusion of the spirit of emancipation, first sought in the wilds of America. It was there that was first lighted that spark which is now animating and stimulating the nations of the old world to become free and happy like ourselves. The unshackled genius of the new world is now exerting itself with gigantic vigour, aided by the infinite treasures of nature, to strengthen its powers, increase its commerce, its resources, and its wealth. No other quarter of the globe, much less a single nation, will eventually be able to dispute the empire of the seas, with the new world.

We shall devote the remainder of this article to a consideration of events which have occurred in Europe since the publication of the work before us, which richly merits a better translation, as well as a republication in this country. This course is necessary to our purpose, although it is our humble opinion, that the writers and publications of this country, give a disproportionate attention to the affairs of other people, and of consequence, neglect our own. Let us look to ourselves; preserve the purity of the national manners and institutions—foster our natural and accidental advantages, and observe, and gather lessons of wisdom as well as moderation from the folly and excesses of rulers and people in the old superannuated world. Above all, let us ever bear in mind and continue to act upon the sentiment of Daniel Webster, and be careful that *"while other nations are moulding their governments after ours, we do not break the pattern."*

The present state of Europe, we think, offers additional probabilities to the theory laid down in the work of the Danish philosopher. Two great principles are now approaching to a struggle, which will, in all human probability, ere long, produce not only wars, but the worst of wars, internal dissensions, aggravated by external struggles with foreign powers. Although the principle of emancipation is common to the revolution of America, and the revolutionary spirit now at work in Europe, all other circumstances are essentially different. With us, it was throwing off a dominion seated at a vast distance beyond the seas, and only known among us by its representatives. In Europe, on the contrary, it is a central power existing in the heart, and pervading every portion of the body politic. A revolution then, must overturn thrones, church establishments, standing armies, hereditary orders, and prejudices hallowed by ages of reverence and submission. The whole frame and organization of society must be dissolved, changed into new elements, and be arranged into new forms.

The enemies of *statu quo*, and the genius of change, are now arraying their respective powers, and in proportion as the people have been debarred from all participation in the government, will be their ardour to govern without controul. Such a struggle cannot end in a day, or in a year,—nor will it be decided in all probability, except through a long series of gradations, which will finally rest at last on a basis suitable to the present state of the human mind. We cannot, therefore, but anticipate heavy times for Europe. A long course of internal and external wars, is fatal to the great interests of a state. Commerce decays, and seeks other more peaceful climes—agriculture is robbed of its labourers, and of the products of labour, to recruit and feed the armies,—and manufacturers are deprived of their foreign purchasers. The powers of the intellect, too, are diverted from the pursuits of science and literature, into the bloody paths of warfare,—and thus it has ever happened, that a long continuance of national struggles, produces a neglect of the arts of peace, and an approach to barbarism.

Insecurity of property is one of the inevitable consequences of civil wars. The products of the land are the common stock of plunder for both parties, and the land itself becomes a prey to confiscation. At this day, a vast portion of the wealth of Europe is vested in stocks, which are still more fatally operated upon by civil wars. Their value, in fact, becomes, in such a state of things, merely nominal; and it depends upon the success of one or other of the parties in the struggle, whether they again attain to their original prices, or become worthless. Such a crisis seems fast approaching in Europe. When once the conflicting elements of anarchy and despotism commence their warfare, who shall say where and when it will end? Prophecy, in this case, would be presumption,—when it does end, the result will be equally uncertain. Whether a chastened freedom, guarantied by a fair representation of the people in the governments, a despotism without limits, or an anarchy without controul, is beyond the reach of human foresight to predict.

One thing, however, we think, is certain. This unsettled state of life, liberty and property, in Europe, will produce a vast accession of wealth and population in the new world, and accelerate its progress to the sceptre of intellect and power, hitherto, for so long a time, wielded by the old. The neighbouring nations of Europe, being all nearly in the same state of internal insecurity, afford no safe refuge to fugitives or property, from each other—even if their national antipathies did not present a barrier to emigration. The United States, on the contrary, with nothing to disturb their tranquillity, but the peaceable struggles of an election, and stretching out a hand of welcome to all nations, and all ranks of mankind, from the exiled monarch to the mechanic or peasant, coming in search of employment and bread, will present a safe deposit for the wealth of Europe,—a sanctuary where the persecuted, the harassed, and the timid spirit, may find repose from the storms that vex his native land.

Thus, to our native energy, intelligence, and resources, will be added a large portion of those of the other quarter of the world, and the united result, in all human probability, *must* be the fulfilment of the great prophecy, that the empire of the world was travelling towards the setting sun. The sceptre will depart from the east, and be wielded by the west. Power, dominion, science, literature, and the arts, hitherto the satellites of despotism, will become the bright and beautiful handmaids of a brighter goddess than themselves, and the glory of Europe, like that of Asia, be preserved in her history and her traditions.

The anticipation is as rational as glorious to an American. Look at the state of Europe once more, and separate it into its constituent parts. Let us begin with France. What has she gained by her revolution of July but a branch of the same tree, in the room of the rotten trunk? Has she won freedom or repose? Not even the freedom of complaint,—nor any other repose, but the repose of the National Guards. What is the cry of the people of Paris? Not liberty alone, but "give us employment and bread." Thus irritated by a feeling of disappointment on one hand, and goaded on by hunger, can they stop where they are? Certainly not; it is not in the nature of man, nor the nature of things. Two such impulses can only be satisfied by the grant of their demands, and only quelled by force.

Look at the great rival of France on the opposite side of the channel. The same mighty evils are at work there—discontent aggravated by hunger. At the moment we are writing, a question is depending in the Parliament of England, which agitates the island to its centre, and the decision of which, either one way or other, is acknowledged by both parties to amount to the signal of a revolution. The opponents of the Bill of Reform maintain, that, if carried, it will destroy the basis of the government; and the advocates assert, that, if not carried, it will produce a revolution, originating in the disappointment and indignation of the people.

Will the aristocracy of England—the most wealthy and powerful aristocracy in the world—voluntarily, and without a mighty struggle, divest themselves of one of their chief sources of power in the state. Will they sacrifice their parliamentary influence, which constitutes one of the regular modes and means of providing for younger sons and poor relations? Nay, which enables them to dictate to their sovereign? We believe not. Will the people remain quiet under the disappointment of their newborn hopes, aggravated as it will be by poverty and distress, among so large a number? Perhaps they will, so long as there is an army of sixty or eighty thousand men, disposed so happily for the protection of order in the *United* Kingdom, that every breath of discontent is met by a bayonet. But let the monarchs who maintain *order* in Europe, by means of standing armies, recollect the lesson of history, which teaches us, that throughout all ages, and countries, the power which sustained the throne by force, in the end by force overthrew it. There is but one solid permanent support of power, and that is, the attachment of the people.

In the present state of Europe, we incline to the opinion that the safest course for kings to take, would be to identify themselves with the people, and become the organs of their wishes. We see no other means for the present King of England to make head successfully against the weight of the opposition of the church and nobility, in case he decisively sustains the present ministry in their plans of parliamentary reform, than to make common cause with his people, and say to them honestly, "I have become your champion, do you become my supporters." The government of England is acknowledged on all hands to be a mixed government of king, lords, and commons. Who represents the commons of England? The House of Commons. But can it do this effectually, while a large portion of the members are returned by the House of Lords? We should think not. The spirit and purity of the system can only be preserved by the commons, and the commons alone, selecting their representatives in their own house, and not the nobility. Does the House of Commons interfere in the same way in the creation of the members of the House of Lords? They have no voice or influence in the business. Why, then, should the House of Lords interfere in the election, or appointment rather, of the members of the House of Commons? In this point of view, therefore, we can perceive no sort of foundation for the argument of the opponents of reform, that the measure will operate to destroy the balance of the government. We rather think it will restore the balance, and bring it back to the true old theory of three distinct powers—king, lords, and commons.

We believe that the people will be satisfied with this reform for a time, if it take place. When they shall see, as no doubt they will see, that the burthens of the state, and consequently their own, remain the same, or perhaps increase with the increase of those who require relief, and the decrease of those who are able to bestow it; when they shall find that a reform in Parliament will not give them liberal wages, or feed their suffering families, then will they become more dissatisfied than ever. Then, too, will the result disclose where the shoe of reform pinched the opponents of reform. The increased representation of the people will then enable the people to *make* themselves heard and felt, and to force the government into measures that may indeed destroy the constitution of England, if there be any such invisible being. Whichever way we look, therefore, we perceive the same causes of discontent, the same spirit of emancipation at work, that agitates the continent of Europe; and so long as this state of things continues, it requires no spirit of prophecy to predict, that England, so far from advancing in power or intelligence, will, in all probability, invincibly slide from the summit of power, and become the victim of internal weakness at last.

The state of Holland and Belgium, of Italy and Germany, and Russia and Prussia, and Spain and Poland, is still more unfavourable to arts, science, commerce, literature, and agriculture. The rulers are employed in schemes for keeping the people in subjugation, and the people in wresting the promised privileges from their rulers. In such a state of things, the one party has no time to devise schemes for enriching or enlightening the people, but is employed, on the contrary, in placing them, as far as possible, in ignorance and poverty. The other is so taken up with politics, that its habits of economy, steadiness, and enterprise, are forgotten by degrees in the whirlpool of turbulent excitement. Each and all of these countries, with the exception perhaps of Russia, instead of advancing, will gradually recede in wealth and intelligence, not only from internal dissensions, but on account of the large portion of both, that will from time to time, as long as this state of things shall last, direct its course to the new world.

The change from old to new times; from the inapplicable maxims of the past, to the practical truths of the present, has, every where, and in all past ages, been a period of suffering to the human race. The approaches to this state of regeneration, are marked by turbulent disaffection on one hand, inflexible severity on the other; its progress is marked by the dissolution of the social ties, and its crisis with blood and tears. The people have to encounter the most formidable difficulties, under which they probably sink many times, before they rise at last and make the great successive effort. These evils are aggravated and perpetuated as long as possible, by the stern inflexible rigidity of old-established institutions, worthless in proportion to their obstinacy, aided by the blind besotted pride of kings, who seem never to have learnt the lesson of yielding to the changes produced by time and circumstance, and sacrificing gracefully, what will otherwise be taken from them by force.

But all that is great, or good, or valuable, in this world, must be attained by labour, perseverance, courage, and integrity. Liberty is too valuable a blessing to be gained or preserved without the exercise of these great virtues. It must have its victims, and its charter must be sealed with blood. A people afraid of a bayonet, are not likely to be free while Europe swarms with standing armies, having little or no community of interests or feeling with those who maintain them by the sweat of their brow. When the oppressed states of Switzerland, sent forth patriots who made a breach in the forest of German bayonets opposed to them, by circling them in their arms, and receiving them into their bosoms, they deserved to be free—they became free, and their liberties are still preserved. But so long as a host often thousand brawling and hungry malcontents, can be quieted and dispersed by the sound of a bugle, the clattering of a horse's hoofs, or the glittering of a musket barrel, can such people expect to be free? Assuredly not, we think. No where will despotism or aristocracy peaceably resign their long established preponderance without a struggle, and like our own revolution, the contest will at last come to the crisis—*"we must fight, Mr. Speaker, we must fight,"* as said the intrepid Patrick Henry,—and we did fight. So must Europe if it expects emancipation. All the governments of that quarter of the globe, are now sustained by a military force—and by force only can they be overthrown or modified, to suit the great changes which have taken place in the feelings and relative situation of the different orders of society.

That the present state and future prospects of that renowned and illustrious quarter of the globe, are ominous of a continued succession of storms and troubles, we think appears too obvious. The night that is approaching, will be long and dark, in all human probability—it may end in a total regeneration—in a confirmed and inflexible despotism; or in that precise state of things which characterized what are called, the dark ages of Europe—in the establishment of a hundred petty states, governed by a hundred petty tyrants, eternally at variance, and agreeing in nothing but in oppressing the people. Great standing armies are at present the conservators of the great powers of Europe, and public sentiment is no longer the sole or principal cement of empires; when these are gone, as they must be, ere the nations which they oppress can be free, then all the little sectional and provincial jealousies and antipathies, every real or imaginary opposition of interests, and even feelings of personal rivalry, will have an opportunity of coming into full play, and the result may very probably be, the erection of a vast many petty states, which will never be brought to act together in any great system of policy. Thus situated, they will never be able to make head against the growing power of the vast states of the new world, which whatever may be their minor causes of difference, will naturally unite in those views of commercial policy, which being common to all, will be sought by a common effort.

The South American states, it is true, have not yet realized the blessings of emancipation, partly owing to their inexperience in the practical secrets of civil liberty; partly to the want of public virtue in the people, and their rulers, and partly, as we are much inclined to suspect, to the secret intrigues of more than one European power. But their natural and inevitable tendency is, we believe, towards a stable government, combining a complete independence of foreign powers, with such a portion of civil liberty as may suit their present circumstances and situation. They are serving their apprenticeship—they will soon be out of their time, and may safely set up for themselves.

But, however doubtful may be the final result of the great struggle between the kings and the people—or of the aristocracy and the people—for this seems to be the real struggle after all—whatever may be its final result, one thing is certain as fate. While it continues, it must inevitably arrest the prosperity of Europe, such as it is, and force it to retrograde for a time. Instead of devoting their attention to the interests of the nation abroad, and encouraging the industry and intelligence of the people at home, kings will be employed in watching and restraining their subjects. Fearing the intelligence and wealth, as the means of increasing their discontents as well as their power, they will seek to diminish both by new restraints or new exactions; and thus the best ends of government will be perverted to purposes of ignorance and oppression. This is the history of the degradation, and consequent internal weakness of all nations, and a perseverance in such a course in Europe, will only afford another example, that the same effects proceed from similar causes, every where, and at all times.

In the mean while, as oppression, civil wars, internal disaffection, anarchy, and expatriation of wealth and numbers, all combined, are gradually undermining the strength of Europe, and draining her veins, the new world will be, in all human probability, every day acquiring what the old is losing. If she once pass the other, if it be only by the breadth of a single hair, it is scarcely to be anticipated that age and decrepitude will ever be able to regain the vantage ground, against the primitive energies of vigorous youth. Once ahead, and the new world will remain so, until the ever revolving course of time, and the revolutions it never fails to accomplish, shall perhaps again transfer to Asia the sceptre of arts, science, literature, power, and dominion, which was wrested from her by Europe.

To realize these bold anticipations, nothing seems necessary but for the people of the United States to bear in mind, that they are the patriarchs of modern emancipation—that the spark which animates the people of Europe was caught from them—that they led the way in the *great common cause of all mankind*—that the eyes of the world are upon them—and that they stand under a solemn obligation to do nothing themselves, to suffer their leaders to do nothing, which shall bring the sacred name of liberty into disgrace, or endanger the integrity of our great confederation. *"While other nations are moulding their governments after ours, may we not destroy the pattern."*

ART. VII.

WEBSTER'S SPEECHES,

Speeches and Forensic Arguments, by Daniel Webster: 8vo. pp. 520. Boston:
1830.

It has often enough been objected to books written and published in the United States, that they want a national air, tone, and temper. Unhappily, too, the complaint has not unfrequently been well founded; but the volume before us is a striking exception to all such remarks. It consists of a collection of Mr. Webster's Public Addresses, Speeches in Congress, and Forensic Arguments, printed chiefly from pamphlets, already well known; and it is marked throughout, to an uncommon degree, with the best characteristics of a generous nationality. No one, indeed, can open it, without perceiving that, whatever it contains, must have been the work of one born and educated among our free institutions, — formed in their spirit, and animated and sustained by their genius and power. The subjects discussed, and the interests maintained in it, are entirely American; and many of them are so important, that they are already become prominent parts of our history. As we turn over its pages, therefore, and see how completely Mr. Webster has identified himself with the great institutions of the country, and how they, in their turn, have inspired and called forth the greatest efforts of his uncommon mind, we feel as if the sources of his strength, and the mystery by which it controuls us, were, in a considerable degree, interpreted. We feel that, like the fabulous giant of antiquity, he gathers it from the very earth that produced him; and our sympathy and interest, therefore, are excited, not less by the principle on which his power so much depends, than by the subjects and occasions on which it is so strikingly put forth. We understand better than we did before, not only why we have been drawn to him, but why the attraction that carried us along, was at once so cogent and so natural.

When, however, such a man appears before the nation, the period of his youth and training is necessarily gone by. It is only as a distinguished member of the General Government, — probably in one of the two Houses of Congress, that he first comes, as it were, into the presence of the great mass of his countrymen. But, before he can arrive there, he has, in the vast majority of cases, reached the full stature of his strength, and developed all the prominent peculiarities of his character. Much, therefore, of what is most interesting in relation to him, — much of what goes to make up his individuality and momentum, and without which, neither his elevation nor his conduct can be fully understood or estimated, is known only in the circle of his private friends, or, at most, in that section of the country from which he derives his origin. In this way, we are ignorant of much that it concerns us to know about many of our distinguished statesmen; but about none, probably, are we more relatively ignorant than about Mr. Webster, who is eminently one of those persons, whose professional and political career cannot be fairly or entirely understood, unless we have some acquaintance with the circumstances of his origin, and of his early history, taken in connection with his whole public life. We were, therefore, disappointed, on opening the present volume, not to find prefixed to it a full biographical notice of him. We were, indeed, so much disappointed and felt so fully persuaded, that neither the contents of the volume itself, nor the sources of its author's power, nor his position before the nation, could be properly comprehended without it, that we determined at once to connect whatever we should say on any of these subjects, by such notices of his life, as we might be able to collect under unfavourable circumstances. We only regret that our efforts have not been more successful,—and that our notices, therefore, are few and imperfect.

Mr. Webster was born in Salisbury, a farming town of New-Hampshire, at the head of the Merrimack, in 1782. His father, always a farmer, was a man of a strongly marked and vigorous character,—full of decision, integrity, firmness, and good sense. He served under Lord Amherst, in the French war, that ended in 1763; and, in the war of the Revolution, he commanded a company chiefly composed of his own towns-people and friends, who gladly fought under his leading nearly every campaign, and at whose head he was found, in the battle of Bennington, at the White Plains, and at West-Point, when Arnold's treason was discovered. He died about the year 1806; and, at the time of his death, had filled, for many years, the office of Judge of the Court of Common Pleas, for the state of New-Hampshire.

But, during the early part of Mr. Webster's life, the place of his birth, now the centre of a flourishing and happy population, was on the frontiers of civilization. His father had been one of the very first settlers, and had even pushed further into the wilderness than the rest, so that the smoke sent up amidst the solitude of the forest, from the humble dwelling in which Mr. Webster was himself born, marked, for some time, the ultimate limit of New England adventure at the North. Undoubtedly, in any other country, the sufferings, privations, and discouragements inevitable in such a life, would have precluded all thought of intellectual culture. But, in New England, ever since the first free school was established amidst the woods that covered the peninsula of Boston, in 1636, the school-master has been found on the border line between savage and civilized life, often indeed with an axe to open his own path, but always looked up to with respect, and always carrying with him a valuable and preponderating influence.

It is to this characteristic trait of New England policy, that we owe the first development of Mr. Webster's powers, and the original determination of his whole course in life; for, unless the school had sought him in the forest, his father's means would not have been sufficient to send him down into the settlements to seek the school. The first upward step, therefore, would have been wanting; and it is not at all probable, that any subsequent exertions on his own part, would have enabled him to retrieve it. The value of such a benefit cannot, indeed, be measured; but it seems to have been his good fortune to be able in part, at least, to repay it; for no man has explained with such simplicity and force as he has explained them, the very principles and foundations on which the free schools of New England rest, or shown, with such a feeling of their importance and value, how truly the free institutions of our country must be built on the education of all. We allude now to his remarks in the Convention of Massachusetts, where, speaking of the support of schools, he says:—

> "In this particular we may be allowed to claim a merit of a very high and peculiar character. This commonwealth, with other of the New England states, early adopted, and has constantly maintained the principle, that it is the undoubted right, and the bounden duty of government, to provide for the instruction of all youth. That which is elsewhere left to chance, or to charity, we secure by law. For the purpose of public instruction, we hold every man subject to taxation, in proportion to his property, and we look not to the question, whether he, himself, have or have not children to be benefited by the education for which he pays. We regard it as a wise and liberal system of police, by which property, and life, and the peace of society are secured. We seek to prevent, in some measure, the extension of the penal code, by inspiring a salutary and conservative principle of virtue, and of knowledge, in an early age. We hope to excite a feeling of respectability, and a sense of character, by enlarging the capacity, and increasing the sphere of intellectual enjoyment. By general instruction, we seek, as far as possible, to purify the whole moral atmosphere; to keep good sentiments uppermost, and to turn the strong current of feeling and opinion, as well as the censures of the law, and the denunciations of religion, against immorality and crime. We hope for a security, beyond the law, and above the law, in the prevalence of enlightened and well principled moral sentiment. We hope to continue and to prolong the time, when, in the villages and farm houses of New England, there may be undisturbed sleep, within unbarred doors. And knowing that our government rests directly on the public will, that we may preserve it, we endeavour to give a safe and proper direction to that public will. We do not, indeed, expect all men to be philosophers, or statesmen; but we confidently trust, and our expectation of the duration of our system of government rests on that trust, that by the diffusion of general knowledge, and good and virtuous sentiments, the political fabric may be secure, as well against open violence and overthrow, as against the slow but sure undermining of licentiousness." pages 209, 210.

> "I rejoice, Sir, that every man in this community may call all property his own, so far as he has occasion for it, to furnish for himself and his children the blessings of religious instruction and the elements of knowledge. This celestial, and this earthly light, he is entitled to by the fundamental laws. It is every poor man's

undoubted birth-right, it is the great blessing which this constitution has secured to him, it is his solace in life, and it may well be his consolation in death, that his country stands pledged, by the faith which it has plighted to all its citizens, to protect his children from ignorance, barbarism and vice." p. 211.

How Mr. Webster's education was advanced immediately after he left these primary schools, is, we believe, not known. It was, however, with great sacrifices on the part of his family, and severe struggles on his own. At last, when he was fifteen or sixteen years old, after a very imperfect preparation, he was entered at Dartmouth College; at least, so we infer, for he was graduated there in 1801. What were his principal or favourite pursuits during the three or four years of his academic life, we do not know. We remember, however, to have met formerly, one of his classmates, who spoke with the liveliest interest of the generous and delightful spirit he showed among his earliest friends and competitors, in the midst of whom, he manifested, from the first, aspirations entirely beyond his condition, and, when the first year was passed, developed faculties which left all rivalship far behind him. Indeed, it is known, in many ways, that, by those who were acquainted with him at this period of his life, he was already regarded as a marked man; and that, to the more sagacious of them, the honours of his subsequent career have not been unexpected.

Immediately after leaving college, he began the study of the law in the place of his nativity, with Mr. Thompson, soon afterwards a member of Congress; a gentleman who, from the elevation of his character, was able to comprehend that of his pupil and contribute to unfold its powers. But the *res augustæ domi* pressed hard upon him. He was compelled to exert himself for his own support; and his professional studies were frequently interrupted and impaired by pursuits, which ended only in obtaining what was needful for his mere subsistence.

Circumstances connected with his condition and wants at this time, led him to Boston, and carried him, when there, into the office of Mr. Gore. This was, undoubtedly, one of the deciding circumstances of his life. Mr. Gore was a lawyer of eminence, and a *gentleman*, in the loftiest and most generous meaning of the word. His history was already connected with that of the country. He had been appointed district attorney of the United States for Massachusetts, by Washington; he had served in England as our commissioner under Jay's treaty; and he was afterwards governor of his native state, and its senator in Congress. His whole character, private, political, and professional, from its elevation, purity and dignity, was singularly fitted to influence a young man of quick and generous feelings, who already perceived within himself the impulse of talents and the stirrings of an ambition whose direction was yet to be determined. Mr. Webster felt, that it was well for him to be there; and Mr. Gore obtained an influence over his young mind, which the peculiarly kind and frank manners of the instructer permitted early to ripen into an intimacy and friendship that were interrupted only by death.

Mr. Webster finished the study of his profession in Boston, and was there admitted to the bar in 1805;—Mr. Gore, who presented him, venturing, at the time, to make a prediction to the court respecting his pupil's future eminence, which has been hardly more than fulfilled by all his present fame. At first, he began the practice of his profession in Boscawen, a small village adjacent to the place of his birth; but in 1807, he removed to Portsmouth, where, no doubt, he thought he was establishing himself for life.

As a young lawyer, about to lay the foundations for future success, his portion could, perhaps, hardly have been rendered more fortunate and happy than it was now in Portsmouth. He rose rapidly in general regard, and was, therefore, almost at once, ranked with the first in his profession in his native state. Of course, his associations and intercourse were with the first minds. And, happily for one like him, the presiding judge of the highest tribunal in New-Hampshire was then Mr. Smith, afterwards governor of the state, whose native clearness of perception, acuteness, and power, united to faithful and accurate learning in his profession, and the soundest and most practical wisdom in the fulfilment of his duties on the bench, and in his intercourse with the bar, gave him naturally and necessarily great influence over its younger members. Mr. Webster, as the most prominent among them, came much in contact with him, and profited much from his sagacious foresight and wise and discriminating kindness. He came, too, still more in contact with Mr. Mason, afterwards a senator in Congress, and then and still the leading counsel in New-Hampshire. Mr. Mason was his senior by several years, but there was no other adversary capable of encountering him; and the intellect with which Mr. Webster was thus called to contend on equal terms was one of the highest order, of ample resources, and of the quickest penetration; whose original reach, firm grasp, and unsparing logic, left no safety for an adversary, but in a vigour, readiness and skill, which could never be taken unprepared or at disadvantage. It was a severe school; but there is little reason to doubt, Mr. Webster owes to its stern and rugged discipline much of that intellectual training and power, which render him, in his turn, so formidable an adversary. He owes to it, also, notwithstanding their uniform and daily opposition in court, the no less uniform personal friendship of Mr. Mason in private life.

It was in the midst, however, of this period, both of discipline and success as a lawyer, in New-Hampshire, that he entered public life. In the government of his native state, we believe, he never took office of any kind; and his first political place, therefore, was in the thirteenth Congress of the United States. He was chosen in 1812, soon after the declaration of war; and as he was then hardly thirty years old, he must have been one of the youngest members of that important Congress. His position there was difficult, and he felt it to be so. He was opposed to the policy of the war; he represented a state earnestly opposed to it; and he had always, especially in the eloquent and powerful memorial from the great popular meeting in Rockingham, expressed himself fully and frankly on the whole subject. But he was now called into the councils of the government, which was carrying on the war itself. He felt it to be his duty, therefore, to make no factious opposition to the measures essential to maintain the dignity and honour of the country; to make no opposition for opposition's sake; though, at the same time, he felt it to be no less his duty, to take good heed that neither the constitution, nor the essential interests of the nation, were endangered or sacrificed — *ne quid detrimenti respublica accipiat.*

This, indeed, seems to have been his motto up to the time of the peace; and his tone in relation to it is always manly, bold, and decisive. When Mr. Monroe's bill for a sort of conscription was introduced, he joined with Mr. Eppes, and other friends of the administration, in defeating a project, which, except in a moment of great anxiety and excitement, would probably have found no defenders. But when, on the other hand, the bill for "encouraging enlistments" was before the house, he held, in January 1814, the following strong and striking language, in which, now the passions of that stormy period are hushed, all will sympathize.

"The humble aid which it would be in my power to render to measures of government, shall be given cheerfully, if government will pursue measures which I can conscientiously support. If, even now, failing in an honest and sincere attempt to procure a just and honourable peace, it will return to measures of defence and protection, such as reason, and common sense, and the public opinion, all call for, my vote shall not be withholden from the means. Give up your futile projects of invasion. Extinguish the fires that blaze on your inland frontiers. Establish perfect safety and defence there by adequate force. Let every man that sleeps on your soil sleep in security. Stop the blood that flows from the veins of unarmed yeomanry, and women and children. Give to the living time to bury and lament their dead, in the quietness of private sorrow. Having performed this work of beneficence and mercy on your inland border, turn, and look with the eye of justice and compassion on your vast population along the coast. Unclench the iron grasp of your embargo. Take measures for that end before another sun sets upon you. With all the war of the enemy on your commerce, if you would cease to make war upon it yourselves, you would still have some commerce. That commerce would give you some revenue. Apply that revenue to the augmentation of your navy. That navy, in turn, will protect your commerce. Let it no longer be said, that not one ship of force, built by your hands since the war, yet floats upon the ocean. Turn the current of your efforts into the channel, which national sentiment has already worn broad and deep to receive it. A naval force, competent to defend your coast against considerable armaments, to convoy your trade, and perhaps raise the blockade of your rivers, is not a chimera. It may be realized. If, then, the war must continue, go to the ocean. If you are seriously contending for maritime rights, go to the theatre, where alone those rights can be defended. Thither every indication of your fortunes points you. There the united wishes and exertions of the nation will go with you. Even our party divisions, acrimonious as they are, cease at the water's edge. They are lost in attachment to the national character, on the element where that character is made respectable. In protecting naval interests by naval means, you will arm yourselves with the whole power of national sentiment, and may command the whole

abundance of the national resource. In time, you may be enabled
to redress injuries in the place where they may be offered; and, if
need be, to accompany your own flag throughout the world with
the protection of your own cannon."[5] Speech, pp. 14, 15.

Later in the same Congress, the subject of the establishment and principles of
a national bank came into discussion, and the finances of the country being then
greatly embarrassed, this subject rose to paramount importance, and absorbed
much of the attention of Congress up to the moment when the annunciation of
peace put a period, for the time, to all such debates. On the whole matter of the
bank and the currency, Congress was divided into three parties. First, those who
were against a national bank under any form. These persons consisted chiefly of
the remains of the old party, which had originally opposed the establishment of
the first bank in Washington's time, in 1791, and in 1811 had prevented the renewal of its charter. They were, however, generally, friends of the existing administration, whose position now called strongly for the creation of a new bank;
and, therefore, while they usually voted on preliminary and incidental measures
with the favourers of a bank, they voted, on the final passage of the bill, against
it; so that it was much easier to defeat the whole of any one project, than to carry
through any modification of it. Second, there was a party consisting almost entirely of friends of the administration, who wished for a bank, provided it were such
a one as they thought would not only regulate the currency of the country, and
facilitate the operations of the government, but also afford present and important
aid by heavy loans, which the bank was to be compelled to make, and to enable
it to do which, it was to be relieved from the necessity of paying its notes in specie;—in other words, it was a party that wished to authorize and establish a paper
currency for the whole country. The third party wished for a bank with a moderate
capital, compelled always to redeem its notes with specie, and at liberty to judge
for itself, when it would, and when it would not, make loans to the government.

The second party, of course, was the one that introduced into Congress the
project for a bank at this time. The bill was originally presented to the Senate; and
its main features were, that the bank should absorb a large amount of the depre-

[5] These are the last words of the speech; and the sentiment they contain in favour of
a navy and naval protection, has been maintained with great earnestness by Mr. Webster
for nearly thirty years, on all public occasions. In an oration delivered July 4th, 1806, and
printed at Concord, N. H., he says, "an immense portion of our property is in the waves.
Sixty or eighty thousand of our most useful citizens are there, and are entitled to such
protection from the government as their case requires." In another oration, delivered in
1812, and printed at Portsmouth, he says, "a navy sufficient for the defence of our coasts
and harbours, for the convoy of important branches of our trade, and sufficient, also, to
give our enemies to understand, when they injure us, that *they* too are vulnerable, and that
we have the power of retaliation as well as of defence, seems to be the plain, necessary,
indispensable policy of the nation. It is the dictate of nature and common sense, that means
of defence shall have relation to the danger." These doctrines in favour of a navy were extremely unwelcome to the nation when they were delivered; the first occasion referred to,
being just before the imposition of the embargo; and the second, just before the capture of
the Guerriere. How stands the national sentiment now? Who doubts the truth of what Mr.
Webster could not utter in 1806 and 1812 without exciting ill-will to himself?

ciated public debt of the United States, and grant to the government heavy loans on the security of a similar debt to be created; that its capital should consist of fifty millions of dollars, of which five millions only were to be specie, and the rest depreciated government securities; and that the bank, when required, should lend the government thirty millions. At the time when this plan was brought forward, all the numerous state banks south of New-England had refused to redeem their notes, or, as it was called "to ears polite," had "suspended specie payments," in consequence of which, their notes had fallen in value from 10 to 25 per cent., and specie, of course, had risen proportionally in value, and disappeared from circulation entirely. To afford the contemplated national bank any chance for carrying on its operations, or even for beginning them, it was to be authorized "to suspend specie payments," which meant, that it was to be authorized never to begin them; for, without this authority, their specie would be drained the moment their notes should be issued equal to its amount. On the other hand, all the taxes and revenues of the government were to be receivable in the paper of the bank, however much it might fall in value. In short, the whole scheme was one of those vast Serbonian bogs, where, from the days of Laws's Mississippi Company, armies whole of legislators and projectors have sunk, without leaving even a monument behind them to warn their followers of their fate.

We must not, however, be extravagantly astonished, that a project which we now know was in its nature so wild and dangerous, should have found favourers and advocates. The finances of the country were then in a critical, and even distressing position; and all men were anxious to devise some means to relieve them. A large part of the nation, too, sincerely entertained the chimerical notion, now universally exploded, that it was practicable to establish and maintain a safe and stable paper currency, even when not convertible into specie at the pleasure of the holder; and the example of England and its national bank was referred to with effect, though, from its history since, the same example could now be referred to with double effect on the other side of the discussion. After an earnest and able debate, then, the bill, on the whole, passed the Senate, and it was understood that a considerable majority of the House of Representatives was in its favour.

When brought there on the 9th of December, 1814, it excited a very animated discussion, which, with various interruptions from the forms and rules of the House, references to committees, and occasional adjournments, was continued till the 2d of January. In this protracted debate Mr. Webster took a conspicuous part; and his efforts, of which the speech now published is but an inconsiderable item, did much to avert the threatened evil, and to establish his reputation, not merely as an eloquent and powerful debater, which had already been settled in the previous session, but as a sagacious and sound statesman.

His principal opposition to the bill was made on the last day of its discussion. He then introduced a series of resolutions, bringing the bank proposed within the limits of the specie-paying principle, and taking off from it the restraints, which placed it too much within the power of the government to make it useful as a monied institution, either to the finances or to the commerce of the country. The objections to the plan then before Congress, and the disasters that would probably follow its adoption, he portrayed in the following strong language, which none, however, will now think to have been too strong.

"The capital of the bank, then, will be five millions of specie, and forty-five millions of government stocks. In other words, the bank will possess five millions of dollars, and the government will owe it forty-five millions. This debt from government, the bank is restrained from selling during the war, and government is excused from paying until it shall see fit. The bank is also to be under obligation to loan government thirty millions of dollars on demand, to be repaid, not when the convenience or necessity of the bank may require, but when debts due to the bank, from government, are paid; that is, when it shall be the good pleasure of government. This sum of thirty millions is to supply the necessities of government, and to supersede the occasion of other loans. This loan will doubtless be made on the first day of the existence of the bank, because the public wants can admit of no delay. Its condition, then, will be, that it has five millions of specie, if it has been able to obtain so much, and a debt of seventy-five millions, no part of which it can either sell or call in, due to it from government.

"The loan of thirty millions to government, can only be made by an immediate issue of bills to that amount. If these bills should return, the bank will not be able to pay them. This is certain, and to remedy this inconvenience, power is given to the directors, by the act, to suspend, at their own discretion, the payment of their notes, until the President of the United States shall otherwise order. The President will give no such order, because the necessities of government will compel it to draw on the bank till the bank becomes as necessitous as itself. Indeed, whatever orders may be given or withheld it will be utterly impossible for the bank to pay its notes. No such thing is expected from it. The first note it issues will be dishonoured on its return, and yet it will continue to pour out its paper, so long as government can apply it in any degree to its purposes.

"What sort of an institution, sir, is this? It looks less like a bank, than a department of government. It will be properly the paper-money department. Its capital is government debts; the amount of its issues will depend on government necessities; government, in effect, absolves itself from its own debts to the bank, and by way of compensation absolves the bank from its own contracts with others. This is, indeed, a wonderful scheme of finance. The government is to grow rich, because it is to borrow without the obligation of repaying, and is to borrow of a bank which issues paper, without liability to redeem it. If this bank, like other institutions which dull and plodding common sense has erected, were to pay its debts, it must have some limits to its issues of paper, and therefore, there would be a point beyond which it could not make loans to government. This would fall short of the wishes of the contrivers of this system. They provide for an unlimited issue of paper, in an entire exemption from payment. They found their bank, in the first place, on the discredit of government, and then hope to enrich government out of the insolvency of their bank. With them, poverty itself is the main source of supply, and bankruptcy a mine of inexhaustible treasure." Pp. 224-5.

The resolutions proposed by Mr. Webster, and supported in this speech, were not passed. Probably he did not expect them to pass, when he proposed them; but the same day, the main question was taken upon the passage of the bill itself; and, as it was rejected by the casting vote of the speaker, there can be no reasonable doubt, that without his exertions this portentous absurdity would not have been defeated. It is but justice, however, to the supporters of the measure, to say, that the mischievous consequences of its adoption, were by no means so apparent then as they are now. We have since had no little experience on the whole matter. It required all the power and influence of the general government, and of the present sound and specie-paying Bank of the United States, acting vigorously in concert for several years after the war, to relieve the country from the flood of depreciated notes of the state banks with which it was inundated, and to restore a safe and uniform currency. When or how this evil could have been remedied, if, at the very close of the war, it had been almost indefinitely increased by the establishment of a vast machine, issuing every day as much irredeemable paper as would be taken at any and every discount, and thus co-operating with the evil itself, instead of opposing it, is more than any man will now be bold enough to conjecture. We should, no doubt, have been in bondage to it to this hour, and probably left it as a yoke upon the necks of our children.

But, at the time referred to, the necessities of the government were urgent; and, on motion of Mr. Webster, the rule that prevented a reconsideration at the same session of a subject thus disposed of, was suspended the very next day, and a bill for a bank was on the same day, January 3, recommitted to a select committee. On the 6th, the committee reported a specie-paying bank, with a much diminished capital, which was carried in the house, with the fewest possible forms, on the 7th; Mr. Webster and most of his friends voting for it. It passed the senate, too, though with some difficulty; but was refused by the president, on the ground, that it was not sufficient to meet the exigencies of the case, which, indeed, we now know, no bank would have been able to meet. This project, however, being thus rejected, another was immediately introduced into the senate, the basis of which was to be laid, like that of the first bank proposed, in a paper currency. It passed that body; but on being brought into the house met a severe and determined opposition, which ceased only when, on the 17th, the news of peace being received, the bill was indefinitely postponed.

Mr. Webster's exertions, however, on the subject of the currency, did not cease with the overthrow of the paper bank system. He was re-elected to New-Hampshire for the fourteenth Congress, and sat there during the sessions of 1815-16; and 1816-17. The whole state of things in the nation was now changed. The war was over, and the great purpose of sound statesmanship was therefore to bring the healing and renovating influences of peace into the administration and finances of the country. The present bank was chartered in April 1816, and was placed, substantially on the principles maintained in Mr. Webster's resolutions of the preceding year. But still it seemed doubtful whether this institution, however wisely managed, would alone have power enough to restore a sound currency. The small depreciated notes of the state banks south of New-England, still filled the land with their loathed intrusion; and, what was worse, the revenue of the general government, receivable at the different custom-houses, was collected in this degraded paper, to the great injury of the finances of the country, and to the still greater injury of the property of private individuals, who, in different states, paid, of course, different rates of duties to the treasury, according to the value of the paper medium in which it happened to be received. Mr. Webster foresaw the mischiefs that must follow from this state of things, if a remedy were not speedily applied. He, therefore, in the same month of April 1816, introduced a resolution, the effect of which was, to require the revenue of the United States to be collected and received only in the legal currency of the United States, or in bills equal to that currency in value.

In stating the nature of the evil, after showing by what means the paper of the state banks south of New-England had become depreciated; he says,—

> "What still farther increases the evil is, that this bank paper being the issue of very many institutions, situated in different parts of the country, and possessing different degrees of credit, the depreciation has not been, and is not now, uniform throughout the United States. It is not the same at Baltimore as at Philadelphia, nor the same at Philadelphia as at New-York. In New-England, the banks have not stopped payment in specie, and of course their paper has not been depressed at all. But the notes of banks which have ceased to pay specie, have nevertheless been, and still are, received for duties and taxes in the places where such banks exist. The consequence of all this is, that the people of the United States pay their duties and taxes in currencies of different values, in different places. In other words, taxes and duties are higher in some places than they are in others, by as much as the value of gold and silver is greater than the value of the several descriptions of bank paper which are received by government. This difference in relation to the paper of the District where we now are, is twenty-five per cent. Taxes and duties, therefore, collected in Massachusetts, are one quarter higher than the taxes and duties which are collected, by virtue of the same laws, in the District of Columbia." Pp. 233-4.

A little further on, after showing that if this state of things is not changed by the government, it will be likely to change the government itself, he adds,—

"It is our business to foresee this danger, and to avoid it. There are some political evils which are seen as soon as they are dangerous, and which alarm at once as well the people as the government. Wars and invasions therefore are not always the most certain destroyers of national prosperity. They come in no questionable shape. They announce their own approach, and the general security is preserved by the general alarm. Not so with the evils of a debased coin, a depreciated paper currency, or a depressed and falling public credit. Not so with the plausible and insidious mischiefs of a paper money system. These insinuate themselves in the shape of facilities, accommodation, and relief. They hold out the most fallacious hope of an easy payment of debts, and a lighter burden of taxation. It is easy for a portion of the people to imagine that government may properly continue to receive depreciated paper, because they have received it, and because it is more convenient to obtain it than to obtain other paper, or specie. But on these subjects it is, that government ought to exercise its own peculiar wisdom and caution. It is supposed to possess on subjects of this nature, somewhat more of foresight than has fallen to the lot of individuals. It is bound to foresee the evil before every man feels it, and to take all necessary measures to guard against it, although they may be measures attended with some difficulty and not without temporary inconvenience. In my humble judgment, the evil demands the immediate attention of Congress. It is not certain, and in my opinion not probable, that it will ever cure itself. It is more likely to grow by indulgence, while the remedy which must in the end be applied, will become less efficacious by delay.

"The only power which the general government possesses of restraining the issues of the state banks, is to refuse their notes in the receipts of the treasury. This power it can exercise now, or at least it can provide now for exercising in reasonable time, because the currency of some part of the country is yet sound, and the evil is not universal. If it should become universal, who, that hesitates now, will then propose any adequate means of relief? If a measure, like the bill of yesterday, or the resolutions of to-day, can hardly pass here now, what hope is there that any efficient measure will be adopted hereafter?" pp. 235-6.

The doctrine of this speech is as important as it is true. A sound and uniform currency is essential, not only for the convenient and safe management of the fiscal concerns of a government; but, no less so, for the security of private property. It is, indeed, at once the standard and basis of all transfer and exchange; and, whenever the circulating medium has become much deranged in any country, it has been found an arduous, and sometimes a dangerous task, to restore it to a sound state. The effort almost necessarily brings on a conflict between the two great classes of debtor and creditor, into which every community is divided,—the creditor claiming the highest standard of value in the currency, and the debtor the lowest; and the results of such a conflict have not unfrequently been found in changes, convulsions, and political revolution. From such a conflict we were saved in this country, by the defeat of the paper-currency bank proposed in 1814,—by the establishment of the present specie paying bank, and by the adoption of Mr. Webster's resolution, which was approved by the President on the 30th of April, 1816.

It was at this period, however, that Mr. Webster determined to change his residence, and, of course, to retire for a time at least, from public life. He had now lived in Portsmouth nine years; and they had been to him years of great happiness in his private relations, and, in his relations to the country, years of remarkable advancement and honour. But, in the disastrous fire, which, in 1813, destroyed a large part of that devoted town, he had sustained a heavy loss, which the means and opportunities offered by his profession in New Hampshire were not likely to repair. He determined, therefore, to establish himself in a larger capital, where his resources would be more ample, and, in the summer of 1816, removed to Boston, where he has ever since resided.

His object now was professional occupation, and he devoted himself to it for six or eight years exclusively, with unremitting assiduity, refusing to accept office, or to mingle in political discussion. His success corresponded to his exertions. He was already known as a distinguished lawyer in his native state; and the two terms he had served in Congress, had placed him, notwithstanding his comparative youth, among the prominent statesmen of the country. His rank as a jurist, in the general regard of the nation, was now no less speedily determined. Like many other eminent members of the profession, however, who have rarely been able to select at first what cases should be entrusted to them, it was not for him to arrange or determine the time and the occasion, when his powers should be decisively measured and made known. We must, therefore, account it for a fortunate accident, though perhaps one of those accidents granted only to talent like his, that the occasion was the well known case of Dartmouth College; and, we must add, as a circumstance no less fortunate, that the forum where he was called to defend the principles of this great cause, and where he did defend them so triumphantly, was that of the Supreme Court of the United States, at Washington.

There is, indeed, something peculiar in this grave national tribunal, especially with regard to the means and motives it offers to call out distinguished talent, and try and confirm a just reputation, which is worth notice. The judges themselves, selected from among the great jurists of the country, as above ignorance, weakness, and the temptations of political ambition,—with that venerable man at their head, who for thirty years has been the ornament of the government, and, in whose wisdom has been, in no small degree, the hiding of its power—constitute a tribunal, which may be truly called solemn and august. The advocates, too, who appear before it, are no less a chosen few, full of talent and skill, and eager with ambition, who go there from all the ends of the country, to discuss the gravest and most important interests both public and private,—to settle the conflicts between domestic and foreign jurisprudence, or the more perilous conflicts between the authority of the individual states, and that of the general government;—in short, to return constantly upon the first great principles of national and municipal adjudication, and take heed, that, whatever is determined shall rest only on the deep and sure foundations of truth, right, and law. And, finally, if we turn from the bench and the bar, to the audience which is collected around them, we shall find again much that is remarkable, and even imposing. We shall find, that, large as it is, it is gathered together from a city not populous, where every thing, even the resources of fashion, must have a direct dependence on the operations of government; and where the senators themselves, and the representatives of foreign powers, no less than the crowds collected during the session of Congress, by the solicitations of an enlightened curiosity, or of a strenuous indolence, can, after all, discover no resort so full of a stirring interest and excitement, as that of the Supreme Court, into whose arena such practised and powerful gladiators daily descend, rejoicing in the combat. Taking it in all its connexions, then, we look upon this highest tribunal of the country, not only to be solemn and imposing in itself, but to be one of peculiar power over the reputations of these jurists and advocates, who appear before it, and who must necessarily feel themselves to be standing singularly in presence of the nation, represented there as it is, in almost every way, and by almost every class, from the fashion and beauty lounging on the sofas in the recesses of the court-room, up to the eager antagonists, who are impatiently waiting their time to contend for the mastery on some great interest or principle, and the judges who are ultimately to decide it.

Mr. Webster had already appeared once or twice before this tribunal;—but not in any cause which had called seriously into action the powers of his mind. The case of Dartmouth College, however, was one that might well task the faculties of any man. That institution, founded originally by charter from the king of Great Britain, had been in successful operation nearly half a century, when, in 1816, the Legislature of New Hampshire, from some movements in party politics, was induced, without the consent of the college, to annul its charter, and, by several acts, to give it a new incorporation and name. The trustees of the college resisted this interference; and, in 1817, commenced an action in the state courts, which was decided against them. A writ of error was then sued out by the original plaintiffs, to remove the cause for its final adjudication, to the Supreme Court of the United States; and it came on there for argument in March, 1818.

The court room was excessively crowded, not only with a large assemblage of the eminent lawyers of the Union, but with many of its leading statesmen,—drawn there no less by the importance of the cause, and the wide results that would follow its decision, than by the known eloquence of Mr. Hopkinson and Mr. Wirt, both of whom were engaged in it. Mr. Webster opened it, on behalf of the college. The question turned mainly on the point, whether the acts of the Legislature of New-Hampshire, in relation to Dartmouth College, constituted a violation of a contract; for, if they did, then they were contrary to the Constitution of the United States. The principles involved, therefore, went to determine the extent to which a legislature can exercise authority over the chartered rights of all corporations; and this of course gave the case an importance at the time, and a value since, paramount to that of almost any other in the books. Mr. Webster's argument is given in this volume at p. 110, et seq.; that is, we have there the technical outline, the dry skeleton of it. But those who heard him, when it was originally delivered, still wonder how such dry bones could ever have lived with the power they there witnessed and felt. He opened his cause, as he always does, with perfect simplicity in the general statement of its facts; and then went on to unfold the topics of his argument, in a lucid order, which made each position sustain every other. The logic and the law were rendered irresistible. But, as he advanced, his heart warmed to the subject and the occasion. Thoughts and feelings, that had grown old with his best affections, rose unbidden to his lips. He remembered that the institution he was defending, was the one where his own youth had been nurtured; and the moral tenderness and beauty this gave to the grandeur of his thoughts; the sort of religious sensibility it imparted to his urgent appeals and demands for the stern fulfilment of what law and justice required, wrought up the whole audience to an extraordinary state of excitement. Many betrayed strong agitation; many were dissolved in tears. When he ceased to speak, there was a perceptible interval before any one was willing to break the silence; and, when that vast crowd separated, not one person of the whole number doubted, that the man who had that day so moved, astonished, and controlled them, had vindicated for himself a place at the side of the first jurists of the country.

From this period, therefore, Mr. Webster's attendance on the Supreme Court at Washington has been constantly secured by retainers, in the most important causes; and the circle of his professional business, which has been regularly enlarging, has not been exceeded, if it has been equalled, by that of any other lawyer who has ever appeared in the national forum. The volume before us contains few traces of all this. It contains, however, two arguments upon constitutional questions of great interest and wide results. One is the case of Gibbons *vs.* Ogden, in 1824, involving the question, how far a state has authority to grant the exclusive right of navigating the tide-waters within its territorial limits; refusing that right to all persons belonging to other states, as well as to its own citizens. This question struck, of course, at the great steam-boat monopoly granted by the state of New-York, from motives of public munificence, to Mr. Fulton, the admirable first mover of that national benefit, and Chancellor Livingston, its early and adventurous patron. The case was argued by Mr. Webster and Mr. Wirt against the monopoly, and by Mr. Oakley and Mr. Emmet for it; so that probably as much ability was brought into the discussion on each side, as has been called for by any single cause in our judicial annals. The result was, that the monopoly was declared to be unconstitutional; and thus another great national blessing was obtained, hardly less important than the original invention, — that of throwing open the right to steam-navigation to the competition of the whole Union.

There were circumstances which gave uncommon interest to this cause, independently of its great constitutional importance, and the wide consequences involved in it. It had been litigated, during a series of years, in every form, in the state courts of New-York, where the monopoly had triumphed over all opposition. And it need hardly be said, that the state courts of New-York have maintained as proud a reputation for learning, research, and talent, as any in the Union. What lawyer has not sat gladly at the feet of Chancellor Kent, and Chief Justice Spencer? And what state, in relation to her jurisprudence, can so boldly say—

"Quæ regio in terris nostri non plena laboris?"

Mr. Webster's argument in the opening of this case,—which was closed with great power by the Attorney-General, Mr. Wirt,—furnishes, even in the meagre outline still preserved, p. 170-184, a specimen of some of the characteristics of his mind. We here see his clearness and downright simplicity in stating facts; his acute suggestion and analysis of difficulties; his peculiar power of disentangling complicated propositions, and resolving them into elements so plain, as to be intelligible to the simplest minds; and his wariness not to be betrayed into untenable positions, or to spread his forces over useless ground. We see him, indeed, fortifying himself, as it were, strongly within the narrowest limits of his cause, concentrating his strength, and ready at any moment to enter, like a skilful general, at all the weak points of his adversary's position. This argument, therefore, especially as it was originally pronounced in court, we look upon, as a whole, to have been equally remarkable for depth and sagacity; for the choice and comprehensiveness of the topics; and for the power and tact exhibited in their discussion. Yet we are carried along so quietly by its deep current, that, like Partridge in Tom Jones, when he saw Garrick act Hamlet, all seems to us so spontaneous, so completely without effort, that we are convinced, nay, we feel sure, there is neither artifice nor mystery, extraordinary power nor genius, in the whole matter. But, to those who are familiar with Mr. Webster, and the workings of his mind, it is well known, that, in this very plainness; in this earnest pursuit of truth for truth's sake, and of the principles of law for the sake of right and justice, and in his obvious desire to reach them all by the most direct and simple means, is to be found no small part of the secret of his power. It is this, in fact, above every thing else, that makes him so prevalent with the jury; and, not only with the jury in court, but with the great jury of the whole people.

The same general remarks are applicable to his argument in the case of Ogden against Saunders, in 1827, which we notice now, out of the regular series of events, in order to finish at once the little we can say of his professional career as a lawyer. The case to which we now refer, involved the question of the constitutionality of state insolvent laws, when they purported to absolve the party from the obligation of the *contract*, as well as from personal *imprisonment*, on execution. In a legal and constitutional point of view, this has always been thought one of Mr. Webster's ablest and most convincing arguments. With the court he was only half successful; there being a remarkable diversity of opinion among the judges. But, taken in connexion with the opinion of Chief Justice Marshall, delivered in the case, with which Mr. Webster's argument coincides, both in reasoning and in conclusion, it seems absolutely to have exhausted the whole range of the discussion on that side, and to furnish all that future inquirers can need to master the question.

But, during the years we have just passed over, Mr. Webster's success was not confined to the bar. In the year 1820-21, a convention of delegates was assembled in Boston, to revise the constitution of Massachusetts. As it was one of those primary assemblies, where no office disqualifies from membership, and as the occasion was one of the rarest importance, the talent and wisdom, the fortunes and authority of that commonwealth were, to a singular degree, collected in it. The venerable John Adams, then above eighty-five years old, represented his native village; Mr. Justice Story, of the Supreme Court of the United States, was a delegate from Salem; Judge Davis, of the District Court of the United States, and the greater part of the judicial officers of the state were there, as well as a large number of the leading members of the Massachusett's bar, and a still larger number of its wealthiest or most prominent land-holders and merchants. No assembly of equal dignity and talent was ever collected in that commonwealth. Mr. Webster was one of the delegates from Boston. What influence he exerted, or how beneficial, or how extensive it was, can be entirely known only there where it was put forth. But, if we may judge from the important committees on which he served; the prominent interests and individuals his duty called him occasionally to defend, to encounter, and to oppose; and the business-like air of his short remarks, which are scattered up and down through the whole volume of the "Journal of Debates and Proceedings" of this convention, published soon afterwards, we should be led to believe, that, though he was then but a newly adopted child of Massachusetts, he had already gained a degree of confidence, respect and authority, to which few in that ancient commonwealth could lay claim. The fruits of it all, in the present volume, are, a short speech on "Oaths of Office;" another on "the removal of Judges upon the address of two-thirds of each branch of the Legislature;" and a more ample and very powerful one on the "Principle of representation in the Senate." They are all strong and striking; and it would be easy to extract something from each, characteristic of its author; but we have not room, and must content ourselves with referring, for a specimen of the whole, to the remarks on the free schools of New-England, from the speech in the Senate, which we have already cited; adding merely, that, to this remarkable speech of Mr. Webster, and to another of great beauty and force, by Mr. Justice Story, was ascribed, at the time, a change in the opinions and vote of the convention, which, considering the importance of the subject, and the long discussion it had undergone, was all but unprecedented.[6]

While this convention was still in session, a great anniversary came round at the north. The two hundredth year from the first landing of the Pilgrims at Plymouth, was completed on the 22d of December, 1820; and every man born in New-England, or in whose veins stirred a drop of New-England blood, felt that he had an interest in the event it recalled, and demanded its grateful celebration. Preparations, therefore, for its commemoration, on the spot where it occurred, were made long beforehand; and, by the sure indication of the public will, and at the special invitation of the Pilgrim Society, Mr. Webster was summoned as the man who should go to the Rock of Plymouth, and there so speak of the centuries past, as that the centuries to come should still receive and heed his words. Undoubtedly he amply fulfilled the expectations that waited on this great occasion. His address, which opens the present volume, is one of the gravest productions it contains. He seems to feel that the ground on which he stands is holy; and the deep moral sensibility, and even religious solemnity, which pervade many parts

[6] North American Review, 1821. Vol. xii. p. 342.

of this striking discourse,—where he seems to have collected the experience of all the past, in order to minister warning and encouragement to all the future,—is in perfect harmony with the scene and the occasion, and produced its appropriate effect on the multitude elected, even at that inclement season, from the body of the New-England states, to offer up thanksgivings for their descent from the Pilgrim fathers. The effect, too, at the time, has been justified by a wider success since; and the multiplied editions of the printed discourse, while they have carried it into the farm-houses and hearts of the New-England yeomanry, are at the same time ensuring its passage onward to the next generation and the next, who may be well satisfied, when the same jubilee comes round, if they can leave behind them monuments equally imposing, to mark the lapse and revolutions of ages.

It would not be difficult to select eloquent passages from this discourse. We prefer, however, to take one containing what was then a plain and adventurous prediction; but what is now passing into history before our very eyes. We allude to the remarks on the principle of the subdivision of property in France, as affecting the permanency of the French government, which Mr. Webster ventured to call in question, on the same general grounds, on which he undertook to prove the permanency of our own.

> "A most interesting experiment of the effect of a subdivision of property on government, is now making in France. It is understood, that the law regulating the transmission of property, in that country, now divides it, real and personal, among all the children, equally, both sons and daughters; and that there is, also, a very great restraint on the power of making dispositions of property by will. It has been supposed, that the effects of this might probably be, in time, to break up the soil into such small subdivisions, that the proprietors would be too poor to resist the encroachments of executive power. I think far otherwise. What is lost in individual wealth, will be more than gained in numbers, in intelligence, and in a sympathy of sentiment. If, indeed, only one, or a few landholders were to resist the crown, like the barons of England, they must, of course, be great and powerful landholders with multitudes of retainers, to promise success. But if the proprietors of a given extent of territory are summoned to resistance, there is no reason to believe that such resistance would be less forcible, or less successful, because the number of such proprietors should be great. Each would perceive his own importance, and his own interest, and would feel that natural elevation of character which the consciousness of property inspires. A common sentiment would unite all, and numbers would not only add strength, but excite enthusiasm. It is true, that France possesses a vast military force, under the direction of an hereditary executive government, and military power, it is possible, may overthrow any government. It is in vain, however, in this period of the world, to look for security against military power, to the arm of the great landholders. That

notion is derived from a state of things long since past; a state in which a feudal baron, with his retainers, might stand against the sovereign, who was himself but the greatest baron, and his retainers. But at present, what could the richest landholder do, against one regiment of disciplined troops? Other securities, therefore, against the prevalence of military power must be provided. Happily for us, we are not so situated as that any purpose of national defence requires, ordinarily and constantly, such a military force as might seriously endanger our liberties.

"In respect, however, to the recent law of succession in France, to which I have alluded, *I would, presumptuously, perhaps, hazard a conjecture, that if the government do not change the law, the law, in half a century, will change the government; and that this change will be not in favour of the power of the crown, as some European writers have supposed, but against it.* Those writers only reason upon what they think correct general principles, in relation to this subject. They acknowledge a want of experience. Here we have had that experience; and we know that a multitude of small proprietors, acting with intelligence, and that enthusiasm which a common cause inspires, constitute not only a formidable, but an invincible power." Pp. 47-8.

In less than six years from the time when this statesman-like prediction was made, the King of France, at the opening of the Legislative Chambers, thus strangely and portentously echoed it,

"Legislation ought to provide by successive improvements, for all the wants of society. *The progressive partitioning of landed estates essentially contrary to the spirit of a monarchical government* would enfeeble the guaranties which the charter has given to my throne and to my subjects. Measures will be proposed to you, gentlemen, to establish the consistency which ought to exist between the political law and the civil law; and to preserve the patrimony of families, without restricting the liberty of disposing of one's property. The preservation of families is connected with, and affords a guaranty to political stability, which is the first want of states, and which is especially that of France after so many vicissitudes."

But the discovery came too late. The foundations, on which to build or sustain the cumbrous system of the old monarchy, were already taken away; and the events of the last summer, while they would almost persuade us, that the "Attendant Spirit" so boldly given by the orator in this very discourse to one of the great founders of our government, had opened to him, also, on the Rock of Plymouth, "a vision of the future;"[7]—these events, we say, can leave little doubt in the mind of any man, that the speaker himself may live long enough,—as God grant he may!—to witness the entire fulfilment of his own extraordinary prophecy, and to see the

[7] See the beautiful passage respecting the fortune and the life of John Adams at p. 44.

French people erecting for themselves a sure and stable government, suited to the foundation, on which alone it can now rest.

In 1825, Mr. Webster was called to interpret the feelings of New-England, on another great festival and anniversary. Fifty years from the day, when the grave drama of the American Revolution was opened with such picturesque solemnity, as a magnificent show on Bunker's Hill, witnessed by the whole neighbouring city and country, clustering by thousands on their steeples, the roofs of their houses, and the hill-tops, and waiting with unspeakable anxiety the results of the scene that was passing before their eyes,—fifty years from that day, it was determined to lay, with no less solemnity, the corner stone of a monument worthy to commemorate its importance. An immense multitude was assembled. They stood on that consecrated spot, with only the heavens over their heads, and beneath their feet the bones of their fathers; amidst the visible remains of the very redoubt thrown up by Prescott, and defended by him to the very last desperate extremity;[8] and with the names of Warren, Putnam, Stark, and Brooks, and the other leaders or victims of that great day frequent and familiar on their lips. In the midst of such a scene and with such recollections, starting like the spirits of the dead from the very sods of that hill-side, it may well be imagined, that words like the following, addressed to a vast audience,—composed in no small degree of the survivors of the battle, their children, and their grandchildren,—produced an effect, which only the hand of death can efface.

> "We know, indeed, that the record of illustrious actions is most safely deposited in the universal remembrance of mankind. We know, that if we could cause this structure to ascend, not only till it reached the skies, but till it pierced them, its broad surfaces could still contain but part of that, which, in an age of knowledge, hath already been spread over the earth, and which history charges itself with making known to all future times. We know, that no inscription on entablatures less broad than the earth itself, can carry information of the events we commemorate, where it has not already gone; and that no structure, which shall not outlive the duration of letters and knowledge among men, can prolong the memorial. But our object is, by this edifice, to show our own deep sense of the value and importance of the achievements of our ancestors; and, by presenting this work of gratitude to the eye, to keep alive similar sentiments, and to foster a constant regard for the principles of the Revolution. Human beings are com-

---

[8] In an able article on the battle of Bunker's Hill, which is found in the North American Review, 1818, VII. 225-258, and is understood to have been written by Mr. Webster, he says,—"In truth, if there was any commander-in-chief in the action, it was Prescott. From the first breaking of the ground to the retreat, he acted *the most important part*; and if it were now proper to give the battle a name from any distinguished agent in it, it should be called, Prescott's battle." We have no doubt this is but an exact measure of justice to one of those who hazarded all in our revolution, when the hazard was the greatest. The whole review is strong, and no one hereafter can write the history of the period it refers to, without consulting it. The opening description of the battle is beautiful and picturesque.

posed not of reason only, but of imagination also, and sentiment; and that is neither wasted nor misapplied which is appropriated to the purpose of giving right direction to sentiments, and opening proper springs of feeling in the heart. Let it not be supposed that our object is to perpetuate national hostility, or even to cherish a mere military spirit. It is higher, purer, nobler. We consecrate our work to the spirit of national independence, and we wish that the light of peace may rest upon it for ever. We rear a memorial of our conviction of that unmeasured benefit, which has been conferred on our own land, and of the happy influences, which have been produced, by the same events, on the general interests of mankind. We come, as Americans, to mark a spot, which must for ever be dear to us and our posterity. We wish, that whosoever, in all coming time, shall turn his eye hither, may behold that the place is not undistinguished, where the first great battle of the Revolution was fought. We wish, that this structure may proclaim the magnitude and importance of that event, to every class and every age. We wish, that infancy may learn the purpose of its erection from maternal lips, and that weary and withered age may behold it, and be solaced by the recollections which it suggests. We wish, that labour may look up here, and be proud, in the midst of its toil. We wish, that, in those days of disaster, which, as they come on all nations, must be expected to come on us also, desponding patriotism may turn its eyes hitherward, and be assured that the foundations of our national power still stand strong. We wish, that this column, rising towards heaven among the pointed spires of so many temples dedicated to God, may contribute also to produce, in all minds, a pious feeling of dependence and gratitude. We wish, finally, that the last object on the sight of him who leaves his native shore, and the first to gladden his who revisits it, may be something which shall remind him of the liberty and the glory of his country. Let it rise, till it meet the sun in his coming; let the earliest light of the morning gild it, and parting day linger and play on its summit." Pp. 58-9.

The last formal address delivered by Mr. Webster on any great public occasion, was unexpectedly called from him in the summer of 1826, in commemoration of the services of Adams and Jefferson;—an occasion so remarkable, that what was said and felt on it, will not pass out of the memories of the present generation. We shall, therefore, only make one short extract from Mr. Webster's address at Faneuil Hall—the description of the peculiar eloquence of Mr. Adams, in giving which, the speaker becomes, himself, a living example of what he describes.

"The eloquence of Mr. Adams resembled his general character, and formed, indeed, a part of it. It was bold, manly, and energetic; and such the crisis required. When public bodies are to be addressed on momentous occasions, when great interests are at stake, and strong passions excited, nothing is valuable, in speech, farther than it is connected with high intellectual and moral endowments. Clearness, force, and earnestness are the qualities which produce conviction. True eloquence, indeed, does not consist in speech. It cannot be brought from far. Labour and learning may toil for it, but they will toil in vain. Words and phrases may be marshalled in every way, but they cannot compass it. It must exist in the man, in the subject, and in the occasion. Affected passion, intense expression, the pomp of declamation, all may aspire after it—they cannot reach it. It comes, if it come at all, like the outbreaking of a fountain from the earth, or the bursting forth of volcanic fires, with spontaneous, original, native force. The graces taught in the schools, the costly ornaments, and studied contrivances of speech, shock and disgust men, when their own lives, and the fate of their wives, their children, and their country, hang on the decision of the hour. Then words have lost their power, rhetoric is vain, and all elaborate oratory contemptible. Even genius itself, then feels rebuked, and subdued, as in the presence of higher qualities. Then, patriotism is eloquent; then, self-devotion is eloquent. The clear conception, outrunning the deductions of logic, the high purpose, the firm resolve, the dauntless spirit, speaking on the tongue, beaming from the eye, informing every feature, and urging the whole man onward, right onward to his object—this, this is eloquence; or rather it is something greater and higher than all eloquence, it is action, noble, sublime, god-like action." page 84.

During a part, however, of the period, over which we have thus very slightly passed, Mr. Webster was again in public life. He was elected to represent the city of Boston, in the seventeenth Congress, and took his seat there in December, 1823. Early in the session, he presented a resolution in favour of appointing a commissioner or agent to Greece; and the resolution being taken up on the 19th of January following, Mr. Webster delivered the speech, which usually passes under the name of "the Greek Speech." His object, however, in presenting the resolution, did not seem, at first, to be well understood. It was believed, that, seeing the existence of a warm public sympathy for the suffering Greeks, and solicited by the attractions of the subject itself, and of the classical associations awakened by it, his object was to parade a few sentences and figures, and so make an oration or harangue, which might usher him, with some *éclat*, a second time, upon the theatre of public affairs. The galleries, therefore, were thronged with a brilliant and fashionable audience. But the crowd was destined to be disappointed;—Mr. Webster, after a graceful and conciliating introduction, in which he evidently disclaimed any such purpose, addressed himself at once to the subject, and made, what he always makes, a powerful, but a downright business speech. His object, instead of being the narrow one suggested for him, was apparent, as he advanced, to be the broadest possible. It was nothing less, than to take occasion of the Greek revolution, and the conduct pursued in regard to it by the great continental powers, in order to exhibit the principles laid down and avowed by those powers, as the basis on which they intended to maintain the peace of Europe. In doing this, he went through a very able examination of the proceedings of all the famous Congresses, beginning with that of Paris, in 1814, and coming down to that of Laybach, in 1821;—the principles of all which were, that the people hold their fundamental rights and privileges, as matter of concession and indulgence from the sovereign power; and that all sovereign powers have a right to interfere and controul other nations, in their desires and attempts to change their own governments:—

> "The ultimate effect of this alliance of sovereigns, for objects personal to themselves, or respecting only the permanency of their own power, must be the destruction of all just feeling, and all natural sympathy, between those who exercise the power of government, and those who are subject to it. The old channels of mutual regard and confidence are to be dried up, or cut off. Obedience can now be expected no longer than it is enforced. Instead of relying on the affections of the governed, sovereigns are to rely on the affections and friendship of other sovereigns. They are, in short, no longer to be nations. Princes and people no longer are to unite for interests common to them both. There is to be an end of all patriotism, as a distinct national feeling. Society is to be divided horizontally; all sovereigns above, and all subjects below; the former coalescing for their own security, and for the more certain subjection of the undistinguished multitude beneath." page 249.

But, as he says afterwards,—

> "This reasoning mistakes the age. The time has been, indeed, when fleets, and armies, and subsidies, were the principal reliances even in the best cause. But, happily for mankind, there has arrived a great change in this respect. Moral causes come into consideration, in proportion as the progress of knowledge is advanced; and the *public opinion* of the civilized world is rapidly gaining an ascendency over mere brutal force. It is already able to oppose the most formidable obstruction to the progress of injustice and oppression; and, as it grows more intelligent and more intense, it will be more and more formidable. It may be silenced by military power, but it cannot be conquered. It is elastic, irrepressible, and invulnerable to the weapons of ordinary warfare. It is that impassable, unextinguishable enemy of mere violence and arbitrary rule, which, like Milton's angels,

'Vital in every part,
Cannot, but by annihilating, die.'

> "Until this be propitiated or satisfied, it is vain for power to talk either of triumphs or of repose. No matter what fields are desolated, what fortresses surrendered, what armies subdued, or what provinces overrun. In the history of the year that has passed

by us, and in the instance of unhappy Spain, we have seen the vanity of all triumphs, in a cause which violates the general sense of justice of the civilized world. It is nothing, that the troops of France have passed from the Pyrenees to Cadiz; it is nothing that an unhappy and prostrate nation has fallen before them; it is nothing that arrests, and confiscation, and execution, sweep away the little remnant of national resistance. There is an enemy that still exists to check the glory of these triumphs. It follows the conqueror back to the very scene of his ovations; it calls upon him to take notice that Europe, though silent, is yet indignant; it shows him that the sceptre of his victory is a barren sceptre; that it shall confer neither joy nor honour, but shall moulder to dry ashes in his grasp. In the midst of his exultation, it pierces his ear with the cry of injured justice, it denounces against him the indignation of an enlightened and civilized age; it turns to bitterness the cup of his rejoicing, and wounds him with the sting which belongs to the consciousness of having outraged the opinion of mankind.

"In my own opinion, Sir, the Spanish nation is now nearer, not only in point of time, but in point of circumstance, to the acquisition of a regulated government, than at the moment of the French invasion. Nations must, no doubt, undergo these trials in their progress to the establishment of free institutions. The very trials benefit them, and render them more capable both of obtaining and of enjoying the object which they seek." page 253.

How completely does the mighty drama now passing before our eyes on the great theatre of Europe, justify these hold and sagacious predictions! A great revolution has just taken place in France, and a distinguished prince, out of the regular line of succession, has been invited to the throne, *on condition* of governing according to the constitution prescribed by the representatives of the popular will. Belgium is doing the same thing. Devoted Poland has attempted it. Italy is in confusion,—and Germany disturbed and uneasy;—so that, it seems already no longer to be in the power of any conspiracy of kings or Congresses, to maintain permanently in Western Europe, a government not essentially founded on free institutions and principles. We will only add, that Mr. Webster has, on hardly any other occasion, entered into the discussion of European politics; and the consequence has been, that, if this speech has found less favour at home than some of his other efforts, it is one, that has brought him great honour abroad; since, besides being printed wherever the English tongue is spoken, it has been circulated through South America, and published in nearly every one of the civilized languages of Europe, including the Spanish and the Greek.

In April, 1824, he took a part in the great discussion of the tariff question; and his speech on that occasion, as well as the one he delivered on the same subject in May, 1828, are both given in the volume before us. But the whole matter is so fresh in the recollections of the community, and Mr. Webster's constant defence of a tariff adapted to the general interests of the country, encouraging alike the cause of American manufactures and the interests of commerce, are so well known, from the first tariff of 1816, to the present moment, that it cannot be needful to speak of them. We would remark, however, that, in the speech of 1824, two subjects are discussed with great ability;—the doctrine of exchange, and the balance of trade. Both of them had been drawn into controversy in Congress, on previous occasions, quite frequently, calling forth alternately "an infinite deal of nothing," and the crudest absurdities; but, from the period of this thorough and statesmanlike examination of them, they have, we believe, hardly been heard of in either house. The great points involved in both of them, have been considered as settled.

We have thus far spoken of Mr. Webster almost entirely as a public orator and debater, or as a jurist. But there is another point of view, in which he is less known to the nation, but no less valued at Washington. He has few equals in the diligence of the committee-rooms. Reputation in and out of Congress, is, in this respect, very differently measured. Nothing is more common in either House than moderately good speakers, prompt in common debate, and sufficiently well instructed not to betray themselves into contempt with the public. Because they *can* speak and *do* speak; and especially because they speak *often* and *vehemently*, they obtain a transient credit abroad for far more than they are worth, and far more than they are, at last, able to maintain. It may, indeed, be said, as a general truth, that those who speak most frequently in Congress are least heeded, and least entitled to distinction. Members of real ability speak rarely; and, when they do speak, it is from the fulness of their minds, after a careful consideration of the subject, and with a deference for the body they address, and a regard to the public service, which does not permit them to occupy more time than the development of their subject absolutely requires. They are, therefore, always heard with attention and respect; and often with the conviction, that they may be safely followed.

But there is another class in Congress, less known to the public at large, and yet whose services are beyond price. We speak now of those excellent men, who, as chairmen and members of the committees, in the retired corners of the capitol, are doing the real business of legislation, and giving their days and nights to maturing schemes of wise policy and just relief; men who are content, week after week, and month after month, to sacrifice themselves to the negative toil of saving us from the follies of indiscreet, meddlesome, and ignorant innovators, or from the more presumptuous purposes of those who would make legislation the means of furthering and gratifying their own private, unprincipled ambition. Such business-men,—who should be the heads of the working party, if such a party should ever be formed,—are well understood within the walls of Congress. They are marked by the general confidence that follows them; and when they speak, to propose a measure, they are listened to; nay, it may almost be said, they are obeyed.

Mr. Webster has long been known as an efficient labourer in these noiseless toils of the committee-rooms and of practical legislation; and we owe to his hand not a few important improvements in our laws. The most remarkable is, probably, the Crimes-Act of 1825, which, in twenty-six sections, did so much for the criminal code of the country. The whole subject, when he approached it, was full of difficulties and deficiencies. The law in relation to it remained substantially on the foundation of the first great Act of 1790, ch. 36. That act, however, though deserving praise as a first attempt to meet the wants of the country, was entirely unsuited to its condition, and deficient in most important particulars. Its defects, indeed, were so numerous, that half the most notorious crimes, when committed where the general government alone could have cognizance of them, were left beyond the reach of human law and punishment;—rape, burglary, arson and other malicious burnings in forts, arsenals, and light-house establishments, together with many other offences, being wholly unprovided for. Mr. Webster's Act, which, as a just tribute to his exertions, already bears his name, cures these gross defects, besides a multitude of others; and it was well known at the time, that he wished to go much further, and give a competent system to the country on the whole criminal code, but was deterred by the danger of failure, if he attempted too much at once. Indeed, the difficulty of obtaining a patient hearing for any bill of such complexity and extent, is well understood in Congress; and it is not, perhaps, an unjust reproach upon our national legislature to confess, that even the most experienced statesmen are rarely able to carry through any great measure of purely practical improvement. Temporary projects, and party strifes, and private claims, and individual jealousies, and, above all, the passion for personal display in everlasting debate, offer obstacles to the success of mere patriotism and statesmanship, which are all but insurmountable. Probably no man, at that time, but Mr. Webster, who, in addition to his patient habits of labour in the committee-room, possessed the general confidence of the House, and had a persevering address and promptitude in answering objections, could have succeeded in so signal an undertaking. Sir Samuel Romilly and Mr. Peel have acquired lasting and merited reputations in England for meliorations of their criminal code. But they had a willing audience, and an eager support. Mr. Webster, without either, effected as much in his Crimes-Act of 1825, as has been effected by any single effort of these statesmen, and is fairly to be ranked with them among those benefactors of mankind, who have enlightened the jurisprudence of their country, and made it at once more efficient and more humane.

At the same session of Congress, the great question of internal improvements came up, and was vehemently discussed in January, on the appropriation made for the western national road. Mr. Webster defended the principle, as he had already defended it in 1816; and as he has defended it constantly since, down to the last year and the last session, without, so far as we have seen, receiving any sufficient answer to the positions he took in debate on these memorable occasions. Perhaps the doctrine he has so uniformly maintained on this subject, is less directly favourable to the interests of the northern than of the western states; but it was high-toned and national throughout, and seems in no degree to have impaired the favour with which he was regarded in New-England. At any rate, he was re-elected, with singular unanimity, to represent the city of Boston in the nineteenth Congress, and took his seat there anew in December, 1825.

In both sessions of this Congress, important subjects were discussed, and Mr. Webster bore an important part in them; but we can now only suggest one or two of them. As chairman of the Judiciary Committee, he introduced the bill for enlarging the number of judges of the Supreme Court of the United States. His views in relation to it are contained in the remarks he made on the occasion, and had great weight with the House; but the bill was afterwards lost through an amendment of the Senate. So, too, on the question of the Panama mission, involving the points that were first moved in 1796 in the House of Representatives, on occasion of the British Treaty, Mr. Webster has left on record his opinions, doctrines, and feelings, in a speech of great beauty and power, which will always be recurred to, whenever the right of the House of Representatives to advise the executive in relation to the management of foreign missions may come under discussion. But we are compelled to abstain from any further notice of them both, by want of room.

In 1826, he had been elected, we believe, all but unanimously, to represent the City of Boston, in the House of Representatives; but, before he took his seat, a vacancy having occurred in the Senate, he was chosen to fill it by the Legislature of Massachusetts, of which, a great majority in both its branches, besides the council and the governor, belonged to the old republican party of the country. He was chosen, too, under circumstances, which showed how completely his talents and lofty national bearing had disarmed all political animosities, and how thoroughly that commonwealth claimed him as her own, and cherished his reputation and influence as a part of her treasures. There was no regular nomination of him from any quarter, nor any regular opposition; and he received the appointment by a sort of general consent and acclamation, as if it were given with pride and pleasure, as well as with unhesitating confidence and respect.

How he has borne himself in the Senate during the four sessions he has sat there, is known to the whole country. No man has been found tall enough to overshadow him; no man has been able to attract from him, or to intercept from him, the constant regard of the nation. He has been so conspicuous, so prominent, that whatever he has done, and whatever he has said, has been watched and understood throughout the borders of the land, almost as familiarly and thoroughly as it has been at Washington.

But though the eyes of all have thus been fastened on him in such a way, that nothing relating to him can have escaped their notice, there is yet one occasion, where he attracted a kind and degree of attention, which, as it is rarely given, is so much the more honourable when it is obtained. We refer now, of course, to the occasion, when, in 1830, he overthrew the Doctrines of Nullification. Undoubtedly, in one sense of the word, Mr. Webster was taken completely by surprise, when these doctrines, for the first time in the history of the country, were announced in the Senate; since he was so far from any particular preparation to meet or answer them, that it was almost by accident he was in his place, when they were so unexpectedly, at least to him and all his friends, brought forth. In another and better sense of the phrase, he was not taken by surprise at all; for the time was already long gone by, when, on any great question of national interest or constitutional principle, he could be taken unprepared or unarmed. We mean by this, that the discussion of the most important points in the memorable debate alluded to, came on incidentally; or rather that these points were thrust forward by a few individuals, who seemed predetermined to proceed under cover of them, to the ultimate limits of personal and party violence.

Mr. Foot's resolution to inquire respecting the sales and the surveys of western lands, was the innocent cause of the whole conflict. It was introduced on the 29th of December, 1829; and was not then expected by its author, or, perhaps, by any body else to excite much discussion, or lead to any very important results. When it was introduced, Mr. Webster was absent from Washington. Two days afterwards he took his seat. The resolution had, indeed, called forth a few remarks, somewhat severe, the day after it was presented, and then had been postponed to the next Monday; but, apparently from want of interest in its fate, or from the pressure of more important business, it was not called up by the mover till January 13. From this time, a partial discussion began; but it lingered rather lifelessly, and, in fact, really rose even to skirmishing only one day, until the 19th, when General Hayne, a distinguished senator from South Carolina, in a vehement and elaborate speech, attacked the New-England States for what he considered their selfish opposition to the interests of the West; and endeavoured to show that a natural sympathy existed between the Southern and Western States, upon the distribution and sales of the public lands, which would necessarily make them a sort of natural allies. With this speech, of course, the war broke out.

While it was delivering, Mr. Webster entered the Senate. He came from the Supreme Court of the United States; and the papers in his hands showed how far his thoughts were from the subjects and the tone, which now at once reached him. As soon as General Hayne sat down, he rose to reply; but Mr. Benton of Missouri, with many compliments to General Hayne, and apparently willing the Senate should have all the leisure necessary to consider and feel the effects of his speech, moved an adjournment; Mr. Webster good naturedly consented. Of course, he had the floor the next day; and in a speech, which will not be forgotten by the present generation, poured out stores of knowledge long before accumulated, in relation to the history of the public lands and to the legislation concerning them; defending the policy of the government towards the new states; showing the dangerous tendency of the doctrines respecting the Constitution, current at the South, and sanctioned by General Hayne; and repelling the general charges and reproaches cast on New-England, especially the charge of hostility to the West, which,—if there was meaning in words or acts,—he proved to be distinctly applicable to the language and votes of the South Carolina delegation in the House of Representatives in 1825. The war was thus, at once, carried into the enemy's country.

The next day, January 21, it being well known that Mr. Webster had urgent business, which called him again into the Supreme Court of the United States, one of the members from Maryland moved an adjournment of the debate. It would, perhaps, have been only what is customary and courteous, if the request had been granted. But General Hayne objected. "The gentleman," he said, "had discharged his weapon, and he (Mr. H.) wished for an opportunity to return the fire." To which Mr. Webster having replied;—"I am ready to receive it; let the discussion go on;"—the debate was resumed. Mr. Benton then concluded some important remarks he had begun the day before; and Mr. Hayne rose, and opened a speech, which occupied the Senate the remainder of that day, and the whole of the day following. It was a vigorous speech, embracing a great number of topics and grounds;—calling in question the fairness of New-England, the consistency of Mr. Webster, and the patriotism of the State of Massachusetts;—and ending with a bold, acute, and elaborated exposition and defence of the doctrines now, for the first time, formally developed in Congress, and since well known by the name of the *Doctrines of Nullification*. The first part of the speech was caustic and personal; the latter part of it grave and argumentative;—and the whole was delivered in presence of an audience, which any man might be proud to have collected to listen to him.

Mr. Webster took notes during its delivery; and it was apparent to the crowd, which, for two days, had thronged the senate-chamber, that he intended to reply. Indeed, on this point, he was permitted no choice. He had been assailed in a way, which called for an answer. When, therefore, the doors of the senate-chamber were opened the next morning, the rush for admittance was unprecedented. Mr. Webster had the floor, and rose. The first division of his speech is in reply to parts and details of his adversary's personal assault,—and is a happy, though severe specimen of the keenest spirit of genuine debate and retort;—for Mr. Webster is one of those dangerous adversaries, who are never so formidable or so brilliant, as when they are most rudely pressed;—for then, as in the phosphorescence of the ocean, the degree of the violence urged, may always be taken as the measure of the brightness that is to follow. On the present occasion, his manner was cool, entirely self-possessed, and perfectly decided, and carried his irony as far as irony can go. There are portions of this first day's discussion, like the passage relating to the charge of sleeping on the speech, he had answered; the one in allusion to Banquo's ghost, which had been unhappily conjured up by his adversary; and the rejoinder respecting "one Nathan Dane of Beverly, in Massachusetts,"—which will not be forgotten. The very tones in which they were uttered, still vibrate in the ears of those who heard them. There are, also, other and graver portions of it,—like those which respect the course of legislation in regard to the new states; the conduct of the North in regard to slavery, and the doctrine of internal improvements,—which are in the most powerful style of parliamentary debate. As he approaches the conclusion of this first great division of his speech, he rises to the loftiest tone of national feeling, entirely above the dim, misty region of sectional or party passion and prejudice:—

> "The eulogium pronounced on the character of the state of South Carolina, by the honourable gentleman, for her revolutionary and other merits, meets my hearty concurrence. I shall not acknowledge that the honourable member goes before me in regard for whatever of distinguished talent, or distinguished character, South Carolina has produced. I claim part of the honour, I partake in the pride, of her great names. I claim them for countrymen, one and all. The Laurenses, the Rutledges, the Pinckneys, the Sumpters, the Marions—Americans, all—whose fame is no more to be hemmed in by state lines, than their talents and patriotism were

capable of being circumscribed within the same narrow limits. In their day and generation, they served and honoured the country, and the whole country; and their renown is of the treasures of the whole country. Him, whose honoured name the gentleman himself bears—does he esteem me less capable of gratitude for his patriotism, or sympathy for his sufferings, than if his eyes had first opened upon the light of Massachusetts, instead of South Carolina? Sir, does he suppose it in his power to exhibit a Carolina name, so bright, as to produce envy in my bosom? No, Sir, increased gratification and delight, rather. I thank God, that, if I am gifted with little of the spirit which is able to raise mortals to the skies, I have yet none, as I trust, of that other spirit, which would drag angels down. When I shall be found, Sir, in my place here, in the Senate, or elsewhere, to sneer at public merit, because it happens to spring up beyond the little limits of my own state, or neighbourhood; when I refuse, for any such cause, or for any cause, the homage due to American talent, to elevated patriotism, to sincere devotion to liberty and the country; or, if I see an uncommon endowment of Heaven—if I see extraordinary capacity and virtue in any son of the South—and if, moved by local prejudice, or gangrened by state jealousy, I get up here to abate the tithe of a hair from his just character and just fame, may my tongue cleave to the roof of my mouth!

"Sir, let me recur to pleasing recollections—let me indulge in refreshing remembrance of the past—let me remind you that in early times, no states cherished greater harmony, both of principle and feeling, than Massachusetts and South Carolina. Would to God that harmony might again return! Shoulder to shoulder they went through the revolution—hand in hand they stood round the administration of Washington, and felt his own great arm lean on them for support. Unkind feeling, if it exist, alienation and distrust, are the growth, unnatural to such soils, of false principles since sown. They are weeds, the seeds of which that same great arm never scattered.

"Mr. President, I shall enter on no encomium upon Massachusetts—she needs none. There she is—behold her, and judge for yourselves. There is her history: the world knows it by heart. The past, at least, is secure. There is Boston, and Concord, and Lexington, and Bunker Hill—and there they will remain forever. The bones of her sons, falling in the great struggle for independence, now lie mingled with the soil of every state, from New England to Georgia; and there they will lie forever. And, Sir, where American liberty raised its first voice; and where its youth was nurtured and sustained, there it still lives, in the strength of its manhood and full of its original spirit. If discord and disunion shall wound it—if party strife and blind ambition shall hawk at and tear it—if folly and madness—if uneasiness, under salutary and necessary restraint—shall succeed to separate it from that union, by which alone its existence is made sure, it will stand, in the end, by the side of that cradle in which its infancy was rocked: it will stretch forth its arm with whatever of vigour it may still retain, over the friends who gather round it; and it will fall at last, if fall it must, amidst the proudest monuments of its own glory, and on the very spot of its origin." pages 406, 407.

The next day, Mr. Webster went into a grave and formal examination of *the doctrines of nullification*, or the right of the state legislatures to interfere, whenever, in their judgment, the general government transcends its constitutional limits, and to arrest the operation of its laws. Four days had hardly elapsed, since this doctrine had been announced with an air of assured success in the Senate; and these four days had been filled with active debate and contest. Of course, here again, there had been neither time nor opportunity for especial preparation. Happily, too, there was no need of it. The fund, on which the demand was so triumphantly made, was equal to the draft, great and unexpected as it was. Mr. Webster's mind is full of constitutional law and legislation. On all such subjects, he needs no forecast, no preparation, no brief;—and, on this occasion, he had none. He but uttered opinions and arguments, which had grown mature with his years and his judgment, and which were as familiar to him as household words. We have, therefore, no elaborate, documentary discussion,—no citation of books or authorities. It is with principles, great constitutional principles, he deals; and it is in plain, direct arguments, which all can understand, that he defends them. There is nothing technical, nothing abstruse, nothing indirect, either in the subject or its explanation. On the contrary, all is straight forward—obvious—to the purpose. For instance, after stating the question at issue to be, "*whose prerogative is it, to decide on the constitutionality or unconstitutionality of the laws?*" he goes on:—

"This leads us to inquire into the origin of this government, and the source of its power. Whose agent is it? Is it the creature of the state legislatures, or the creature of the people? If the government of the United States be the agent of the state governments, then they may control it, provided they can agree in the manner of controlling it; if it be the agent of the people, then the people alone can control it, restrain it, modify, or reform it. It is observable enough, that the doctrine for which the honourable gentleman contends, leads him to the necessity of maintaining, not only that this general government is the creature of the states, but that it is the creature of each of the states severally; so that each may assert the power, for itself, of determining whether it acts within the limits of its authority. It is the servant of four and twenty masters, of different wills and different purposes, and yet bound to obey all. This absurdity (for it seems no less) arises from a misconception as to the origin of this government and its true character. It is, Sir, the people's constitution, the people's government,—made for the people,—made by the people,—and answerable to the people. The people of the United States have declared that this constitution shall be the supreme law. We must either admit the proposition, or dispute their authority. The states are, unquestionably, sovereign, so far as their sovereignty is not affected by this supreme law. But the state legislatures, as political bodies, however sovereign, are yet not sovereign over the people. So far as the people have given power to the general government, so far the grant is unquestionably good, and the government holds of the people, and not of the state governments. We are all agents of the same supreme power, the people.—The general government and the state governments derive their authority from the same source. Neither can, in relation to the other, be called primary, though one is definite and restricted, and the other general and residuary. The national government possesses those powers which it can be shown the people have conferred on it, and no more. All the rest belongs to the state governments, or to the people themselves. So far as the people have restrained state sovereignty, by the expression of their will, in the constitution of the United States, so far, it must be admitted, state sovereignty is effectually controlled. I do not contend that it is, or ought to be controlled farther. The sentiment to which I have referred, propounds that state sovereignty is only to be controlled by its own "feeling of justice;" that is to say, it is not to be controlled at all; for one who is to follow his own feelings is under no legal control.—Now, however men may think this ought to be, the fact is, that the people of the United States have chosen to impose control on state sovereignties. There are those, doubtless, who wish they had been left without restraint; but the constitution has ordered the matter differently. To make war, for instance, is an exercise of sovereignty; but the constitution declares that no state shall make war. To coin money is another exercise of sovereign power; but no state is at liberty to coin money. Again, the constitution says that no sovereign state shall be so sovereign as to make a treaty. These prohibitions, it must be confessed, are a control on the state sovereignty of South Carolina, as well as of the other states, which does not arise "from her own feelings of honourable justice." Such an opinion, therefore, is in defiance of the plainest provisions of the constitution." pages 410, 411.

Again, what can be more sure and convincing than such plain reasoning as this:—

"I maintain, that, between submission to the decision of the constituted tribunals, and revolution, or disunion, there is no middle ground—there is no ambiguous condition, half allegiance, and half rebellion. And, Sir, how futile, how very futile it is, to admit the right of state interference, and then attempt to save it from the character of unlawful resistance, by adding terms of qualification to the causes, and occasions, leaving all these qualifications, like the case itself, in the discretion of the state governments. It must be a clear case, it is said, a deliberate case; a palpable case; a dangerous case. But then the state is still left at liberty to decide for herself, what is clear, what is deliberate, what is palpable, what is dangerous. Do adjectives and epithets avail any thing? Sir, the human mind is so constituted, that the merits of both sides of a controversy appear very clear, and very palpable, to those who respectively espouse them; and both sides usually grow clearer as the controversy advances. South Carolina sees unconstitutionality in the tariff; she sees oppression there, also; and she sees danger. Pennsylvania, with a vision not less sharp, looks at the same tariff, and sees no such thing in it—she sees it all constitutional, all useful, all safe. The faith of South Carolina is strengthened by opposition, and she now not only sees, but *resolves*, that the tariff is palpably unconstitutional, oppressive, and dangerous: but Pennsylvania, not to be behind her neighbours, and equally willing to strengthen her own faith by a confident asseveration, *resolves*, also, and gives to every warm affirmative of South Carolina, a plain, downright, Pennsylvania negative. South Carolina, to show the strength and unity of her opinion, brings her assembly to a unanimity, within seven voices; Pennsylvania, not to be outdone in this respect more than others, reduces her dissentient fraction to a single vote. Now, Sir, again, I ask the gentleman, what is to be done? Are these states both right? Is he bound to consider them both right? If not, which is in the wrong?—or rather, which has the best right to decide? And if he, and if I, are not to know what the constitution means, and what it is, till those two state legislatures, and the twenty-two others, shall agree in its construction, what have we sworn to, when we have sworn to maintain it? I was forcibly struck, Sir, with one reflection, as the gentleman went on in his speech. He quoted Mr. Madison's resolutions, to prove that a state may interfere, in a case of deliberate, palpable, and dangerous exercise of a power not granted. The honourable member supposes the tariff law to be such an exercise of power; and that, consequently, a case has arisen in which the state may, if it see fit, interfere by its own law. Now, it so happens, nevertheless, that Mr. Madison deems this same tariff law quite constitutional. Instead of a clear and palpable violation, it is, in his judgment, no violation at all. So that, while they use his authority for a hypothetical case, they reject it in the very case before them. All this, Sir, shows the inherent—futility—I had almost used a stronger word—of conceding this power of interference to the states, and then attempting to secure it from abuse by imposing qualifications, of which the states themselves are to judge. One of two things is true; either the laws of the Union are beyond the discretion, and beyond the control of the states; or else we have no constitution of general government, and are thrust back again to the days of the confederacy." pp. 416, 417.

This is a striking fact about Mr. Madison; but one still more striking occurred after the publication of the speech. His great name and authority had been constantly and confidently appealed to, not only in this debate, by General Hayne, but, on previous occasions, by other favourers of the South Carolina doctrines, until at last it began to be almost feared, that Mr. Madison sustained the positions of the nullifiers. But as he had already shown that the tariff law was quite constitutional, so, now, with no less promptness and power, he came out against the whole doctrine of nullification, and showed that his resolutions of 1798, on which its friends had rested the wild fabric of their argument, as its main pillars, had nothing to do with it; and thus, in conjunction with what had been done in the Senate, brought down the whole temple they had built with such pains and cost, upon the heads of their uncircumcised presumption and extravagance. His letter, indeed, on this subject, is one of the most characteristic efforts of his great wisdom, and one of the most important results of this discussion, since it took from the advocates of nullification all the support of his authority—the *magni nominis umbra*—the shade and shelter of his great name.

But to return to Mr. Webster; the general tone of the last half of his speech is uncommonly grave and imposing; but there is one passage in which a lighter accent is assumed. It is that in which he runs out General Hayne's nullifying doctrine into practice, and sets him, as a military man, to execute his own nullifying law. The argument of this passage is the more efficacious, because it is concealed under so much wit and good-humour.

> "And now, Mr. President, let me run the honourable gentleman's doctrine a little into its practical application. Let us look at his probable *modus operandi*. If a thing can be done, an ingenious man can tell *how* it is to be done. Now, I wish to be informed, *how* this state interference is to be put in practice. We will take the existing case of the tariff law. South Carolina is said to have made up her opinion upon it. If we do not repeal it, (as we probably shall not,) she will then apply to the case the remedy of her doctrine. She will, we must suppose, pass a law of her legislature, declaring the several acts of Congress, usually called the Tariff Laws, null and void, so far as they respect South Carolina, or the citizens thereof. So far, all is a paper transaction, and easy enough. But the collector at Charleston, is collecting the duties imposed by these tariff laws—he, therefore, must be stopped. The collector will seize the goods if the tariff duties are not paid. The state authorities will undertake their rescue; the marshal, with his posse, will come to the collector's aid, and here the contest begins. The

militia of the state will be called out to sustain the nullifying act. They will march, Sir, under a very gallant leader: for I believe the honourable member himself commands the militia of that part of the state. He will raise the *Nullifying Act* on his standard, and spread it out as his banner. It will have a preamble, bearing that the tariff laws are palpable, deliberate, and dangerous violations of the Constitution! He will proceed, with his banner flying, to the custom-house in Charleston;

'All the while,
Sonorous metal blowing martial sounds.'

Arrived at the custom-house, he will tell the collector that he must collect no more duties under any of the tariff laws. This, he will be somewhat puzzled to say, by the way, with a grave countenance, considering what hand South Carolina herself had in that of 1816. But, Sir, the collector would, probably, not desist, at his bidding. He would show him the law of Congress, the treasury instruction, and his own oath of office. He would say, he should perform his duty, come what might. Here would ensue a pause: for they say that a certain stillness precedes the tempest. The trumpeter would hold his breath awhile, and before all this military array should fall on the custom-house, collector, clerks, and all, it is very probable some of those composing it, would request of their gallant commander-in-chief, to be informed a little upon the point of law; for they have, doubtless, a just respect for his opinions as a lawyer, as well as for his bravery as a soldier. They know he has read Blackstone and the Constitution, as well as Turrene and Vauban. They would ask him, therefore, something concerning their rights in this matter. They would inquire, whether it was not somewhat dangerous to resist a law of the United States. What would be the nature of their offence, they would wish to learn, if they, by military force and array, resisted the execution in Carolina of a law of the United States, and it should turn out, after all, that the law *was constitutional*? He would answer, of course, treason. No lawyer could give any other answer. John Fries, he would tell them, had learned that some years ago. How, then, they would ask, do you propose to defend us? We are not afraid of bullets, but treason has a way of taking people off, that we do not much relish. How do you propose to defend us? 'Look at my floating banner,' he would reply, 'see there the *nullifying law!*' Is it your opinion, gallant commander, they would then say, that if we should be indicted for treason, that same floating banner of yours would make a good plea in bar? 'South Carolina is a sovereign state,' he would reply. That is true—but would the judge admit our plea? 'These tariff laws,' he would repeat, 'are unconstitutional, palpably, deliberately, dangerously.' That all may be so; but if the tribunal should not happen to be of that opinion, shall we swing for it? We are ready to die for our country, but it is rather an awkward business, this dying without touching the ground! After all, that is a sort of *hemp*-tax, worse than any part of the tariff.

Mr. President, the honourable gentleman would be in a dilemma, like that of another great general. He would have a knot before him which he could not untie. He must cut it with his sword. He must say to his followers, defend yourselves with your bayonets; and this is war—civil war." pp. 421, 422.

After this his tone becomes even more grave and solemn than before, until, when he approaches the conclusion, he bursts forth with the expression of feelings of attachment to the Union and the Constitution, which it seemed no longer possible for him to suppress. We should quote the passage, but that it has been quoted every where, and is familiar to every body.

We forbear to pursue this debate any further. Mr. Hayne replied in a short speech, which he afterwards expanded in the newspapers into a long one; and Mr. Webster rejoined with a syllogistic brevity, exactness, and power, which carried with them the force and conclusiveness of a demonstration; and thus ended the discussion as between these two. It was afterwards continued, however, for several weeks, and a majority, or nearly a majority, of the whole Senate took part in it; but whenever it is now recollected or referred to, the contest between the two principal speakers, from the 19th to the 23d of January, is, we believe, generally intended.

The results of this memorable debate are already matter of history. The vast audience that had contended for admission to the senate-chamber, till entrance became dangerous, were the first to feel and make known its effect; for, with his peculiar power of explaining abstruse and technical subjects, so that all can comprehend them, Mr. Webster there expounded a great doctrine of the constitution, which had been powerfully assailed, so that all might feel the foundations on which it rests, to have been consolidated rather than disturbed by the attempt to shake them. Their verdict, therefore, was given at the time, and heard throughout the country. But since that day, when the crowd came out of the senate-chamber rejoicing in the victory which had been achieved for the constitution, nearly twenty editions of the same argument have been called for in different parts of the country, and thus scattered abroad above an hundred thousand copies of it, besides the countless multitudes that have been sent forth by the newspapers, until almost without a metaphor, it may be said to have been carried to every fire-side in the land. The very question, therefore, which was first submitted to an audience in the capitol,—comprising, indeed, a remarkable representation of the talents and authority of the country, but still comparatively small,—has since been submitted by the press to the judgment of the nation, more fully, probably, than any thing of the kind was ever submitted before; and the same remarkable plainness, the same power of elucidating great legal and constitutional doctrines till they become as intelligible and simple as the occupations of daily life, has enlarged the jury of the senate-chamber till it has become the jury of the whole people, and the same verdict has followed. What, therefore, Chancellor Kent said in relation to it, is as true as it is beautiful;—"Peace has its victories as well as war;"—and the triumph which Mr. Webster thus secured for a great constitutional principle, he may now well regard, as the chief honour of his life.

Indeed, a man such as he is, when he looks back upon his past life, and forward to the future, must needs feel, that his fate and his fortunes, his fame and his ambition, are connected throughout with the fate and the fortunes of the constitution of his country. He is the child of our free institutions. None other could have produced or reared him;—none other can now sustain or advance him. From the days when, amidst the fastnesses of nature, his young feet with difficulty sought the rude school-house, where his earliest aspirations were nurtured, up to the moment when he came forth in triumph from the senate-chamber, conscious that he had overthrown the Doctrines of Nullification, and contended successfully for the Union of the States, he must have felt, that his extraordinary powers have constantly depended for their development and their exercise on the peculiar institutions of our free governments. It is plain, indeed, that he has thriven heretofore, by their progress and success; and it is, we think, equally plain, that in time to come, his hopes and his fortunes can be advanced only by their continued stability and further progress. We think, too, that Mr. Webster feels this. On all the great principles of the constitution, and all the leading interests of the country, his opinions are known; his ground is taken; his lot is cast. Whoever may attack the Union on any of the fundamental doctrines of our government, he must defend them. *Prima fortuna salutis monstrat iter.* The path he has chosen, is the path he must follow. And we rejoice at it. We rejoice, that such a necessity is imposed on such a mind. We rejoice, that, even such as he cannot stand, unless they sustain the institutions that formed them; and that, what is in itself so poetically just and so morally beautiful, is enforced by a providential wisdom, which neither genius nor ambition can resist or control. We rejoice, too, when, on the other hand, a man so gifted, faithfully and proudly devotes to the institutions of his country the powers and influence they have unfolded and fostered in him, that, in his turn, he is again rewarded with confidence and honours, which, as they can come neither from faction nor passion, so neither party discipline nor political violence can diminish nor impair them. And, finally, and above all, we rejoice for the great body of the people, that the decided and unhesitating support they have so freely given to the distinguished Senator, with whose name "this land now rings from side to side," because he has triumphantly defended the Union of the States and the principles of the Constitution;—we rejoice, we say, *for the people*, because, such a support given by them for such a cause, not only strengthens and cements the very foundations of whatever is most valuable in our government; but at the same time, warns and encourages all who would hereafter seek similar honours and favours, to consult for the course they shall follow, neither the indications of party nor the impulses of passion, but to address themselves plainly, fearlessly, calmly, directly to the intelligence and honesty of *the whole nation*, "and ask no omen but their country's cause."

ART. VIII.

POLAND.

1. —*Histoire de Pologne par M. Zielinski, Professeur au Lycée de Varsovie. Tome premier, pp. 383. Tome second, pp. 422: Paris: 1830.*

2. —*Polen, zur Zeit der zwey letzten Theilungen dieses Reichs: Historisch, Statistisch, und Geographisch beschrieben, &c. &c. Poland, at the time of the two last divisions of this kingdom; Historically, Statistically, and Geographically, described, with a map, exhibiting the divisions of Poland, in the years 1772, 1793, and 1795: pp. 551.*

3. —*Histoire de l'Anarchie de Pologne, par M. Rulhiere.*

4. —*Spittler's Entwurf der Geschichte Polens, Miteiner Fortsetrung bis auf die neuesten Zeiten verslhen von Georg Sartorius, in Spittler's Essay at the History of the European States. Vol. II. pp. 460-546: Third edition: Berlin: 1823:*

We venture to invite public attention to a review of the history of Poland. The subject excites a deep but melancholy interest; we dread to hear the result of the glorious but unhappy conflict, in which that devoted country is engaged. We know, indeed, that the Poles will be faithful to their cause; we know, that they are encouraged by the sincere prayers of all who desire the permanent and extended welfare of the world; we know, that though single-handed, hemmed in by hostile powers, and all unprovided as they are with the means of conducting war, they will sustain the terrible struggle with fearless intrepidity. But Warsaw, like the Carthage of old, must fall at last; though the excited spirit of patriotism may cover its fall, with a glory which will not fade. But we fear almost to read of partial successes. The generous enthusiasm of the Poles for political independence, is identified with the best interests, the security and permanent repose of Europe; it has not failed to achieve brilliant actions in its contest against the fearful odds of an immense empire; it may perform yet more honourable deeds upon the great theatre of the contest; but all these temporary advantages fail to excite in us a thrill of triumph. We fear for the result. The brave opposition which has been made, displays the more fully the merits of the nation which is doomed as a victim, and we almost shrink from admiring the gallantry which will eventually render more bloody and more severe the sacrifice that must at last be offered on the unholy altars of despotism. The nationality of Poland has excited the struggle; has animated her sons to battle; and has armed them in the panoply of an heroic despair. That nationality will be utterly destroyed by the impending successes of Russia. The alarum was rung too late for the devoted people; they rallied to the watchword of liberty, but their glory and strength were already departed. Its name will be erased from the list of nations; and the beautiful plains on which the proud cavalry of its nobles used to assemble in the haughty exercise of their elective rights, will be confounded with the great mass of lands, which constitute the vast empire of the North.

Before our remarks can meet the eyes of our readers, perhaps, this result will have been accomplished. There was a short interval in the history of our age, when the monarchs, in their resistance to Napoleon, made their appeal to their people, acknowledged the power and aroused the enthusiasm of the many, and seemed inclined to give durability to their institutions by conciliating the general good will. It was during that short period, that the residue of Poland, having by the fortunes of war become occupied by Russian troops, was annexed to Russia, not as an integral part of its empire, but as a coordinate and independent kingdom. No such system had ever before been pursued; but Alexander was for a while seized with the general love of constitutions, and believed them still consistent with his independent sway. In consequence, Poland, that is, the small remaining portion of the ancient kingdom, received its separate existence, and under a free constitution. But the absolute politicians soon discovered that this would prove in their doctrines an anomaly. It soon became evident that the liberties of Poland were inconsistent with the abject submission of Russia; and since we cannot hope, that the latter will as yet claim a change in its government, it seems assured, that the Poles will be compelled to submit to the same servitude. Such appears to us the necessary issue of the present conflict; Polish nationality will be entirely subverted; and the kingdom of Poland be merged in the consolidated empire.

We regard such an issue, as one deeply to be deplored. The favorite poet of Italy, in searching for objects to illustrate the general decay of human affairs, and to pourtray the insignificance of personal sufferings, as compared with the larger proofs of the instability of fortune, exclaims with pathetic truth;

> "Cadono le città, cadono i regni
> E l'uom d'esser mortal par che si sdegni."

Of the ruin of a realm, we have a most appalling example. In the places of many of the old Polish cities, it is said, that dense forests have now sprung up; that the traveller, as he makes his way through their interminable shades, finds the pavement of streets and the relics of deserted towns in the midst of a lifeless solitude. And now, that the sum of evils may be full, the nation of the Poles seems destined to a fall, from which there will be to them no further resurrection.

Yet the former history of Poland hardly palliates the position which the sovereigns and states of Europe have assumed towards her. In the days of her republican pride, was she not the chosen ally of France and the rightful mistress of Prussia? The crowns of Sweden and of Bohemia have at separate times been worn by her kings; the Danube was hardly the limit of her southern frontier; the coasts of the Euxine were hers; and when Vienna itself was about to yield to the yoke of Turkish barbarism, it was a Polish king that stayed the wave and rescued Christendom from the danger of Turkish supremacy. If France had on the one side saved Europe from the Saracens, Poland had in its turn protected it against the Turks; and John Sobieski alone deserves to be named with Charles Martel, as the successful defenders of Christendom in the moments of its greatest danger.

But in the foreign politics of European powers, generosity and gratitude have usually prevailed no more than other moral considerations. The interests of the state have sometimes disputed the ascendency with the intrigues of courtiers, or the cabals of ecclesiastics; but the voice of justice has rarely been heard in its own right. Political vice has usually been counteracted by political vice; and if the right of the stronger has been sometimes resisted, it was only from the multiplication of jealousies. Thus, we shall see, that the crisis of Poland was delayed, not by its intrinsic strength, but by the collision of foreign interests.

A consideration of the revolutions in Polish history is full of instruction for our nation. The inquirer finds, that the causes of the decline of that unhappy country were deeply rooted in its constitution; that it yielded to foreign aggression, only because it had been reduced to anarchy by the licentious vehemence of domestic feuds. The Poles themselves struck the wounds of which their republic bled; and their efforts at resistance would have been ample and effectual, if they had not continued their factions till the ruin was complete; if the alarums which aroused them to united action, had not been the knell of their country.

The Poles are a branch of the great Slavonian family of nations. No history reveals, no tradition reports their origin. The plains upon the Vistula were at a very early period the seat of their abode; and when, in the seventh century, the Bulgarians excited movements on the Danube, new tribes crossed the Carpathian mountains, and perhaps contributed to the development of the political condition among their brethren whom they joined.

The name itself of Poles, does not occur till the end of the tenth century; but fable has not omitted to lend an aspect of romance to the early fortunes of the nation. Shall we repeat the wonderful tale of the hospitable peasant Piast, who is said have been chosen in 840 to be the Polish king? His descendants are said to have been kings in Poland till the time of Casimir III.; and so late as 1675 were princes in Silesia. It was owing to the virtues of this plebeian monarch, that the natives among the Poles, when elected to be kings, were called Piasts.

The German kings were zealous to diffuse Christianity beyond the Vistula; and Mjesko, who was baptized in 964, was the first of the Polish chiefs who embraced Christianity, and at the same time became the vassal of the German king. Yet it is hard to assign a fixed character to the government during this earliest historical period. As Poland is a plain, its natural aspect invited aggressions from all sides; and it was in its turn fond of war as a profession. Its limits were uncertain, and the power of its chiefs ill defined. Nor was its relation to Germany established. International law was but faintly developed; nor could it be said, whether the masters of Poland did homage for the whole, or only for a portion of their territory. Indeed, it was sometimes utterly refused. To the peremptory demand of tribute, on the part of the Emperor Henry V., the Polish Duke replied, "no terror can make me own myself your tributary, even to the amount of a penny; I had rather lose my whole country, than possess it in ignominious peace." Unsuccessful in the field, the emperor relied on his treasures to make his supremacy acknowledged. "See here," said he to the Polish deputation, opening his chest, "the resources which shall enable me to crush you." A Polish envoy immediately drew from his finger a ring of great value, and throwing it in, exclaimed, "add this to your gold."[9] Venality was not in fashion in those days, and the emperor suffered a complete overthrow.

So it was, that for the four first centuries in Polish history, prowess in the field rendered the nation glorious and passionately fond of war. The pressure of external force at last led to the formation of a permanent territory, and an acknowledged form of government, after a long subdivision of the country among various chiefs, and a confused political condition, eminently favourable to the leaders of a barbarous aristocracy.

The first permanent mass that arose out of the chaos of separate principalities, was Great Poland, on the Wartha; and this was at last united under the same master with Little Poland, on the Vistula. The nation desired a king, as their only refuge from anarchy and invasions. The Pope John XII. had been desired to appoint the king; he pleaded the principle of nonintervention, and bade the nation execute its own laws and its own will. In consequence, Ladislaus was crowned with great solemnity at Cracau, in 1320, and the series of Polish kings is from that time uninterrupted. But the period of aristocratic anarchy had impressed a character upon the government and the nation. There existed no established laws, no rising commerce, no pure religious worship. The bravery of the Poles in the field was brilliant, but barren. Their enthusiasm won victories, but could not turn them to the advantage of the country. And when, at the epoch we have named, a king was chosen for the whole state, his power was already limited, not by a fair representation of the interests of the nation, but solely by the high aristocracy. Without their consent no laws could be established, nor wars declared, nor government administered, nor justice decreed.

And yet the ensuing period of Polish history is that of greatest national prosperity. The vices of the constitution were not fully developed till the close of the sixteenth century. Indeed, Casimir the Great, the immediate successor of Ladislaus, was able, like Augustus of Rome, during a reign of thirty-seven years, to establish something like justice and tranquillity in his kingdom. If he lost territory on the one side, he gained large provinces from Russia on the other. But his greatest merit consisted in his functions as a law-giver. His code was written in the Latin, expressed in neat and clear language, and was favourable to the industry and prosperity of the country. The Polish historians delight to recount the magnificence which his economy enabled him to maintain; and applying to him what used to be said of the Roman, declare that he found Poland of wood, and left it of brick.

But the seeds of evil were also planted by him. According to his desire, Lewis,

[9] The emperor in no wise confused, is said to have replied, "much obliged to you," and retained the present.

the king of Hungary, was elected his successor. The consent of the nobles could be purchased only by concessions; and in order to secure the royal dignity in his family to one of his daughters, he was compelled to enter into terms with the oligarchy. Freedom from taxation was the great point demanded and promised. All towns, castles, and estates, belonging to the nobles, were freed from taxation forever; and no services of any kind were to be required. In case of war, the nobles were to take the field on horseback, for the defence of the country; but if necessity required the employment of troops abroad, it was to be at the charge of the king. Thus the paternal ambition of the king, uniting with the avarice of the nobles, laid the foundation of anarchy and weakness, by concessions wholly at variance with the existence of an equitable liberty. The people, having no means of making their rights heard, were abandoned entirely to the tyranny of their immediate masters. Such was the origin of the *pacta conventa*, and such the first venal bargain, by which the energies of Poland were bartered away, and aristocratic tyranny made the basis of the constitution.

Fatal as was this arrangement for the political progress of Poland, it was yet favourable for the extension of its territory. Hedwiga, the daughter of Lewis, succeeded to the throne; and by accepting for her husband Jagellon, the grand duke of Lithuania, she annexed that dutchy to Poland, and was the means of converting its inhabitants from paganism. It was in 1386 that the grand duke was baptized, and with him the celebrated family of the Jagellons obtained the Polish crown.

The Lithuanians were converted to Christianity, not by fire and sword, nor by any process of argument. It was the will of their prince; and besides, excellent woollen coats and leather shoes, were distributed to the neophytes. He who could repeat the *pater noster* and the decalogue, was received as a Christian. They were a barbarous race, — yet, like the Poles, formed a part of the Slavonian family, and had gradually become an independent nation. The complete union of the two countries did not take place for nearly two centuries.

The family of the Jagellons, for seven successive reigns, extending through 186 years, obtained the throne. The praises of that period form the theme of eulogy among the patriotic writers of Poland. It was the period of the greatest harmony between the kings and the nation. They were admired for the fidelity with which they maintained their covenants; the crown of Sweden was repeatedly proffered to them, — and they had conferred on Poland, the lasting benefit of uniting to it a country, which before had been the theatre of constant hostilities. But yet so far as the sovereigns themselves are observed, not one of them displayed the highest excellence of a ruler. They were abundantly distinguished for the virtues which constitute personal worth; but they were not of the persevering energy, or prudent discernment, which could alone have given a sure foundation to the Polish government.

The first in the line, to secure the accession of his son, confirmed the privileges of the nobles. The peasantry was forgotten; the class of citizens hardly remembered, but the personal rights and the property of the nobles was sacredly assured. It was further stipulated, that none but natives should be appointed to the high offices of the state. A stipulation of that sort, would have rendered the genius of

Peter the Great inadequate to the reforms which he planned and executed; the limitation in Poland undoubtedly retarded the progress of culture.

The second in the series, a minor at his accession, was elected king of Hungary also; and he had hardly begun to exercise his power and display his valour, before he fell in the famous battle of Varna, in the effort to save the Greek empire from the Turks. His brother and successor, Casimir IV., had two powerful enemies, the Teutonic knights, and the Polish nobility. The latter war was the more formidable,—for, as the power of his foreign adversaries compelled him to resort frequently to the diets, of which he convoked no less than forty-five, it is not strange, that the nobles wrung some new privilege from every occurrence, which rendered their co-operation necessary. At length it was established, that no new law should be enacted, nor any levy of troops be made, without the consent of the general diet. The custom of sending deputies now became prevalent, because the frequency of the diet rendered a general attendance troublesome. The number of delegates was at first fixed by no rule, and the whole form grew up as chance, as gradual usage prescribed; but, as the excessive power of the nobility increased, the rights of the peasantry were impaired. The code of Casimir the Great, had left the labourer the choice of his residence; it was now decreed, that the peasant should be considered as attached to the soil, and the fugitive might be pursued and recovered as a run-a-way slave. A third estate was hardly known; and, if the deputies of cities sometimes appeared in a convention, their chief privilege was to kiss the new king's hand, or sign decrees, on which they were not invited to deliberate. Polish politics established the rule, that none but nobles were citizens.

While the general diet thus received its character as the representation of the nobility, elected in the provincial assemblies, another body now gradually assumed an active existence. The highest civil and religious officers of the kingdom formed a senate; and they were constituted members, not because they were great proprietors, but in consequence of the office, to which they had been named by the king.

Casimir was succeeded by his three sons. Under the first, John Albert, the power of the oligarchy was confirmed, and not a semblance of an independent prerogative remained to the crown. Under Alexander, it was further decreed by the diet, that nothing should in future be transacted, except *communi consensu*. The nobility had already usurped all the sovereign authority; they now in their zeal to confirm their usurpations, introduced the ambiguous clause, which was afterwards to be perverted to their own ruin. A dismal inadvertence failed to insert, that the will of the majority should be binding; and hence it became possible at a later day to interpret the law, as investing each deputy with a tribunicial authority. Under Sigismund, the third son of Casimir, all attempts to restore the royal authority were futile. The equality of the nobles was established by law;—yet a portion of them already began to look with contempt on their less wealthy peers, and would gladly have separated themselves from the great mass of "the plebeian nobility."

With Sigismund Augustus, the son of Sigismund, the race of the Jagellons expired. At that time, Poland was still powerful; the Prince of Stettin and the Prince of Prussia were its vassals; the palatines of Wallachia and Moldavia owed allegiance to it; the Duke of Courland did it homage; Livonia was incorporated among its territories. Nothing but a government was wanting to render it one of the most brilliant states of Europe. Copernicus had already rendered it illustrious in science; and, in no part of Europe was the knowledge of the Latin language so generally diffused.

Now that the royal dynasty was at an end, the succession to the throne, which had hitherto been in part hereditary, became necessarily elective. But no forms had been prescribed for the occasion. It was not known who were the rightful depositaries of power during the interregnum, nor who were possessed of a voice in the election of king. At length the right of convoking the diet was assigned to the primate, and the elective franchise was decided to appertain in an equal degree to each of the nobles, without the intervention of electors.

To maintain religious peace was the next concern. The reformation had made its way to Poland,—but not merely under the forms of Calvinism and Lutheranism. The Socinians existed also as a powerful party. Those who were not Catholics, were at variance with each other; the diet, therefore, with great consideration, decreed, that no one should be punished or persecuted for his religious opinions. The term, *dissidents*, was originally used of them all, as expressing their mutual differences; in process of time, it was, however, applied exclusively to those who were out of the Roman church.

At length the day for the election arrived. The Polish nobility, each on his war-horse, appeared at the appointed place in countless troops, and it seemed as though an army had been assembled, rather than an electoral body. The candidates were proposed,—the ambassadors of the leading foreign powers admitted to address the electors, and freedom given to any Pole to offer himself as a candidate, for the suffrages of his countrymen. Yet, before proceeding to the election, a constitution was formed, embodying all the privileges of the oligarchy, and conferring on that order, the unequivocal sovereignty. After this work was accomplished, the vote was taken, and Henry of Anjou was chosen king.

It was wise for the nation, which showed a spirit of religious tolerance, to exact of their new king, a pledge in favour of religious peace. An oath was not too strong a guarantee to be required of him, who was a leader in the massacre of St. Bartholomy's night! It was wise, also, to require money and other advantageous stipulations of France. But the Poles felt still greater satisfaction in the law which was now established, prohibiting the choice of a successor, during the lifetime of the king.

The Duke of Anjou left the siege of Rochelle for the Polish crown; and four months after his coronation, he fled from Poland by night, as a fugitive, on horseback, accompanied by seven attendants. The Poles, dismayed and humiliated by the procedure, fixed a limit for his return, and when that period had expired, they declared the throne to be vacant, and proceeded to a new election.

Stephen Bathory, the duke of Transylvania, was the successful candidate. Under his short reign, Poland saw the last years of its prosperity; and from the epoch of his death, the spirit of faction prevailed over every sentiment of justice or patriotism. The king had no further authority to concede; and internal feuds, sustained by the most bitter passions, now divided the nobility.

It was in 1586 that king Stephen died. At that time Poland extended from Brandenburgh and Silesia to Esthonia; its power along the Baltic was undisputed; and the shores of the Euxine had as yet submitted to no other dominion. Wallachia and Hungary were its southern limits; while, in the east, it still contended with Russia for an extended frontier. Its soil was productive of the most valuable returns; its plains were intersected by navigable rivers; its population amounted to sixteen millions, and its resources seemed to promise the means of easily sustaining more than three-fold that number. The principle of religious equality was recognized by its law; and it believed itself to possess a greater degree of liberty than any nation of Europe. How could such a state, so magnificent in its resources, so commanding in its actual strength, so celebrated for daring valour, sink into the gloom and debility of anarchy? How could such a nation in its glory submit to unconnected activity, and, like the fabled Titan, suffer the birds of prey to gorge upon its vitals, without one effectual struggle in self-defence?

The wildest spirit of party was displayed at the next election of a king. The factions were respectively led by two powerful and ambitious families; and to the former evils in the state were now added those political feuds, fostered by the passion for aggrandizement, and rendered virulent by the excess of personal hatred. The dominant party declared Sigismund III. to be elected the king of Poland.

The new king was, unluckily, first, an imbecile and narrow-minded man, with all the obstinacy belonging to weakness; next, he was heir to the Swedish throne; thirdly, he was a bigotted Catholic; and, lastly, and for Poland the saddest of all, he lived to reign forty-five years. His blind stupidity left the storms of party to rage unrestrained, and the usurpations of the nobility to proceed unchecked: his hereditary claim on Sweden, which wisely rejected his right, and preferred Gustavus Adolphus, led to a war, in which Poland was the chief sufferer; his bigotry prevented him from healing the intestine divisions by wise toleration; and, finally, his long life gave almost every one of his neighbours an opportunity of aggrandizement by aggressions on his realm. The dismemberment of the Polish dominions began. The Porte secured Moldavia; the Swedes took possession of Livonia and Courland; and, though the short anarchy in Russia led to some success in that quarter, it was a greater loss that the Elector of Brandenburgh, contrary to the stipulations of ancient treaties, claimed and obtained the succession to the fief of the Prussian Dutchy. In short, the reign of Sigismund was marked by deadly errors of policy, and foolish obstinacy of character. The continued oppression of the peasantry, and the constant recurrence of eventual losses in wars, were in no degree compensated by the display of warlike virtues on the part of a democratic nobility.

It was of little advantage to the Poles, that Ladislaus IV., the son and successor of Sigismund, was a man of distinguished merit. At his accession the nobles devised a new condition. Hitherto they had guarded themselves against taxation; they now proceeded to tax the king. For a long period, one quarter of the income of the royal domains had been set apart for the military service, especially for the artillery; they now demanded a concession of a full moiety. But, it may be asked, what was done for the people? The answer would be, absolutely nothing. It did not seem to be imagined, that the labouring class had any rights; not a law was proposed for the benefit of the millions, who cultivated the soil. Even the peasants on the estates of the king were equally oppressed;—why? It was the nobles who farmed the royal domains.

Every thing stagnated. Every thing, do we say? The natural instinct of freedom in the Cossacks could brook their abject servitude no longer. They reclaimed their partial independence, complained that their rights were infringed, and found demagogues, who were desirous and were able to lead them.

At this crisis the king died, and his brother, John Casimir, a man tried by misfortunes, who, having been the inmate of a French dungeon, afterwards, from disappointment and chagrin, became a Jesuit and a Cardinal, was elected his successor.

The powers and the revenues of the king had been plundered; one thing more was alone wanting to give full development to the Polish constitution. In the year 1652, a diet was dissolved by the opposition of a single deputy; this was remarkable enough; but it was still more strange, that what had been once effected by passion, should remain an acknowledged right; and that while the country rung with curses against the deputy who had set the example, the power should still have been claimed as a sacred privilege. No redress could be obtained except by confederations; and it was now the height of anarchy, that public law recognized these separate assemblies. Indeed, the days of the *liberum veto* were necessarily the days of legalized insurrection. It was a sort of dictatorship, invented for the new contingency. Only the misery was, that there could be as many confederations as there were separate factions.

Poland had, all this while, formidable foreign enemies to encounter. The Swedes, the Czar, the Porte, were all greedy for aggrandizement. This was no time for domestic dissensions. The only wonder is, that the nation could have resisted its enemies at all. As it was, several provinces were lost; in 1657, the Duke of Prussia seized the opportunity of freeing himself altogether from his relation as vassal to the Polish crown.

The melancholy Casimir could not endure all this. He held a diet in 1661, and told the deputies plainly: "First or last, our state will be divided by our neighbours. Russia will extend itself to the Bug, and perhaps to the Vistula; the Elector of Brandenburgh will seize upon Great Poland and the neighbouring districts; and Austria will not remain behind, but will take Cracau and other places." The prophecy was uttered in vain; and a few years after, the philosophic monarch, having buried his wife, for whose sake alone he had been willing to reign, resigned the crown, and removed to France.

This was a new state of things. A diet of election was convened, and the decree ratified, that *henceforward no king of Poland should be allowed to resign*. One would think the decree very flattering to the nation!

The next object was the choice of a king. We have seen, that the Poles had usually elected a member of the previous royal family. They had adhered to the Jagellons, and now also to the Sigismunds, until the families were extinct. The field was therefore open; and this time the division lay, not between contending factions of the high aristocracy, but between the high aristocracy, on the one hand, and the "plebeian nobility," on the other. The party of "the many" prevailed; and the electoral vote was given to Michael Wisniowiecki, a man of great private worth, poor, as to his fortunes, modest, and retiring. The joy of the inferior nobility was at its height; and the shouts of the noble multitude, and the salutes from the artillery, proclaimed aloud the triumphs of equality. Poor Michael declined the honour, in vain. He entreated, with tears in his eyes, to be released from it. His tears were equally vain. He made his escape from the electoral field on horseback; the deputies pursued him and compelled him to be king.

From the commencement of his reign the faction of the high aristocracy opposed him. The first diet which he convened was broken up; the senate was openly discontented; the enthusiasm of the nobility grew cool; and it was found that a mistake had been committed. The Cossacks were tumultuous; the Turks pursued a ruinous war, terminated only by a disgraceful peace. The nation was indignant; a new war was decreed; when, fortunately for himself and the state, the king died. John Sobieski, the leader of the aristocracy, succeeded.

The relief of Vienna, in 1683, is the crowning glory of Sobieski. His subsequent campaigns were unsuccessful; for he had neither sufficient troops, nor money, nor provisions, nor artillery. Nor was he happy in his family. The great champion of Christendom was governed by his wife, and the nation sneered at his weakness. His ambition as a father led him to desire, during his lifetime, the election of his son as successor. Unable to accomplish this, he took to avarice, not a very respectable passion for a private man, but a very dangerous one for a prince. But in avarice he had able auxiliaries in his wife and the Jews. Every thing was venal; and the king grew rich, without growing happy. As a last resort, he tried retirement and letters. But the pursuit of letters, in itself intrinsically exalted, must be chosen in its own right, if happiness is to be won by it; to the disappointed statesman it is but a mere shield against despair; a sort of philosopher's robe to hide the ghastliness of sullen discontent. Sobieski found in the Latin classics, which he diligently read, no healing "medicine for the soul diseased;" and the atrabilious humours of his wife, and the torment of his station, and his mental discontent, all combined to hasten his death. He passed from this world on the same hour and the same day as his election.

We have traced the progress of the infringements upon the royal authority; we have seen the election of the king decided by a faction in an oligarchy, by a rabble of noblemen, by the high aristocracy; the next election was decided by bribes. Two strong parties only appeared; the French, which declared for Conti, and the Saxon, which advocated the interests of the Elector Augustus. But the French ambassador had distributed all his money, while the Saxon envoy was still in Funds. So each party chose its own king; each made proclamation of its sovereign; each sung its anthem in the Cathedral; but the French party subsided, as soon as the primate, its chief support, could agree upon his price.

Thus the Saxon elector prevailed. He was one of the most dissolute princes of the age; and an unbounded luxury and abandoned profligacy were introduced by him among the higher orders in Poland. The morals of the nobility now became nearly as bad as their political constitution. What need have we to dwell on the personal war which Augustus II. commenced against Charles XII. of Sweden; the defeats he sustained; his forced resignation of the crown; the appointment of Stanislaus in his stead; and his own restoration after the battle of Pultawa? The leading point in his history is this: that with him the Russian ascendency in Poland was established. All the rest of Europe was rapidly advancing in culture; the only change in Poland was the predominance of Russia.

On the death of Augustus II. the majority of the votes was in favour of Stanislaus; but the vicinity of a Russian army sustained the pretensions of Augustus III. His reign, if reign it may be termed, extended through a period of thirty years. They were interrupted by no wars; not because the nation desired or profited by peace, but in consequence of the general inertness, the universal languor, the unqualified anarchy. The king possessed no power, except through the miserable expedients of an intriguing cabinet. The cities were deserted; the regular administration of justice was unknown; and the barbarism of the middle ages reverted. Nothing preserved Poland in existence, but the jealousies of surrounding powers.

The last king of Poland was chosen under the dictation of Russian arms, at the express desire of Catharine the Second. Stanislaus Poniatowski was crowned at Warsaw in 1764, and ascended the throne with philanthropic intentions, but with a feeble purpose. His reign illustrates the vast inferiority of the virtues of the heart to the virtues of the will. The difficulties of his position do not excuse his own imbecility; and while the paralysis of the nation was complete, he was himself deficient in the manly virtues of a sovereign.

Within nine years after his accession to the throne, the first dismemberment of Poland was consummated. The student of human nature might ask, by what mighty armies the division was effected? What overwhelming force could lead a nation of nobles to submit to the degradation? What bloody battles were fought, what victories were won in the struggle? It might be supposed, that all Poland would have started as if electrified; that the ground would have been disputed, inch by inch; that every town would have become a citadel, garrisoned by the stern lovers of independence and national honour.

The fall of Poland was ignominious. Not one battle was fought, not one siege was necessary for effecting the division. Anarchy, intolerance, scandalous dissensions, an imbecile sovereign, these were the instruments which accomplished the ruin of the state.

The personal adherents of Stanislaus had designed to change the form of government from a legal anarchy to a limited monarchy. This patriotic design of the Czartorinskis was defeated by the hot-headed zeal of the republican party, by the influence of Russia, and most of all, by the excesses of intolerable bigotry.

The dissidents had, in the early part of the century, incurred suspicion, as the secret adherents of Sweden. If in England, where culture had made such advances, the Catholics could be disfranchised, is it strange, that in Poland, a vehement party was opposed to the toleration of Protestants? In 1717, unconstitutional enactments had been made to their injury; and at subsequent periods, the religious tyranny had proceeded so far as to exclude the dissident from all civil privileges. They were excluded from the national representation, and declared incapable of participating in any public magistracy whatever.

On the accession of Stanislaus it was hoped that a more moderate and equitable spirit would prevail. Stanislaus himself favoured the cause of religious freedom. The dissidents made a very moderate request for the establishment of freedom of worship, without claiming the restitution of all their franchises. The zealots, strengthened by the opponents of the king, would concede absolutely nothing; and as in politics religious parties have always exhibited the most deadly hostility, so in this case Poland was more distracted than ever.

The Russian ambassador immediately seized the opportunity of making Russian influence predominant under the mask of protecting liberty of conscience. The empress demanded for the dissidents a perfect equality with the Catholics; and amidst scenes of tumultuous discussion and legislative frenzy, the demand was rejected. The highest religious zeal became combined with a detestation of Russian interference, and unbridled passion accomplished its utmost.

The dissidents, unsuccessful in their application to the diet, confederated under Russian protection; and as the proceedings of the king had excited a vague apprehension of some encroachments on the privileges of the nobles, the confederates were joined by the opponents of the king also. In this way a general confederation was formed agreeably to the established usage in Poland; but the whole was under the guidance and control of Repnin, the Russian ambassador.

When the general diet was convened in 1767, so large a Russian army was already encamped in Poland, that Repnin was able to dictate the petitions and the complaints which were to be presented for consideration. No foreign power interfered. France and Austria were exhausted; and Frederic was careful to preserve a good understanding with his great Northern ally.

But with all this, some refractory spirits appeared in the diet. No terrors could subdue the inflexible and impassioned spirit of Soltyk, Zaluski, and the two Rzewuskis. And what was done by an ambassador of the foreign power in the capital of a free and mighty state? Repnin ordered the resolute patriots to be seized by night and transported to Siberia. Horror chilled the nation at the outrage, and the rage of despair filled all but the partisans of Russia. The ambassador of Catharine was now able to dictate to the diet all the decrees relating to the dissidents, and all the other laws which were enacted at the session. It was plain, that he did not understand the wants of the dissidents; but he took care to render the continuance of Russian interference necessary for their security.

It was the misfortune of the Polish patriots, that the defence of their nationality became identified with the most furious form of religious bigotry. The diet had not terminated its session before a new confederation convened at Bar, and contending against the Russians on the one hand, attempted to depose the king on the other. But the confederation was easily dissolved by the Russian army, and its leaders were obliged to fly for refuge beyond the frontier.

Thus the cause of the Poles seemed to be abandoned by all the world. The efforts of the king were insignificant; the nobles were many of them in the pay of Russia, the rest of them divided by civil, religious, and family factions; and England and France were idle spectators of the approaching dissolution of the Polish state.

Yet one power there was, whose ancient maxim would not allow a Russian army in Poland. While all the Christian monarchs neglected or joined to pillage the unhappy land, the Porte declared war against the aggressor. The issue of that contest is well known; and the power of Russia was but the more confirmed by her entire success in the war. Russian ascendancy in the North and East became established, and the last hope of Poland was removed.

When at length the three principal powers invaded Poland, and published their manifesto, proclaiming its dismemberment, the nation submitted almost without a struggle. The blow came as upon one in a lethargy. The revelries of the wealthy nobility, the feuds of the great families, and the wretchedness of the peasantry, continued as before.

It may be asked, who first planned the partition of Poland? We believe it was Frederic. Austria was indeed the first to advance her frontier; but every thing tends rather to show, that the Austrian cabinet insisted upon its share, only because the robbery was at all events to be committed; and Russia had no interest in proposing a division, for she already virtually possessed the whole. Frederic, on the contrary, was earnestly desirous of consolidating and uniting his kingdom, of which the parts were before divided by Polish provinces.

Previous to this first division in 1773, Poland had possessed a territory of about 220,000 miles; her neighbours now left her about 166,000. Prussia and Austria would gladly have taken more; but Russia protected the residue, as prey reserved for herself.

Or rather, the Russian ambassador in Warsaw, was from that time the real sovereign over the land. A secret article in the treaty with Prussia guaranteed the liberties and constitution of Poland, that is, stipulated that the state of anarchy should continue.

And yet it seems surprising, that a nation of fourteen millions, and of proverbial valor should have submitted without a blow. The result can be explained only from the abject state to which the peasantry had become reduced, and the immense gulf which separated the nobility from the people.

But a new epoch was opening in the history of the world. The United States of America had achieved their independence, and established their liberties. The impulse was instantaneously felt throughout Europe, and it extended to Poland. The relative position of the Northern European powers was also changed. The alliance between Russia and Prussia had expired in 1780, nor had the Empress been willing to renew it. On the contrary, the alliance of Austria was preferred, and the new associates combined to engage in a war with the Porte. The purpose of dismembering the Turkish state was avowed, and the Poles foresaw full well, that their own territory would next be coveted. They therefore determined to shake off the intolerable yoke of foreign interference, and, observing that their constitution was absolutely in ruins, they ventured to attempt a reconstruction of their state.

The condition of the public mind in France had its share of influence. The Polish nobility had long been partial to the language and manners of France. Nor were the two countries in situations wholly unlike. Both states were disorganized; one was suffering from anarchy, the other tending to it; and both needed a renewal of their youth. On the Seine and on the Vistula, a new order of things was demanded. The United States had been the first state in the world to introduce a written constitution; Poland was now the first country in Europe to imitate the example.

It was in October, 1788, that the revolutionary diet assembled at Warsaw. It assembled tranquilly: for Austria and Russia were at war with the Porte, and Sweden had also threatened St. Petersburg from the north. Its first decree abolished the *liberum veto*. Henceforward, the will of the majority was to be the law.

But even yet the spirit of faction was unsubdued. A Russian party,—a minority, it is true, yet, under the circumstances, a formidable one, introduced divisions into the diet. The king himself had not lofty independence enough to join heartily with the patriots, but still continued to hope for the political safety of his country, from the clemency of Catharine.

A treaty of alliance with Russia against the Porte, was proposed to the diet and rejected, in part, through the influence of Prussia. It was next voted to raise the Polish army, from 18,000 to 60,000; and, if possible, to 100,000 men. To effect this object, the nobility and clergy voluntarily submitted to taxation. The control of the army was entrusted not to the king, but to a special commission.

Some foreign support was next desired; and the political position of Prussia, gorged though she had been with the spoils of Poland, seemed yet under the reign of its new king to offer a safe and resolute protector. The court of Berlin published to the world its determination to guarantee the independence of Poland, and to avoid all interference in its internal concerns.

Stanislaus wavered, and evidently leaned to the Russian side. The decision of the diet at length won him over to the party of the patriots;—and he agreed to assist in expelling the Russian army from the Polish soil, in forming a constitution, and in soliciting the concurrence of other nations in repressing the unmeasured aggrandizement of Russia. These proceedings were not without effect;—in June of the following year, the ambassador of Catharine announced that her army had left Poland, and would not again cross its boundaries.

The diet now advanced to the work of framing a constitution; while the representatives of the third estate were, in the meanwhile, admitted to a seat in the assembly.

The alliance with Prussia was, however, delayed, partly by means of Russian intrigue, but still more, because Frederic William demanded the cession of Dantzig. On this point, divisions ensued, which were never reconciled. But, in March,

1790, a treaty of peace and alliance between Poland and Prussia was signed, containing a guarantee of each other's possessions, and a mutual pledge of assistance, in case of an attack from abroad. Should any foreign nation attempt interference in the internal concerns of Poland, the court of Berlin pledged itself to render every assistance by means of negotiations, and, if they failed, to make use of its whole military force.

But, alas, for the plighted faith of princes! The time of this treaty was a very critical juncture. Joseph II. of Austria was dead; Prussia was in alliance with the Porte, and of course exposed to a war with Russia; and the negotiations for a general peace in the congress of Reichenbach, were not yet begun. At that congress, Prussia revealed its will to become master of Dantzig and Thorn; and it was not deemed an impossible thing to induce King Frederic William to be false to his word, which had been plighted to the Poles.

The period, during which a diet might legally continue, having expired, a new one was convened December 16th, 1790. It consisted of all who had been members of the former diet, and of an equal number of additional members. The new infusion increased the strength of the patriotic party. In January, 1791, they voted the punishment of death against any who should receive a pension from a foreign power; in April, they extended the right of citizenship to mechanics, and all free people of the Christian religion;—a *habeas corpus* act was passed, protecting all residents in the cities.

Finally, on the 3d of May, 1791, the long desired new Polish constitution was promulgated. The king repaired to the cathedral, and, at the high altar, swore to maintain it; the illustrious nobles imitated the example,—all Warsaw celebrated the day as a memorable festival.

The new constitution made the Roman Catholic religion the ruling religion in Poland,—but conceded full liberty to other forms of worship. It confirmed the privileges of the nobility, and the charters of the cities; it gave to the peasantry the right of making compacts with their over lord, and placed the inhabitants of the open country, under the protection of the laws and the government. Poland was called a republic. The supremacy of the will of the people was distinctly recognized; but, for the sake of civil freedom, order, and security, the government was composed of three separate branches. *The legislative* was divided into two chambers,—that of the deputies and the senators; the former, the popular branch, was esteemed the sacred source of legislation; the latter, under the presidency of the king, could accept a law, or postpone its consideration. The decision was according to a majority of voices. The *liberum veto* was abolished; confederations were prohibited as inconsistent with the genius of the constitution; and it was provided, that, after every quarter of a century, the constitution should be revised and amended. *The executive*, composed of the king and his cabinet, was bound to carry the laws into effect; but it could neither number nor interpret them, nor impose taxes, nor borrow money, nor declare war, nor make peace, nor conclude treaties definitively. The crown ceased to be elective, and was declared to be hereditary in the family of the elector of Saxony. *The judiciary* shared in the general improvement.

The majority of the nation loudly applauded the results of the diet, and the western cabinets of Europe were satisfied. The British Parliament was eloquent in the praises of the new order of things, and Austria and Prussia united in negotiating with Russia for the recognition of the constitution, and the indivisibility of Poland.

Catharine II. preserved an ominous silence, till the peace of Jassy was concluded, and her armies were ready for action. She then rejected the interference of the two powers, who had attempted to check her career,—and, listening to the requests of a few factious and misguided members of the ancient Polish oligarchy, she proceeded to denounce the spirit of revolutions. The Polish diet rejoined with dignity and moderation, expressed its intentions of peace with respect to the rest of Europe, and published its determined resolution to maintain the independence of its country, and its new form of government. It then applied to the neighbouring powers for assistance;—but Lucchesini, the Prussian envoy, gave evasive answers to all questions respecting an impending war, and especially avoided all written communications; and the elector of Saxony, after some wavering, declined the intended honour of the Polish crown for his family.

Meanwhile the war of Austria and Prussia against France had begun; and now the way was open to Russia to invade Poland, Lucchesini, the Prussian envoy, declared, May 4th, 1792, that his king had not participated in framing the new constitution, and was not bound to its defence; while, on the 18th of the same month, Catharine censured the new government "as adverse to Polish liberties," and declared that she made war "to rescue Poland from its oppressors." While a confederation of factious refugees was made at Targowitz, according to the ancient usage of the anarchy, the Russians precipitated themselves upon the distracted kingdom in two great masses. The Poles, under Joseph Poniatowski and Kosciusko, fought with undaunted valour, but unsuccessfully. On the 30th of May, King Stanislaus ordered a general levy of the population. On the 4th of July, he expressed his determination to share the fate of the nation, and to die with it if necessary, rather than survive its independent existence: and oh! the misery of a gallant nation, with a pusillanimous chief, on the 23d of July he declared his adhesion to the confederation of Targowitz. A vehement scolding letter from Catharine had effected the change in his heroism. The movements of the Polish army were stopped by his order; while Joseph Poniatowski and Kosciusko resigned their places. The leading patriots poured out their souls in eloquent regrets at the last assembly of the diet, and travelled abroad.

The innocent confederates having, after the king's adhesion, added many names to their former number, were now assembled at Grodno, fully relying on the magnanimous clemency of Catharine, to maintain the integrity of their state. Just then the German army was returning from its excursion in Champagne, where it had won no laurels; and Prussia, having obtained the reluctant assent of Austria, claimed, as a compensation for its ill success against France, the privilege of a new inroad upon its neighbour; and in January, 1793, its army took possession of Great Poland, under pretence of keeping the Jacobins in order.

The confederates rubbed their eyes and began to awake; but it was only to read the Prussian note of March 25th, 1793, declaring the necessity of incorporating about 17,000 square miles of the Polish territory with Prussia, "in order," as it was kindly intimated, "to give to the republic of Poland limits better suited to its internal strength." Two days after the publication of this note, Dantzig was seized, to check the progress of a dangerous political sect. Two days more, and Russia declared its willingness to incorporate into its empire about 73,000 square miles of Poland, and three millions of inhabitants. The diet at Grodno showed some signs of obstinacy; but was obliged to assent to the terms dictated by their ally and their protector. The confederation of Targowitz was now dissolved; it had done its work.

The anger of the Poles was frenzied. They were indignant at every thing; but to them it was the bitterest of all, that Frederic William should have had a share in the plunder.

There now remained to Poland about 76,000 square miles, and between three and four millions of inhabitants. The neighbouring powers generously renounced all further claims, became joint guarantees of the remainder, and promised that now the diet might make any constitution it pleased. How far the good pleasure of the diet was independent, may be inferred from the treaty concluded in October with Russia; of which the conditions were, that Poland should leave to Russia the conduct of all future wars, allow the entrance of Russian troops, and frame its foreign treaties only under the Russian sanction. The diet of Grodno signed this treaty November 24th, 1793, and adjourned. Igelstrom, the general of the Russian army, was constituted the Russian ambassador in Poland. It is evident, that Catharine proposed no further *division* of Poland; she intended to lay claim to the whole that remained; and as a preparatory step, caused a large part of the Polish army to be disbanded.

The party of the patriots determined upon one final effort; and a new confederation was made at Cracau. Its aims extended to the establishment of the internal and external independence of their country, and the restoration of its ancient limits. Kosciusko was called from his retirement at Leipzig, to be the generalissimo of the Patriot army. A supreme council was established, with plenary authority, till the national independence should be recovered; and then a representative constitution was to be formed by a general convention. The movement was national; the Poles were invited to rise in the defence of their country; and those between eighteen and twenty-seven years of age were to serve in the armies; the elder men to constitute the militia.

Success beamed upon the first efforts in the field; and the victory of Raclawice, April 4th, 1794, breathed inspiration into every heart. The Prussian armies continued their encroachments; the Austrians offered no hope of succour; and the king had declared in favour of the Russians. But the victory of Kosciusko inspired such hopes, that, just as Igelstrom was preparing to exile twenty-six men, whom he could not bend, and to disarm the Polish garrison, the people of Warsaw rose in arms. The Russians were defeated; more than 2000 fell; an equal number were made prisoners; Igelstrom, with the remainder, fled from Warsaw. Thus was Good Friday celebrated in Poland, in 1794.

It was ominous, however, for the eventual success of the patriots, that, though they were joined by Lithuania, the dismembered provinces made no movements towards an insurrection. In the Prussian, a strong military police maintained military quiet; in the Russian, there was still less room for hope, since the peasantry knew nothing about politics, and the nobility having lost nothing in the exchange of allegiance, remained contented. Secret cabals were also active in gaining partisans for the foreign powers; some tendencies to the licentious influence of the passions of the multitude, were observed with apprehension; and the spirit of faction had not yet learnt to yield to the exalted sentiment of general patriotism.

The supreme national council, now established in Warsaw, had neither money nor credit. Cracau surrendered to the Prussians; Lithuania was given up after a hard struggle; and though the Poles could have coped victoriously with the Prussians, yet the advance of Suwarrow seemed to portend a fatal issue. On the 10th of October, the last battle in which Kosciusko commanded, was bravely contested; but in consequence of the faithlessness of one of his generals, Poninski, the Polish cavalry yielded. Kosciusko rallied them, was thrown from his horse, grievously wounded, and made a prisoner by the Cossacks. Finis Poloniæ, was his exclamation as he fell.

The contest now centered round Praga, which was defended by a hundred cannon, and the flower of the Polish army. Suwarrow, whose name is unrivalled as the ruthless stormer of cities, commanded the assault. It ensued on the 4th of November. The bridge over the Vistula was destroyed; more than eight thousand Poles fell in battle; more than twelve thousand inhabitants of the town were murdered, drowned, or burned to death in their houses. On November 6th, the capitulation of Warsaw was signed upon the smoking ruins of Praga.

The third division of Poland was complete. No permission was asked. The three powers signed the treaty of partition, and promised each other aid, in case of attack; but no formal communication of the procedure was made to any foreign country. A declaration only was presented to the German diet. Napoleon could, therefore, truly say, in 1806, that France had never recognised the partition of Poland.

And King Stanislaus? He was angry, and wept, and took up and threw down the pen, and fainted, and wept again; and January, 1795, signed the document of abdication. They agreed to pay him 200,000 ducats a year. It was more than he merited. He would have made a very charitable almoner, a very liberal patron, to second rate artists and men of letters. But excellence of heart, when coupled with debility of purpose, is but a sorry character for every day concerns; in a ruler it becomes the most deadly pusillanimity. And now for the romance; for Catharine loved romance. The letter of abdication was forwarded to St. Petersburg by a courier, who arrived on the very birthday of the empress, and in the midst of the festival, presented it to her in the form of a bouquet. What a commentary on despotism! A nation struck out of existence to grace a gala! If men may thus be sported with in masses, if the concentrated existence of a people may be made the pastime of a woman's fancy, well did the ancient exclaim, how contemptible a thing is man, if we do not raise our view beyond his deeds!

The result of what we have written, established the truth, that the fall of Poland was an event which destiny had been preparing for centuries. In an age of barbarism, a great nation had become resolved into separate principalities, and an aristocracy, not definitely limited, if not absolute, had sprung up. The family of the Jagellons came to the throne by a compromise with that nobility; at the extinction of that family, a tumultuous mob exercised tumultuously, by a sort of general enthusiasm, the privilege of electing a monarch; enthusiasm declining, a faction of the high oligarchy succeeded in the election of Sigismund III.; with Michael, the inferior nobility came into power; with Sobieski was introduced the influence of the high nobility, and of female intrigue; with Augustus II. came the reign of gross and undisguised venality; with Augustus III. the controlling presence of a foreign army and domestic anarchy; with Stanislaus the wild fury of religious bigotry, in collision with the treacherous liberality of foreign influence. Every thing had had its day but the real nation; of them no notice had been taken; and though Poland was called a republic, it was a republic without a people. The royal power, the tumultuous patriotism of a nobility, the oligarchical feuds, the democracy of the nobility, the high aristocracy, downright bribery, the direct presence and interference of foreign troops, each had had its period; and is it strange that the anarchy of Poland had become complete? There was not only no government virtually, but even the forms did not exist, by which a government could be effectually set in motion. Is it strange, then, that the party of the patriots was unable to triumph over the obstacles in their path, since they had to contend with the strongest foreign powers, with a domestic political chaos, and with a destiny, which had for ages doomed their country to destruction? The Russians and their coadjutors could never have accomplished their purpose, if the ancestors of the Poles had not themselves prepared the way.

The world would have heard no more of the Polish state, but for the simultaneous revolution in France. There the issue was as different, as the abuses which required remedy, and the instruments which could be applied for their correction. In Poland there was no middling class; in France the revolution sprung from the middling class; in Poland the contest was against the anarchy of an oligarchy; in France against the impending anarchy of superannuated absolutism. Both nations were fertile in great men; both had patriots disciplined in the school of America; both suffered from internal dissensions; both were attacked by the refugees from their own country, under the banners of foreign monarchs; both suffered from the hesitancy of inefficient kings; both contended with the greatest financial difficulties; but in France there existed a free yeomanry, a free class of mechanics, a free, numerous, and cultivated order of citizens; while in Poland, there was almost no intermediate class between the nobility and the serfs. In that lies the secret of the different issue of their struggles. Poland was the victim of the American revolution; France its monument. Poland was erased from among the nations of the earth; while France put forth a gigantic strength in the triumphant defence of its nationality. Poland, brightly though it had shone for ages in the eastern heavens, was blotted out, while the star of France, rising in a lurid sky, through clouds of blood, was at length able to unveil the peerless light of liberty, and lead the host of modern states in the high career of civil improvement.

After the victories of Napoleon over Prussia, the peace of Tilsit restored a portion of Poland to an independent existence as a Grand Dutchy. The loss of national existence, and the disgust at submitting to foreign forms, had excited discontent; and the race still lived, which had witnessed the two last partitions of their country. Napoleon's answer to the Polish deputies, "that he was willing to see if the Poles still deserved to be a nation," resounded through the provinces; and troops assembled hastily between the Vistula and the Niemen. But in Posen, the French emperor set Austria at rest as to Galicia; and when he became the personal friend of Alexander, nothing could be wrested from Russia. Thus the relations of Napoleon enabled him to dispose only of Polish Prussia; and of that, Bialystock was ceded to the Czar, while Prussia still retained a territory sufficient to connect East-Prussia with Brandenburgh. Thus the new Grand Dutchy of Warsaw, under the hereditary sway of the Saxon king, and constituting a portion of the French empire, contained but less than twenty-nine thousand square miles, and less than two and a half millions of inhabitants. Its constitution was given, July 22, 1807. Slavery was abolished, and equality before the law decreed. Two chambers were created, and a diet was to be convened at least once in two years, for fifteen days. The *initiative* of laws belonged to the Grand Duke; the chamber of deputies was to be renewed, one-third every three years. The code of Napoleon was made the law of the land.

In the peace of 1809, the Grand Dutchy was increased by further restorations from Austria; though Russia took advantage of that emergency to demand from its Austrian ally, also a territory of great value, with a population of four hundred thousand souls.

The great expedition against Russia, in 1812, was called by Napoleon his second Polish war. It was his professed object to restrain Russia, and to circumscribe her limits. A proclamation to the Poles promised the restoration of their state, with larger boundaries even than under their last king; and the Poles rose with their wonted enthusiasm. It was a point of honour with their young men to serve in the army; the middling class would accept no pay, while the rich lavished their fortunes, and the women their ornaments, for the defence and restoration of their nation.

Yet, when in June, Napoleon entered Wilna, the Lithuanians showed little disposition to unite with their brethren of Warsaw; and the emperor's answers, as to the future condition of Poland, were too vague to inspire confidence. The eventual defeat of Napoleon, brought the Russians into the pursuit, and the Grand Dutchy was occupied by their armies.

In the close of 1814, the fate of Poland was at issue on the deliberations of the congress of Vienna. While Prussia demanded the cession of all Saxony, Russia claimed Poland, including Austrian Galicia. Encountering strong opposition, the emperor Alexander in his turn formed a Polish army, and issued a proclamation to the Poles, inviting them to arm under his auspices for the defence of their country, and the preservation of their political independence, while Austria, Great Britain, and France, formed a treaty for resistance. But for the return of Napoleon from Elba, the congress of Vienna would probably have issued in a war between its

members. A compromise ensued, it conformity with which, Russia retained nearly all which in had gained of Prussia in the peace of Tilsit, and of Austria in 1809,
and further acquired all the Grand Dutchy of Warsaw, except Posen, which fell to
Prussia, and Cracau, which was left in neutral independence. Constitutions were
promised to the respective parts, and have been, after a manner, conceded.

The constitution issued for Poland, November 27, 1815, by the emperor Alexander, was an attempt to conciliate the liberal sympathies of the people. Religious equality, freedom of the press, security of personal liberty against arbitrary
procedures, the responsibility of all magistrates, and an assurance of all civil and
military offices in Poland to Poles, were the leading features of the compact. The
power of making treaties, of declaring war, of controlling the armed force, and
of pardoning, was assured to the king; but all his commands were to be counter-
signed by a minister, who should be held responsible in case of any violation of
the constitution. The diet, composed of two chambers, was to be assembled once
in two years; the king had the *initiative* and a *veto*.

At the opening of the diet, April 27, 1817, Alexander declared his intention of
gradually introducing into his immense empire, the salutary influence of liberal
institutions; and promised security of persons, and of property, and freedom of
opinions. "Representatives of Poland," said he, "rise to the elevation on which
destiny has placed you. You are called upon to give a sublime example to Europe,
whose eye is fixed upon you." The Poles have in this latest period of their existence,
shown no reluctance to be true to themselves and to the world; but the revolution
of Spain, and Naples, and Greece, struck terror into the cabinet of Alexander, and
led him to abandon the sympathies which he had professed for ameliorated forms
of government. Accordingly, by an arbitrary decree, February 13, 1825, he abolished the publicity of the assemblies of the diet, and taught the Poles the true value
of an apparently liberal form of government, of which the fundamental principles
might be altered according to the caprices or the fears of an individual.

We have thus endeavoured, by a careful reference to numerous and exact authorities, to which we have had access, to give some historical explanations of
the present Polish question. It seems plain, that there is little room to hope for
the re-establishment of Polish independence. The provinces belonging to Austria,
have most of them been under the Austrian rule for nearly sixty years; and so, too,
a large portion of Polish Prussia has belonged to the Prussian monarchy, since
1773. The still larger parts, which have been incorporated into the Russian monarchy, seem to have learnt acquiescence in their condition. A kindred dialect, and a
sort of national relationship, have always rendered Russian supremacy more tolerable to the Polish provinces, than that of the dynasty of Hapsburg, or the court
of Berlin. It is only in that portion of Poland, where, by the establishment of the
Grand Dutchy of Warsaw under Napoleon, and by the erection of a nominally independent kingdom, a spirit of irritation and change has fostered the honourable
passion for national existence, that the present revolution has been supported with
enthusiasm. The world will do honour to this last effort of determined patriotism;
but the liberties of Poland will be reconquered only by the gradual progress of the
moral power of free-opinions, which is advancing in the majesty of its strength;

over the ruins of centuries and the graves of nations.

ART. IX.

HISTORY OF MARYLAND,

A Historical View of the Government of Maryland, from its Colonization to the present day. By John V. L. M'Mahon. Baltimore: 1831. Vol. 1. pp. 539.

The history of Maryland under the proprietary government is little known, says our author, even to her own people. Yet, as that government was the mould of her present institutions, the school of discipline for her revolutionary men, it is to its history we must go back for just notions of both. The revolution was not wrought by a few master minds, miraculously born for the occasion, but was the natural development of a train of causes which leave us less surprised at our ancestors' manful and accordant resistance of usurpation, than at the strange ignorance of them which seems to have begot the unwise designs of the mother country.

Montesquieu has observed, with his usual antithesis, "In the infancy of societies, it is the leaders that create the institutions; afterwards, it is the institutions which make the leaders." Perhaps, the former event has in truth happened less often than received history would persuade us. The more dim the dawn of tradition, the oftener we find ascribed to the Lycurguses, the Numas, the Alfreds, either such original establishments or such fundamental changes as would seem to have created the civil or religious polity of their people anew. We know not how much they were indebted to precedent and concurrent circumstances; and thus obscurity may magnify their renown, as distant objects, according to a figure of our author's, are exaggerated to the eye in a misty morning. The vulgar, who do not trouble themselves with cavils, resolve the result they perceive into the effort of some moral hero, just as the Greeks referred to Hercules the feats which transcended the ordinary limits of physical prowess.

The same thing takes place in a less degree, at periods whose history is more authentically written. The leaders of revolutions may transmute, so to speak, into personal merit, some of the results which, more narrowly considered, are referrible to the pervading spirit and general movement of the occasion. To weigh justly these elements of their renown, is not invidiously to derogate from it, but only to vindicate the truth of history. It still leaves them the highest merit to which, perhaps, the leaders in any kind of reform can truly lay claim, that of seizing the spirit of their age, and employing and directing it with a just energy and discernment. As it has been said that Luther might have ineffectually preached the Reformation in the twelfth century, and Napoleon, if he had not been, in fact, but "the little corporal," might have been no more than a leader of *Condottieri* in the fourteenth; so our revolutionary sages could hardly, in the circumstances of the crisis, and amidst the men of the age, have been other than what they were. Though they fought in the van of the war, they had, however, their *Triarii* to sustain them, a nation, namely, accustomed to the discipline of liberty. The wave of opinion rolled high, and they had the praise of launching their barks on it, with strength and skill indeed, but yet with a propitious gale and a favouring current. The notices in the volume before us, of the character and history of the colonists of Maryland, show how the principles of liberty which they brought with them to "this rough, uncultivated world," (such is their own description of it,) they maintained with a uniform constancy and understanding. Though colonial dependence has seldom been less burdensome in point of fact than in their case, the abstract doctrines of political right were not on that account guarded with the less vigilance. Thus, in our author's language, "they were fitted for self-government before it came, and when it came, it sat lightly and familiarly upon them;" the first moments of its adoption being marked with little or none of that anarchy and licentiousness which mostly deform political emancipations. Their institutions had moulded them; a conclusion not more apparent from our colonial and revolutionary history, than apposite for estimating at least the immediate results of revolutions effected under moral circumstances less propitious. The political structure has often, as in our own case, been pulled down by an excusable impatience of the people; but seldom has it been repaired with such solidity, and just adaption to their wants.

We have said that the obscurity of history may have magnified the pretensions of some of its heroes; it is certain that it quite quenches the light of others. The state whose early transactions our author records, furnished its full share of the intelligent minds that contributed their impulse to the general movement of their time; and as the execution of his task has led him to a closer contemplation of their influence on its issue, he laments the comparative obscuration of merited fame, even in this brief lapse of time, in individuals who were the theme and boast of contemporaries. This is the law of our fate. As the series of events is prolonged, the greater part of the actors in them sink out of their place in the perspective, though their lesser elevation might be scarcely observable to their own age. In the twilight which falls on all past transactions, the rays of national recollections fade from summit to summit, and linger at length only on a few of the more "proudly eminent." Our author sketches some of these forgotten worthies in the melancholy spirit of a traveller who finds a stately column in the desert. With the reverence of "Old Mortality," he re-touches the inscription to the illustrious dead, that they may not wholly perish.

The first volume of the present work, the only one yet published, brings down the history of Maryland to the establishment of the state government. Besides a historical view of the transactions preceding this era, it contains, in an introduction, a view of the territorial limits of the colony as defined in the first grant to the proprietary, and of the disputes with neighbouring grantees by which they were successively retrenched. Two other chapters of the introduction are occupied with a sketch of the civil divisions of the state, and an essay on the sources of its laws.

Appended to the historical sketch is a view of the distribution of the legislative power, of the organization of the two houses of assembly, their respective and collective powers, and the privileges of their members. This plan involves a critical inquiry into the political laws of the state, and a laborious examination of its records. The diligence with which the writer seems to have executed his task, is a voucher of his accuracy; and the body of information thus collected with painful research, will probably establish his work as one of authentic reference. This original collation of the materials from which history is *distilled*, includes a labour, and deserves a praise, which readers can hardly estimate competently. The writer's style is vigorous, but wants compression; he is occasionally inaccurate, but is often lively and striking; his scriptural phraseology is superabundant. As he understands the period and the men he describes, his views and reflections are just. The narrative would have been enlivened by a little more individuality in the portraits of the actors; but though some of the materials for this were probably at his command, at least as to the more recent ones, we are aware of the reasons which impose on this head, a partial silence on the historian of an age not remote. It is respecting its personages that Christina's saying of history is more emphatically true;—"*Chi lo sa, non scrive; chi lo scrive, no sa.*" —"The one who knows it, does not write; the one who writes it, knows it not." It was this Mr. Jefferson meant, when he said the history of the revolution had never been written, and never would be written. On the whole, Mr. M'Mahon's is a valuable contribution to an interesting theme, and we must increase the obligations we are under to him, by borrowing the copious materials he supplies, for a hasty sketch, or rather some selections of the colonial history of Maryland, in which we shall take the liberty to make, without scruple, free use both of his language and thoughts.

The present state of Maryland is embraced within considerably narrower limits than those described in the original grant. By the charter which bears date the 20th of June, 1632, the province assigned to Cecilius, Lord Baltimore, had the following boundaries. On the south, a line drawn from the promontory on the Chesapeake, called Watkins's Point, to the ocean; on the east, the ocean, and the western margin of Delaware Bay and river, as far as the fortieth degree of latitude; on the north, a line drawn in that degree of latitude west, to the meridian of the true fountain of the Potomac; and thence, the western bank of that river to Smith's Point, and so by the shortest line to Watkins's Point. These limits, it is apparent, embrace the whole of the present state of Delaware; they comprehend also that part of Pennsylvania in which Chester lies, as far north as the Schuylkill, and a very considerable portion of Virginia. It may not be uninteresting to trace the controversies which resulted in this abridgment of territory, especially as it appears from Mr. M'Mahon's deduction of that with Virginia, that Maryland has a subsisting claim to a large and fertile portion of the latter state, lying between the south and north branches of the Potomac.

The proprietary's first contest, was with a personage who makes some figure in the early history of his colony, and who, though painted with little flattery by its chroniclers, seems to have possessed some talents, enterprise, and courage. This was the notorious William Clayborne, who, before the grant to Baltimore was carved out of the limits of Virginia, had made some settlements on Kent Island, in the Chesapeake, under the authority of that province. Clayborne defended his claims with pertinacity for several years, and was not brought to submission to the new grantee, till he had harassed the infant colony with commotions, and even prepared to make depredations. He subsequently gratified his resentment by exciting a rebellion, and driving the proprietary's governor to Virginia. That province also for some time persisted to assert its dominion over Maryland, in defiance of the royal grant; and, when that question was at length decided in the proprietary's favour, it was next necessary to fix the actual boundary between the two provinces, a matter not adjusted till June, 1668, when the existing southern line of Maryland was finally determined.

The proprietary's next territorial controversy had a greater duration, and a less fortunate issue, being prolonged nearly a century, and resulting in the dismemberment of a portion of his fairest and most fertile territory. It must be mentioned, that the charter of Maryland extended its northern boundary to the southern limit of what was then called New England. In the intermediate territory between the actual settlements of the two, the Dutch and the Swedes had planted some colonies and trading-houses on the banks of the Delaware Bay and river, in what is now the state of Delaware. The Swedish establishments were reduced by the Dutch in 1655, and appended, together with their own, in the same quarter, to the government of New Netherlands; on the English conquest of which, and the grant of them by Charles II. to his brother, the Duke of York, the settlements on the Delaware became dependencies on the government of New-York, and, though clearly within the limits of Maryland, being south of the latitude of 40°, remained so until the grant to Penn, and the foundation of Pennsylvania in 1681. The southern boundary of Penn's grant, was somewhat loosely established to be "a circle of twelve miles drawn round New Castle, to the beginning of the fortieth degree of latitude." Penn was eager to adjust his boundary with Maryland; but when it was found, on an interview between his agent and Baltimore, at Chester, then called Upland, that Chester itself was south of the required latitude, and that the boundaries of Maryland would extend to the Schuylkill, he very earnestly applied himself, to obtain from the Duke of York, a grant of the Delaware settlements mentioned above. In contravention of the claims of Baltimore, a conveyance was made to him in 1682, of the town of New Castle, with the district twelve miles round it, and also of the territory extending thence southward to Cape Henlopen.

Thus fortified, Penn was again eager to adjust the disputed boundary. The negotiations for this purpose, proving fruitless, were referred to the Commissioners of Trade and Plantations, to whom Penn submits a case of hardship, more *naïf* than convincing. "I told him, (Baltimore,) that it was not the love of the land, but of the water;—that he abounded in what I wanted,—and that there was no proportion in the concern, because the thing insisted on was ninety-nine times more valuable to me, than to him." It must be recollected, that this reasonable claim involved nothing less than Baltimore's entire exclusion from Delaware Bay, and greatly abridged his territory on the coast of the ocean. Another objection was urged by Penn, which finally governed the award of the commissioners, who, in

1685, decided that Baltimore's grant "included only lands uncultivated, and inhabited by savages;" whereas the territory along the Delaware had been settled by Christians antecedently to his grant,—a decision, by the way, inconsistent with the previous ejectment of Clayborne, and with the determination in Baltimore's favour, of the jurisdiction claimed over his grant by Virginia. They directed also, for the avoidance of future contests, that the peninsula between the two bays, should be divided into two equal parts, by a line drawn from the latitude of Cape Henlopen, to the fortieth degree of latitude,—the western portion to belong to Baltimore, and the eastern to His Majesty, and, by consequence, to Penn. This is the origin of the eastern boundary of Maryland, which was thus cut off from the ocean, on the greater portion of her eastern side.

Her northern boundary still remained to be adjusted; but the embarrassments of both proprietaries with the crown, caused the controversy in this quarter to sleep nearly half a century. The mutual border outrages which meanwhile disturbed the debatable ground, led to the compact of the 10th of May, 1732, between Baltimore and the younger Penns, which provided, in the first place, for the extension of a line northerly, through the middle of the peninsula, so as to form a tangent to a circle drawn round Newcastle, with a radius of twelve miles. The northern boundary of Maryland was also to begin, not at the fortieth degree of latitude, but at a point fifteen miles south thereof; and in case the tangent before described should not extend to that point, it was to be prolonged by a line drawn due north from the point where the tangent met the circle; thus was ascertained the eastern extremity of the northern boundary line, which was thence to be extended due west. New obstacles intervened, however, to the execution of this agreement, which was subsequently carried into chancery, but on which no decision was had until 1750; and in the interval, some frightful excesses were committed by the borderers on both sides. The house of one Cresap, in Maryland, was fired by a body of armed men from Pennsylvania, who attempted to murder him, his family, and several of his neighbours, as they escaped from the flames. In retaliation, a little army of three hundred Marylanders invaded the county of Lancaster, and took summary measures to coerce submission to the government of Maryland. These mutual outrages occasioned, in 1739, an order from the king in council for the establishment of a provisional line; and in 1750, Chancellor Hardwicke pronounced a decree, which ordered the specific execution of the agreement of 1732. But Frederic, Lord Baltimore, the heir of Charles, with whom the agreement had been made, contending that he was protected from its operation by certain anterior conveyances in strict settlement, objected to the execution of the decree, until finally, and pending the chancery proceedings, a new agreement was entered into on the 4th of July, 1760, between himself and the Penns, which adopted that of 1732, and also the decree of 1750. Commissioners were appointed to run the lines accordingly, who in November, 1768, reported their proceedings to the proprietaries, and definitively adjusted the eastern and northern boundaries of Maryland, in the terms of the agreement before described. The northern line, from the names of the surveyors, is commonly known as "Mason and Dixon's line," so often referred to as the demarcation of the slave states from the others.

This controversy was not terminated in the north, when the proprietary found new pretensions to combat in the west. These grew out of the words of his charter, which described "the true fountain of the Potomac" as the common *terminus* of his western and southern boundaries. A subsequent grant from the crown had conveyed to certain persons all the tract between the heads and courses of the Rappahannock and Potomac, and the Chesapeake Bay. This grant, which comprehended what was commonly known as "The Northern Neck" of Virginia, and which carried only the ownership of the soil, the jurisdiction remaining in Virginia, was finally vested solely in Lord Culpepper, and from him descended to his daughter, who marrying Lord Fairfax, the property in it passed to the Fairfax family. As it called only for lands on the south side of the Potomac, there was nothing on the face of it inconsistent with the call of the charter of Maryland; but the under-grants from Fairfax were soon pushed so far west as to raise the question of the true fountain of the Potomac. Commissioners appointed by Virginia to ascertain, as between that state and Fairfax, the limits of their respective ownership, determined the North Branch to be the fountain of that river; whereas, from information given to the council of Maryland, in 1753, by Colonel Cresap, one of the settlers in the eastern extremity of the state, it appeared, from its having the longest course, and from other circumstances, that the South Branch was to be considered the principal stream, and its source the true source of the Potomac. The British council for plantation affairs had, as early as 1745, on the petition of Fairfax, made a report, adopting the North Branch as such; but the proprietary of Maryland, who viewed his rights as disregarded in this decision, continued to assert his claim up to the first fountain of the Potomac, "be that where it might." Various circumstances prevented his bringing the matter before the king in council; and so the question hung, till the Revolution substituted the *state* of Virginia for the British crown, as one party in the controversy, and that of Maryland as the other.

In the constitution of the former, adopted in 1776, there is an express recognition of the right of Maryland "to all the territory contained within its charter;" but the actual boundary was not brought into negotiation till 1795. New delays then interposed, and though Virginia named commissioners in the matter in 1801, she restricted their powers to the adjustment merely of the western line, unwilling to allow even a discussion of her claim to the territory between the two branches. The negociation consequently dropped for the time, and Maryland, wearied, it would seem, with various efforts to reclaim the territory south of the North Branch, agreed, at length, by an act passed in 1818, to adopt as the terminus, the most western source of that stream. But a new obstacle, interposed by Virginia, defeated the adjustment under this concession. Her commissioners were instructed to commence the boundary "at a stone, planted by Lord Fairfax on the head waters of the Potomac," being thus restricted to the old adjustment between Fairfax and the crown; those of Maryland were directed to begin at the true or most western source of the North Branch, be that where it might. Fairfax's stone, our author says, is not planted in fact at the extreme western source. The proffer of Maryland, by the act of 1818, to confine herself to the North Branch, being thus rejected by Virginia, she is remitted apparently to her original rights, which comprehend the sovereignty of all the territory between these two streams of the Potomac, and call for the South Branch as her south-western boundary in that quarter. In a letter of Mr. Cooke, then a distinguished lawyer of Maryland, and one of the commissioners named in 1795, to adjust the point, the territory in contest is stated to contain 462,480 acres; and he remarks, that prior occupancy gives, in such a case, no title to one party, and no length of time can bar the claim of the other.

We have thus abridged the author's copious and distinct account of the territorial wars, which resulted in the defeat of the proprietaries of Maryland on two parts of their frontier, and have left a legacy of debate on a third. We must now return to the era of the first grantee and proprietary, and take up the line of the general events of the colonial history.

Cecilius Calvert had no sooner obtained his grant, for which he is said to have been indebted to the influence of his father, George Calvert, who but for his death would have been himself the grantee, than he prepared for the establishment of a colony. The expedition, which he entrusted to his brother, Leonard Calvert, sailed from the Isle of Wight on the 22d of November, 1633, the emigrants consisting of about two hundred persons, principally Catholics, and many of them gentlemen of family and fortune. They reached Point Comfort, in Virginia, on the 24th of February following, and thence proceeded up the Potomac, in search of an eligible site. Having taken formal possession of the province, at an island which they called St. Clements, they sailed upwards of forty leagues up the river, to an Indian town called Piscataway; but deeming it prudent to establish themselves nearer its mouth, they returned to what is now known as St. Mary's river, (an estuary of the Potomac,) on the eastern side of which, six or seven miles from its mouth, they disembarked, on the 27th of March, 1634. Here, near another Indian town, bearing the uncouth name of Yaocomoco, they laid the foundation of the old city of St. Mary's, and of the state of Maryland. The proprietary had made ample provision for his infant colony, of food and clothing, the implements of husbandry, and the means of erecting habitations; expending in the first two or three years upwards of £40,000, and governing, by all concurring accounts, with much policy and liberality.

The new colony seems to have been looked on a little coldly by Virginia, her next neighbour in the great continental wilderness, and to have had indeed more positive ground of complaint in the connivance given there to Clayborne, who has already been mentioned as the colonizer of Kent Island, and whose fancied or real injuries from the proprietary, made him the persevering foe of the colony during twenty-five years. His first essay was to kindle the jealousies of the natives against the colonists, which, in the beginning of 1642, broke out into an open war, that endured for some time, and was the cause of much expense and distress to the province. The distractions of the great rebellion of 1642, which began at this time to involve the colonies, furnished him the next pretences of disturbance, and with fit associates. Richard Ingle, the most prominent of these, was a known adherent of the parliamentary cause; he had before this time been proclaimed a traitor to the king, and had fled the province. The insurrection promoted, therefore, by these confederates and others, (commonly known as "Clayborne and Ingle's rebellion,") was probably carried on in the name of the Parliament; though the loss of the greater part of the provincial records, anterior and relating to this period, the circumstance from which it acquired its chief notoriety, leaves us little other knowledge of the insurrection itself, than that it was attended with great misrule and rapacity, that it commenced in 1644, and that the proprietary government was suspended till August, 1646; Leonard Calvert, the governor, being compelled meanwhile to seek refuge in Virginia. Quiet was then restored by a general amnesty, from which only Clayborne, Ingle, and one Durnford, were excepted. During two or three years the province maintained this tranquillity, by pursuing a neutral course towards the contending parties in England, varied by the single unadvised act of proclaiming, on the 15th of November, 1649, the accession of Charles II., Governor Stone being absent at the moment. This procedure was followed by very ill consequences to the proprietary. The Parliament, now triumphant, issued a commission for the subjugation of the disaffected colonies, of which, ominously, for Maryland, *Captain* Clayborne was named one, and which, after reducing Virginia, demanded of Stone, the Governor of Maryland, an express recognition of the parliamentary authority. Delaying compliance with this demand, he was threatened with the deprivation of his government; but it was arranged at length that he should continue to exercise it, till the pleasure of the commonwealth government could be known. This trust he seems to have discharged with due fidelity to the Parliament. He required, indeed, the inhabitants of the province to take the oath of allegiance to the proprietary government; an act which does not seem inconsistent with his engagements. It was alleged, however, to be an evidence of disaffection; and as intentions, says our author, are always easy to charge, and difficult to disprove, he was in the end compelled to resign his office to a commission named by Clayborne and his associates. Stone now attempted resistance; but an engagement taking place near the Patuxent, his small force of two hundred men was entirely defeated, and himself taken prisoner. He was condemned to die; but he had, like another Marius, inspired, it seems, such respect and affection in the soldiery, that the party intrusted with his execution refused to proceed in it. A general intercession of the people procured a commutation of his sentence to imprisonment, which was continued, with circumstances of severity, during the greater part of the protectorate. With him the proprietary government fell for the time.

The occasion was seized by Virginia, to urge with the Protector, her old claim of jurisdiction over Maryland. The proprietary's charter was assailed, and the story of Clayborne's wrongs, pathetically told at length. The fanaticism of the Protector was approached, by objecting the religious toleration, which, much to the honour of the proprietary, had consistently characterized his government. The union of the two provinces was urged, among other reasons, on the score of its preventing "the cutting of throats," and restraining the excessive planting of tobacco, thereby making way *for the more staple commodities,* such as *silk.* Cromwell, however, who could lay aside his fanaticism on occasion, but who, on the other hand, probably sought to keep the proprietary in his interests, by holding his rights in suspense, made no decision in the case; and the latter, who at first expected a speedy result in his favour, seems to have resolved at length to regain his province by force. His government had fallen without a crime, and, besides, the pretensions of Virginia had roused the pride and indignation of all parties. He had thus many adherents, among the most conspicuous of whom was Josias Fendall, who having, with a consistency that merits remark, signalized by treachery every measure he was concerned in, played for some years a part in the transactions of the colony, worthy of versatile politicians on a more extensive theatre. He is brought to our notice in 1655, when he was in custody before the provincial court, on a charge of disturbing the government, under a pretended power from the late governor, Stone, and was imprisoned. Being discharged, probably on taking an oath not to disquiet the government, he nevertheless appeared soon after as an open insurgent, acting under the proprietary's commission as his governor. We are uninformed of the particulars of his operations against the commissioners. During a part of 1657 and 1658, there seems to have been a divided empire in the province, the commissioners administering theirs at St. Leonard's, and Fendall and his council sitting at St. Mary's. An arrangement between the proprietary and the Virginian commissioners, then in England, at length put an end to these divisions. The latter ceased to push the claims of Virginia, and it was agreed that his province should be restored to the proprietary. On the 20th of March, 1658, it was formally surrendered to Fendall as his governor, under a stipulation for the security of the acts passed during the defection;—a stipulation which the latter fulfilled, not only by declaring them void, but by causing them to be torn from the records.

Clothed thus with authority, Fendall was enabled to play off a kind of parody of Cromwell's proceedings, by "kicking away the ladder by which he had mounted." At the next convention of the assembly, the lower house transmitted a message to the upper, declaring itself the true assembly, and the supreme court of judicature, and demanding its opinion on this claim. The latter, not acceding with the required good grace and promptness to this new doctrine, which involved a complete independence, not only of itself, but of the proprietary, was visited in a body by the lower house, and ordered to sit no longer apart, with the privilege, nevertheless, of seats in the lower house. To the assembly thus reformed, Fendall surrendered his commission from the proprietary, accepting a new one from itself; and the inhabitants of the province were required to recognize no other authority but that of this new legislature, or of the king. The Restoration cut short the rule of this commonwealth party in the province. Baltimore obtained the countenance and aid of the new government,—and thus fortified, enjoined his brother, Philip Calvert, as his governor, to proceed against the insurgents even by martial law, and especially not to permit Fendall to escape with his life. Fendall, accordingly, with one Hatch, was excepted from the general indemnity, and proclamations were issued for their apprehension;—yet, on a subsequent voluntary surrender, he found means to be quits for a short imprisonment, with a disability to vote or hold office;—a lenity not more impolitic in the government, than unmerited by him, as he not long afterwards attempted to excite another rebellion.

An uninterrupted tranquillity of many years followed the commotions just narrated. In 1675, died Cecilius, Lord Baltimore, the first proprietary, leaving his estate in the province to his son and heir, Charles Calvert. On a visit to England, the new proprietary found himself and his government the subject of complaint to the Crown, from the resident clergy of the Church of England, in the province. They represented that the province was no better than a Sodom,—religion despised,—the Lord's day profaned, and all notorious vices committed;—in short, it was in a deplorable condition for want of an established ministry, the Quakers providing for their speakers, and the Catholics for their priests, but no care taken to build up churches in the Protestant religion. Baltimore represented very honestly, that all religions were tolerated by his laws, and none established,—and was dismissed for the time, with the general injunction to restrain immorality, and provide for a competent number of clergy of the Church of England. But the jealousy of popery, now abroad in England, began to flame up in the colonies, and especially in Maryland, which, peopled chiefly by Protestants, was yet under the dominion of a Catholic. Complaints were poured into Charles's ear, of Catholic partialities in the proprietary administration; and, in reply to a communication from Baltimore, by which it was shown beyond doubt, that his offices were distributed without distinction of religion, and the military power almost exclusively in Protestant hands—"that exemplary monarch," says our author, "gave his commentary on religious liberty, by ordering all offices to be put into the hands of the Protestants." With a singular ill fortune, which must be put to the account of his tolerance, the proprietary, thus controlled by a Protestant king, and menaced, besides, with that then formidable weapon of royalty, a *quo warranto,* did not the less encounter an enemy in his Catholic successor, by whom, in 1687, a *quo warranto* was actually issued. Before judgment was pronounced, indeed, the monarch himself was an exile, by the judgment of his people; but the proprietary was now attacked, on the opposite quarter, by the "Protestant Association of Maryland," which succeeded in overthrowing his government. This revolution marks one era in our author's historical narrative, before we proceed in which, we must pause a moment with him, to mention the condition of the colony, at the time this event occurred.

The two hundred original settlers were increased as early as 1660 to twelve thousand, and in 1671 to nearly twenty thousand; their exact number at the protestant revolution is unknown. The settlements had extended from St. Mary's a considerable distance up the Potomac, and all along the Chesapeake Bay on both sides, and were seated chiefly on its shores, and around the estuaries of its rivers. Excepting St. Mary's, there appears to have been no place entitled to the appellation of a town, unless, says the author, we adopt the same number of houses to make a town, which it requires persons to constitute a riot. The *city* of St. Mary's, which numbered fifty or sixty houses in two or three years from its planting, never much exceeded these humble limits. The colonists were almost universally planters of tobacco, and each plantation, according to an early writer, "was a little town of itself, every considerable planter's warehouse being a kind of shop," where inferior planters and others might obtain the necessary commodities. Tobacco supplied the purposes of gold and silver; but as this currency was in some respects inconvenient, the lords proprietaries struck coin, and imitated more powerful sovereigns by attempting,—and, as may be supposed, with the like success,—to circulate it at a rate beyond its intrinsic value. The act of 1686, making coins a legal tender at a certain advance beyond their real worth, deserves mention as establishing the provincial currency in lieu of sterling. There was also at this time a printing-press and a public printer; a circumstance peculiar to this colony at that early period. *Toleration was coeval with the province.* The oath of office prescribed by the proprietary to his governors, recognising the freedom of religious opinion in the amplest manner, "is in itself a text-book of official duty," and ought to be remembered to the honour of Cecilius Calvert, "when the lustre of a thousand diadems is pale." For the only two departures from this principle, the proprietary government is not responsible. An ordinance of Cromwell's Commissioners prohibited the profession of the Catholic religion; and the unscrupulous Fendall, at another time, banished the Quakers for refusing to subscribe an engagement of fidelity to the government. We are to seek, therefore, other causes than the intolerance of the proprietary for the Protestant revolution which we are now to notice.

A chasm in the colonial records, from November, 1688, to the beginning of 1692, leaves us without accurate information of its reasons and progress. Apparently, the alarm of Popery then general through the empire, was the true cause, and some indiscretions of the proprietary's governors the pretence. The government was at this time in a commission of nine deputies, who by summoning the lower house of assembly to take an oath of fidelity to the proprietary, were deemed to have committed a breach of its privilege. The president of the deputies was a Mr. Joseph, whose address on the opening of the assembly, being a very quaint but clumsy exposition of *jus divinum,* and of its derivation to himself, cannot claim the praise of a happy adaption to the humour of the moment. The house refusing to take the oath, the assembly was prorogued. News now came of the expected invasion of England by the Prince of Orange; and, without any fixed views probably, even as to their own course in the existing distractions, much less against the Protestants of the province, the deputies awaked jealousy, and gave rumour wings by ordering the public arms to be collected, and attempting to check reports which might beget "disaffection to the proprietary government." The whole colony resounded with the cry of a Popish plot; and as a treaty long subsisting with some Indian tribes happened to be renewed about this time, the plot thus engendered by the deputies was to be accomplished, it was asserted, by the aid of the savages and the French. An accidental delay of the proprietary's instructions for proclaiming William and Mary, heightened the alarm, or increased the exasperation; and at length, in April 1689, an association was formed, styling itself, "An Association in arms for the defence of the Protestant Religion, and for asserting the right of King William and Queen Mary to the province of Maryland." The deputies took refuge from the storm in a garrisoned fort at Mattapany, by whose surrender, in August 1689, the Associators gained undisputed possession of the province. The articles of surrender have preserved the names of the leaders, at the head of which is that of John Coode, another personage of colonial celebrity.

The first measure of the Associators was to summon a convention at St. Mary's, which transmitted to the king an exposition of the motives of the recent revolution. Their charges against the provincial government are so much at war with the tenor of its history, under both Cecilius and George Calvert, that we can in reason only impute them to popular exaggeration. It was alleged that all the offices of the province were under the control of the Jesuits, and the churches all appropriated to the uses of popish idolatry; nay, that under connivance, if not permission of the government, all sorts of murders and outrages were committed by Papists upon Protestants. Another topic, not less prevailing, was the reluctant and imperfect allegiance of the proprietary rulers to the crown, which they accordingly solicited to take the province under its immediate guard and administration, William gratified his own wishes as well as theirs, by arbitrarily depriving the proprietary of his province, without even the usual forms of law, and by sending out, in 1692, Sir Lionel Copley as the royal governor. We blush, says our author, to name Lord Holt as having given the opinion, behind whose high authority the crown intrenched itself in this summary procedure. The new governor's message to the assembly, recommending "the making of wholesome laws, and the laying aside of all heats and animosities," was responded to by an act, the second passed after its meeting, "for the service of Almighty God, and the establishment of the Protestant religion in the province." By this act, the Church of England was made the established church, and a poll-tax imposed of forty pounds of tobacco on every taxable, to build churches and support ministers. But the new church was not only to be encouraged; penalties were to be added for the suppression of others. Under the act of 1704, "to prevent the growth of popery," Catholic priests were inhibited by severe penalties from saying mass, or exercising, except in private families, other spiritual functions, or in any manner persuading the people to be reconciled to the Church of Rome. Protestant children of Papists, might also compel their parents to furnish them adequate maintenance. The Quakers, too, shared these persecutions for a time; but the toleration of Protestant dissenters was established some years after; and thus, "in a colony founded by Catholics, and which had grown into power and happiness under the government of Catholics, the Catholic inhabitant was the only victim of religious intolerance." The next attempt was against the revenues and land rights of the proprietary; but these were sustained by the crown.

Another victim of the Protestant revolution seems to have been the ancient city of St. Mary's, which, being in a district inhabited chiefly by Catholics, had always been distinguished by its attachment to the proprietaries. This circumstance was not calculated to lessen the complaints long made of its inconvenient remoteness from the greater part of the present settlements. A natural feeling had nevertheless retained the government at its old seat, (antiquity is comparative,) and in 1674 a state-house was built, at an expense (40,000 pounds of tobacco) which, in our author's opinion, shows it to have been a work of some taste and magnitude. This edifice was habitable till the present year, when its remains, which it would have been better taste to spare at least, if not preserve, were removed to make room for a church, erected on or near its site. Notwithstanding this embellishment of his capital, the proprietary, in 1683, yielded to the wishes of the colonists, and removed the legislature, the courts, and the public offices, to "the Ridge," in Anne Arundel county, and thence to Battle Creek, on the Patuxent; but the want of the necessary accommodations drove them from the first after one session, and from the latter after the shorter experiment of three days. The government was brought back to St. Mary's, and remained there till the Protestant revolution, when its removal was again resolved on. The petition of the ancient city against the measure, and the reply to it, exhibit the usual topics of the two parties which divide the world; on the one side, prescription and ancient privilege; utility, and the progress of events on the other. In vain the citizens expatiated also on their capacious harbour, in which five hundred sail might ride securely at anchor; and offered to keep up, at their own cost, a coach, or caravan, or both, to run daily during the session of the legislature and provincial courts, and weekly at other times; and at least six horses, with suitable furniture, for all persons having occasion to ride post. Neither their representations nor their offers begat any thing more than sarcasms on their leanness and poverty, and the intended removal took place in 1694-5.

The spot selected for the new seat of government, was a point of land at the mouth of the Severn; a town, according to the definition before given, but not yet possessing the qualification required by a colonial statute, entitled by the author "an act to keep the towns off the parish," which denied it the right of sending a delegate to the assembly, till inhabited by as many families as might defray his expenses, without being chargeable to the county. This place, known as "Proctor's," or "the town-land at Severn," was named, at the removal, Anne Arundel town; the following year it acquired the title of the Port of Annapolis; it was erected in 1708 into a city, with the privilege, which it still retains, of sending two delegates to the assembly. Four or five years after it had become the seat of colonial legislation, it is described as containing about forty dwellings, seven or eight of which could afford good lodging and accommodation for strangers. One is curious to know what might have been the accommodations at "the Ridge," and at Battle Creek. Our informant continues, "there is also a statehouse and free-school, built of brick, which make a great show among a parcel of wooden houses; and the foundation of a church is laid, the only brick church in Maryland." He adds, "had Governor Nicholson continued there a few *months* longer, he had brought it to *perfection.*" This perfection it seems not to have acquired even as late as 1711, being then described by one "E. Cooke, gentleman," in his poem called "The Sotweed Factor," yet, by rare accident, extant, as—

> "A city situate on a plain,
> Where scarce a house will keep out rain;
> The buildings, fram'd with cypress rare,
> Resemble much our Southwark Fair;—
> And if the truth I may report,
> It's not so large as Tottenham-court."

This tobacco merchant, as we translate his title, a gentleman apparently of a caustic vein, the prototype of English travellers in America, reflects also on the hospitality of the new capital; an allegation doubtful, considering its source, but at any rate amply refuted at a subsequent day, as this little city, though it never acquired a large population or commerce, was, long before the American revolution, proverbial for the profuse hospitality of its inhabitants, their elegant luxury, and liberal accomplishments. A French writer thus describes it during the revolution, when it may be presumed to have shared the distresses and gloom of the period: "In that very inconsiderable town, of the few buildings it contains, at least three-fourths may be styled elegant and grand. Female luxury here exceeds what is known in the provinces of France. A French hair-dresser is a man of importance among them; and it is said a certain dame here hires one of that craft at one thousand crowns a year. The state-house is a very beautiful building; I think the most so of any I have seen in America."[10] To these habits of profusion, our author is inclined to add others less excusable, and hints at "dangerous allurements," administering neither to happiness nor purity. This early seat of colonial elegance and luxury is still the political metropolis of Maryland. From the lofty dome of its state-house the visiter may still look down on mansions that betoken ancient opulence, and on a landscape of quiet beauty, varied with gardens and ancient trees, and picturesquely watered by winding estuaries of the Chesapeake, whose breeze attempers a climate rich in early flowers and fruits. It was at this time the residence, of course, of the royal governors, of whose administration we find little to record in this hasty narrative. One of them, indeed, Francis Nicholson, though a pliant minister of the crown, seems to have acquired some popularity in the province, his versatility of temper combined with some energy and talent, and a courteous demeanour, enabling him to fall easily into the prevailing humour. Having arrived when the enthusiasm of the Protestant revolution was yet fresh, he became a great patron of the clergy, and promoter of orthodoxy, and in that capacity we find him engaged in proceedings against Coode, though the latter had figured in the events by which the Protestant ascendency had been established, when his services were deemed of such merit as to entitle him to the reward of one hundred thousand pounds of tobacco, and an office. Coode seems not to have elevated his private virtues to the level of his public. He subsequently appears exercising the incompatible functions of a clergyman, a collector of customs, and a lieutenant-colonel of militia, at the same time alleging that religion was a trick, and that all the morals worth having were contained in Cicero's offices. If the orthodoxy of Governor Nicholson was offended by these opinions, his vanity was not less so by intimations from Coode, that as he had pulled down one government, he might assist in overthrowing another. The agitator, on the ground of his being in holy orders, was prevented by the governor from serving as a delegate in the assembly, and was then dismissed from his employments, and indicted for atheism and blasphemy. He fled to Virginia, but afterwards, on the removal of Nicholson from the government, came in and surrendered himself. In consideration of former services, his sentence was suspended; age and adversity probably tamed his unquietness, as thenceforward we hear no more of him in the colonial history. Nicholson's next proceedings were against some persons whose principal offence seems to have been the ascription to him of certain acts of early licentiousness not very consistent with his orthodox zeal, and which, as they have come down to posterity, might, the author says, be entitled the *Memorabilia* of Governor Nicholson. Whatever these *Memorabilia* were, they seem not to have impaired the popularity of his administration, which was also remarkable for the establishment, in 1695, of a public *post*, before unknown in the colonies. The route of this post extended from some point on the Potomac through Annapolis to Philadelphia. The postman was bound to travel the route *eight times a year*, for which he received a salary of 50*l*. The scheme dropped on the death of the first postman in 1698, and appears not to have been revived afterwards. A general post-office for the colonies was

---

[10] New Travels by the Abbé Robin, one of the Chaplains to the French Army in N. America.]

established by the English government in 1710.

Though our author pronounces the administration of the royal governors to have been favourable in general to the liberties and prosperity of the colony, its population and resources appear to have increased extremely little during that era. In 1689 it contained about twenty-five thousand inhabitants, and in 1710 only thirty thousand. Immigration had in a great measure ceased; a circumstance imputable to nothing so probably as the change in its religious policy. Complaints are made of the distressed condition of its husbandry, and the years 1694 and 1695 were years of unusual scarcity, and of surprising mortality among the cattle and swine. The artisans, including the carpenters and coopers, constituted, according to a statement in 1697, only one-sixtieth of the whole population. The colonists depended entirely on England for the most necessary articles; in a few families, coarse clothing was manufactured out of the wool of the province; and some attempts were made in the counties of Somerset, and Dorchester, to manufacture linen and woollen cloths on a more extensive scale. Even these imperfect attempts seem to have offended the commercial jealousy of the mother country; for the difficulty of getting English goods at the time, is mentioned by way of excuse for them. There was an inconsiderable export to the West Indies, and a small trade with New-England for rum, molasses, fish, and wooden wares, for their traffic in which latter article the New-Englanders were already conspicuous. The shipping of the colony was very trifling, the trade with England being carried on entirely in English, and that with the West Indies, chiefly in New-England vessels.

The proprietary government had now been suspended twenty-five years. It had fallen through jealousy of the Catholics, and Charles Calvert, who submitted in his own person to the loss of power for the sake of the religion in which he had grown up, had yielded to the anxieties of a parent, and induced his son and heir, Benedict Leonard Calvert, to embrace the doctrines of the established church. By his own death, in February, 1714, and that of his heir in April, 1715, the title to the province devolved to Charles Calvert, the infant son of the latter, who was also educated in the Protestant faith. The reason for excluding the proprietary family then subsisted no longer; their claims were in fact soon after acknowledged by George I. and their government restored in the person of the infant proprietary, in May, 1715. The only consequence of this event meriting notice, was the imposition of a test-oath, requiring of Catholics the abjuration of the Pretender, and the renunciation of some of the essential points of their faith. Private animosity gave edge to these civil persecutions; Catholics were excluded from social intercourse, *nor permitted to walk in front of the State-House*; swords were worn by them for personal defence. Charles Calvert died in 1751, leaving the province to his infant son Frederic, after acquiring for his administration the praise of moderation and integrity. Yet it was fruitful in internal dissensions, which no policy could have averted. The controversy respecting the extension of the English statutes to the colony, originated in 1722, and was succeeded in 1739 by the disputes relating to the proprietary revenue; controversies full of heat at the time, but which will be more conveniently considered in connexion with some subsequent transactions of the same sort. One dispute may be mentioned here, as indicating the spirit of all the rest. The "Six

Nations," a tribe of Indians, occupying a border position between the French and English colonies, had claims to a considerable portion of the territory of Maryland lying along the Susquehanna and the Potomac, and in 1742 it was resolved to depute commissioners to Albany for the purpose of extinguishing them by treaty. The lower house of assembly claiming, however, to participate in the appointment of the commissioners, and also to restrict the amount of expenditure, a dispute arose on this point of prerogative, which was only adjusted, two years after, by the governor's appointing the commission on his own responsibility, and defraying its charges from the ordinary revenue. The claims in question were extinguished by the Indian treaty of Lancaster, in June, 1744.

Questions of this sort now became frequent between the lower house of the colonial legislature and the proprietary governors. At this period the French settlements in Canada had begun to be formidable, and their fortifications had been extended along the northern lakes, with a view of connecting them by a chain of posts on the Mississippi, with their possessions in Louisiana. They had encountered much resistance in this quarter from the Six Nations, just mentioned, whose hostility to France made them usually the allies of the English, but whose consistent aid was only to be bought. As early as 1692, New-York had asked pecuniary succors of the other colonies, of Maryland among them, for securing the faith of these savage allies, and repelling the common enemy. A general injunction to the like effect was issued by the crown, and this was followed by more particular instructions, defining the respective quotas of the colonies. Thus began the system of "crown requisitions," which, always received with an ill grace, were often entirely disregarded. In the "French war," which began in 1754, a few years after the death of the last mentioned proprietary, Maryland scarcely co-operated, and the want of her aid was seriously felt in several of its campaigns; a course construed by the mother country into a pertinacious and unreasonable opposition to its wishes, and by the sister colonies into a selfish disregard of the obligations of mutual defence. Mr. Pitt himself, the subsequent champion of American liberties, was so highly incensed at the conduct of Maryland, as to avow his resolution to bring the colonies to a more submissive temper. Dr. Franklin appreciated more correctly, and explained, the course of the Maryland assembly. We have his authority, that it voted considerable aids, only rendered abortive by unhappy disputes between the two houses as to the mode of raising the requisite revenue. The popular branch claimed also the privilege of exercising its judgment as to the details of defence, and of directing its efforts with a view to the more immediate interests of Maryland, and to the dangers which seemed most instant. In 1754, it voted £6000, however, for the defence of Virginia; and on the disastrous defeat of Braddock, by which the frontiers of Maryland herself were left defenceless, and the terror of her borderers borne to the very heart of her settlements, her legislature waived the pending disputes, and entered into the extensive plan of operations concerted by a council of the colonial governors at New-York. A supply was voted of £40,000, of which £11,000 were to be applied to the erection of a fort and block-house on her own western frontier.

At this period, the westernmost settlements of the province scarcely extended beyond the mouth of the Conococheague, a tributary of the Potomac, though a few of the more adventurous of the borderers had plunged perhaps a little deeper into the wilderness. The settlement at Fort Cumberland, was not then a settlement of Maryland; and, being separated from the inhabited limits of the latter, by a deep and almost trackless forest of eighty miles, the fort at that place could afford no protection to the frontiers of the colony. Its very situation was, at that not remote day, a subject of conjecture to the good people of Maryland. There were many passes of approach for the Indian foe, beyond its range; and a few stockade forts erected by the settlers were the only retreats for their families in case of these sudden and frightful inroads. A more eligible defensive position was sought, therefore, on the Potomac, a few hundred yards from its bank, and ten or eleven miles above the mouth of the Conococheague. On this spot was erected Fort Frederick, the only monument of ante-revolutionary times remaining in Western Maryland, every vestige of the fortification at Cumberland having disappeared. It was constructed of durable materials, in the most approved manner, and was seen by our author in the summer of 1828, the greater part still standing, in good preservation, in the midst of cultivated fields.

At the peace of Paris, which ended the French war, the population of the province had rapidly increased to about 165,000. The number of convicts alone, imported since the proprietary restoration, was estimated at fifteen or twenty thousand. The annual shipment of tobacco to England, according to the best information obtainable, amounted to 28,000 hogsheads, valued at £140,000, and the other exports, in 1761, to £80,000 currency; the imports, in the same year, to £160,000. Iron was the only manufacture that had made any progress. As early as 1749, there were eight furnaces and nine forges, manufacturing, by an estimate in 1761, 2,500 tons of pig, and 600 of bar iron. Such were the resources of Maryland, at the commencement of the civic struggle for her liberties, beginning with the Stamp Act.

For the honour of originating and sustaining the resistance to this, and the like measures of the British government at this time, our author justly remarks, that there is little room for rivalry among the colonies. They had all brought with them, as a familiar principle of English liberty, their right of exemption from taxes, unsanctioned by their assent, for mere purposes of revenue. There was nothing in the political establishments of Maryland to efface this original impression. Its charter exhibits the most favourable form of proprietary government; and its benignant provisions for the security of rights, were the cause that it retained, till the revolution, the anxious attachment of the colonists. It designed entirely to exclude the taxation of the province by the mother country; and, though the proprietary rights were leniently exercised by a family which seems to have been especially characterized by mildness and moderation, they also were limited and modified by the spirit of the colonists, to a consistency with public welfare, and their broad notions of the privileges of freemen. Several branches of the proprietary revenue proving burdensome, or vexatious in the mode of their collection, were commuted, or partially diverted to the public defence and uses; and, even when the provincial assemblies failed of effecting these objects, their pretensions served to familiarize the people with the principle, that all impositions were illegal, not sanctioned by their consent. Our limits do not permit us to go into the history of these questions, which forms an interesting portion of the present work.

The resistance of the colony to external aggressions was not less resolute. We have noticed her neglect of the royal rescripts in the case of the *quotas*; she opposed with like firmness, the plan originated in 1701, and revived in 1715, for destroying the charters, converting the colonies into royal governments, and forming a confederacy of them, at whose head was to be a royal commissioner, residing at New York. She was as adverse to the plan of colonial union, aiming at much the same object, proposed in 1753. We have already alluded to the controversy respecting the extension of the English statutes to the province, which began in 1722, and lasted ten years. In their session of that, year, the lower House of Assembly adopted a series of resolves assertory of their liberties, and declaring the grounds on which they claimed the benefit of the statutes. These resolves, which became the Magna Charta of the province, and were afterwards substantially re-adopted on every occasion, involving its rights and liberties, declared that the province was not to be regarded as a conquered country, but as a colony planted by English subjects, who had not forfeited by their removal any part of their English liberties; that, as such, they had always enjoyed the common law, and those general statutes of England, which were not restrained by words of local limitation, and such acts of the colonial legislature, as were made to suit the particular constitution of the province; and that this was declared, not from apprehension of the infringement of their liberties by the proprietary, but as an assertion of them, and to transmit their sense thereof, and the nature of their constitution, to posterity. These resolves divided the whole province into two parties, "the court party," consisting of the immediate retainers and adherents of the proprietary, and "the country party," which embraced the lower house, and the great body of the people. On the latter side, were enlisted all the talents of the province; and the papers on this subject proceeding from the lower house, were marked by great ability and research. Some of them are from the pen of the elder Daniel Dulany, the father of another distinguished person of that name, and who transmitted to his son the talents, which, our author remarks, seem to have been the patrimony of the family in every generation. The controversy resulted in the recognition of the pretensions of the assembly, and thenceforth the courts of judicature continued to adopt such statutes as were accommodated to the condition of the province.

The spirit which begat and established these claims, appeared equally in the dissensions which succeeded them, respecting the proprietary revenues. A series of resolves was adopted by the lower house in 1739, denouncing, as arbitrary and illegal, the levying of certain duties, the settling of officers' fees by proclamation or ordinance, and the creation of new offices with new fees, without the assent of the assembly. The act proposing the appointment of an agent to present these grievances to the king was vindicated by a message from the lower house, "worthy to be preserved for its laconic boldness." "The people of Maryland," say they, "think the proprietary takes money from them unlawfully. The proprietary says he has a right to take that money. This matter must be determined by his majesty, who is indifferent to both. The proprietary is at home, and has this very money to enable him to negotiate this affair on his part. The people have no way of negotiating it on theirs, but by employing fit persons in London to act for them. These persons must be paid for their trouble, and this bill proposes to raise a fund for that purpose." Though the measures then adopted did not lead to a definitive suppression of the grievances complained of, some of them were removed in another mode. Thus, fines on alienation were relinquished by the proprietary in 1742; officers' fees were established by law in 1747; but the tobacco and tonnage duties formed a standing subject of complaint till the revolution, and a justification of the refusal of supplies, and of other opposition to the government. In voting supplies during the French war, the lower house had imposed an increased tax on "ordinary licenses," and a duty on convicts transported into the colony. The former was resisted as an invasion of proprietary prerogative; the latter, as in conflict with the acts of Parliament authorizing their importation, according to an opinion obtained from Mr. Murray, afterwards Lord Mansfield. The assembly was not daunted by authoritative names. "Precarious," said they, "and contemptible indeed would the state of our laws be, if the bare opinion of any man, however distinguished in his dignity and office, yet acting in the capacity of private counsel, should be sufficient to shake their authority." "I remember," says Daniel Dulany, in his Considerations on the Stamp-Act, "many opinions of crown lawyers on American affairs. They have generally been very sententious;—they have all declared that to be legal, which the minister, for the time being, has deemed to be expedient." The opinion of Attorney-General Pratt, afterwards Lord Camden, prevailed as little on a subsequent occasion. In it he denied the legality of certain extensions of the taxing power, in a supply bill voted by the lower house. It is chiefly remarkable, however, for the distinction set up by one who was afterwards an advocate of American liberties, between the rights of the House of Commons and of the Colonial Assemblies. The Assembly entertained a very different judgment. "Being desirous," they said, "to pay the opinion all due deference, we cannot but wish it had been accompanied with the state of the facts on which it was founded." In nine successive sessions, the supply bill was passed in nearly its original form. With such exhibitions of the tempers of the colonies, it is a just subject of wonder that the Stamp-Act should ever have been ventured on.

The peace of Paris had now, however, not only secured the safety, and with it the gratitude of the colonies, but also confirmed over them, it was supposed, the authority of the mother country. But if the termination of the French war, says the author, seemed to the government a fair occasion for resuming designs never lost sight of, its progress, however calamitous, had nurtured the free and adventurous spirit of the colonists by privations and dangers, until their minds, as well as their resources, were matured for effectual resistance. Their trade, indeed, was burdened with duties imposed for its regulation and restriction; but no tax had yet been laid for the mere purpose of revenue. Sir Robert Walpole "had sagaciously remarked, that, contenting himself with the benefits of their trade, he would leave the taxation of the Americans to some of his successors, who had more courage, and less regard for commerce." The Stamp-Act, by which the experiment was now to be tried, being stripped of the odious machinery of collection, and operating indirectly, was a well contrived initiatory measure. Coupled with it, however, were certain harsh enforcements of the trade-laws at this time, which had the effect of raising higher the indignation of the colonists, and of confounding the distinction hitherto, though reluctantly admitted, between the right to regulate their commerce, and that of direct taxation.

Circumstances prevented Maryland from expressing her opposition to the measure through her legislature, before, and for some period after its adoption. The act was passed on the 22d of March, 1765, and that body was repeatedly prorogued, from November, 1763, to September, 1765. This delay, at such a juncture, did not escape strong remonstrance. There existed, however, at that time, another mirror of the public feeling, whose respectable antiquity deserves mention. This was a journal at Annapolis, conducted by Jonas Green, under the name of "The Maryland Gazette." It was established in 1745, and has ever since been conducted by his descendants, under the same title. Its pithy appeals to the popular sentiment are amusing at this day; and, though the government paper, its temperate support of colonial rights made it the vehicle of communications on that side, not only from the province, but from other colonies. In one from Virginia, the writer says, "it being well known that the only press we have here is totally engrossed for the vile purposes of ministerial craft, I must therefore apply to you, who have always appeared to be a bold and honest assertor of the cause of liberty." The person selected for the distribution of the stamps in Maryland, was Zachariah Hood, a native of the province, and at one time a merchant residing at Annapolis. His appointment was announced with due mock ceremony in the Gazette, and himself to be a gentleman whose conduct was highly approved by all "court-cringing politicians, since he was supposed to have wisely considered, that, if his country must be *stamped*, the blow would be easier borne from a native than a foreigner." His arrival also was greeted with customary honours; his effigy, according to a circumstantial narrative in the Gazette, being hung to the toll of bells, by the "assertors of British American privileges" at Annapolis, and afterwards at Baltimore, Elk-Ridge, Fredericktown, and other places, in emulation. These significant tokens of the popular temper seem to have been promoted, as acts of deliberate defiance, by men of authority and character; as among the "assertors" at Annapolis was the celebrated Samuel Chase, who, at twenty-four, was already the champion of colonial liberties, and gave promise of that combination of abilities, which afterward elevated him beyond rivalry in the province, as a lawyer and advocate, and a leader both of popular and deliberative assemblies. Talents thus employed would naturally provoke the calumny of opponents. A publication of the municipality of Annapolis, describes him as "a busy, restless incendiary, a ringleader of mobs, and a promoter of their excesses; a foul-mouthed and inflaming son of discord and faction." His reply, "abounding in personal reflections, and savouring too much of coarse invective," shows something of the spirit of a tribune of the people, who, thrown into a tumultuous scene, and into contests with the courtly adherents of power, might deem himself excused for some disdain of reserve, and some bluntness of phrase. I admit, he says, that I was one of those who committed to the flames the effigy of the Stamp-Distributor, and who openly disputed the parliamentary right to tax the colonies; while some of you skulked in your houses, and grumbled in corners, asserting the Stamp-Act to be a beneficial law, or not daring to speak out your sentiments. The reader may be curious to know Hood's subsequent adventures. Not daring to distribute the stamps, and finding the indignation which had been lavished on his effigy, taking a more dangerous direction towards his person, he absconded secretly, and never paused in his flight till he reached New-York, and had taken refuge under the cannon of Fort George. Having gone afterwards to reside on Long Island, a party surrounded the house where he was concealed, requiring the abjuration of his office, on pain of being delivered to the exasperated multitude, and carried back to Maryland, with labels upon him signifying his office and designs. Unwilling to run this gantlet through a country up in arms, he yielded, and was accompanied by upwards of a hundred gentlemen from Flushing to Jamaica, where he swore to his abjuration, and was discharged.

The first measure of the assembly, when at length convened, was to appoint commissioners to a general congress that was to be held in New-York; its next, to make an expression of its sentiments on the existing question. The tone and unanimity of the resolves adopted, sufficiently show, in the author's opinion, that the temper and course of Maryland at this juncture, have been too lightly considered, and may advantageously be compared with those of any other colony. Another of her contributions, and not the least effective, to the common cause, was an essay published at Annapolis, in October, 1765. "A style easy but energetic, perspicuous thoughts, illustrations simple, and arguments addressed to every understanding," betrayed it to be the production of Daniel Dulany, the younger, whom it placed at once in the first rank of political writers. Long signal for talents and professional learning, his "Considerations" earned him the more grateful distinction of the great champion of colonial liberties; and in the joyous celebrations of the repeal of the stamp-act, placed him in remembrance with Camden, and with Chatham, his admirer and eulogist. It is known, that in this essay Mr. Dulany, though bold and decided as to the question of right, urged the disuse of British commodities as the most advisable weapon of resistance. This appeal to the commercial cupidity of England would, also, he thought, be the most effectual. The course, even could it have been perseveringly adopted, was too pacific for the temper of the times.

Political integrity and abilities associated the name of Dulany with the history of Maryland, during the better part of a century. The father of the distinguished person just mentioned, was admitted to the bar of the provincial court in 1710, and for forty years held the first place in the confidence of the proprietary and in the popular affection, being a functionary in the highest post of trusts, and long a leader also of the country party in the assembly. He was a kinsman of the celebrated Delany, the intimate of Swift, some of whose letters to him breathe the tone both of friendship and reverend regard. His son, Daniel Dulany, *the Greater*, (as our author styles him,) came to the bar in 1747, and was named one of the council in 1757; in 1761, he was appointed secretary of the province, and thenceforward held these posts in conjunction, till the Revolution. His legal arguments and opinions, the praise of contemporaries, and the deference of courts, attest him to have been an *oracle* of law; as a scholar and an orator, he was not only highly celebrated at home, but in the judgment of Mr. Pinkney, who saw him but in his "evening declination," unexcelled by the master minds abroad. Suavity of manners, and the graces of the person, combine to complete a most agreeable picture.

The stamp-paper had now arrived. The governor, to whom the lower house had refused all advice as to the disposal of that paper, found it expedient to pursue the suggestion of the upper, to retain it on board of the vessel. By a general consent, the ordinary transactions of business and of the courts proceeded without it, and on the 24th of February, 1766, an association, bearing the name of the "Sons of Liberty," was formed at Baltimore, with the object of compelling the government offices at Annapolis to dispense with it likewise. They assembled at that place on a day assigned, the 31st of March; and the provincial court and other offices, after first a peremptory refusal, and some delay, conceded the point. Thus was the stamp-act virtually annulled in Maryland; it had been repealed in England a few days before, on the 18th of March; so that, in the author's words, "Maryland was never polluted even by an attempt to execute it."

Of the subsequent revival of the scheme of taxing the colonies, the manner and the event are so well known, that we have only to notice the contemporary transactions in Maryland, which fanning the resentment of her people, kept her at an even pace with the other provinces in the march of resistance. The "Proclamation and Vestry Act questions," have lost indeed their momentary interest, but serve to show in how many schools of exercise the champions were trained, who afterward displayed their collected prowess in a more conspicuous arena.

The colonial legislature had always controlled the provincial officers by exercising the right to determine their fees, which, by way of further precaution, they had been in the habit of regulating by temporary acts. An act of this nature, passed in 1763, coming up for renewal in 1770, objections were made to the exorbitance of the fees themselves, abuses in the mode of charging, and the want of a proper system of commutation. Angry discussions were followed by a prorogation of the assembly, and subsequently by a proclamation of Governor Eden, ostensibly to prevent extortion in the officers, but with the real purpose of regulating the fees by the prerogative of his office; accordingly, he re-established the fee-act of 1763. The proclamation begat the usual array of parties for and against prerogative, in which our author includes the established clergy on the government side, and on the popular, the lawyers. In this conflict of influence and abilities, by a turn which is to be lamented, as it threw them into collision with the Revolutionary leaders, and exciting high resentments on both sides, kept him aloof from their measures, Daniel Dulany was, in this question, the prominent partisan of the governor and upper house. The grounds somewhat technical on which he defended their procedure as both legal and expedient, and the more large and comprehensive ones on which it was impugned, were set forth in a series of essays in the Maryland Gazette, in which Mr. Dulany's antagonist was Charles Carroll of Carrollton. The angry excitement of the day gave these essays one feature in common,—strong invective, and personalities,—"of which, some are now unintelligible, and all deserve to be forgotten." Their distinctive characteristics are,—in Mr. Dulany's, "the traces everywhere of a powerful mind, confident in its own resources, indignant at opposition, contemptuous, as if from conscious superiority, yet sometimes affecting contempt to escape from principles not to be resisted;" in his opponent's, the language of a man "confident in his cause, conscious that he is sustained by public sentiment, and exulting in the advantage of this position." When the discussion was dropped by these combatants, it was taken up by others, as vigorous and adroit. In this new controversy, John Hammond, no contemptible reasoner in behalf of the proclamation, found antagonists in Thomas Johnson, the first governor of the *state* of Maryland, Samuel Chase, and his more conciliatory friend and coadjutor, William Paca. In the proceedings of the lower house relative to this subject, we find a sententious description of political liberty, which might serve as the motto of all *Constitutionalists.* "Who," says their address, *"who are a free people? Not* those over whom government is reasonably and equitably exercised, but those who live under a government so constitutionally checked and controlled, that proper provision is made against its being otherwise exercised."

The "Vestry Act" related to *clergy dues,* and the controversy on it arose out of the technical objection, that the law imposing them, which was enacted in 1701-2, was passed by an assembly, which, being dissolved by the demise of the king, had nevertheless been convened with fresh writs of election. The law thus regarded as intrinsically defective, had the farther demerit of being revived, (as in the case of the officer's fees,) in default of an existing enactment, by proclamation of the governor. In this discussion the clergy naturally took a part, and "found in their own body an advocate of extraordinary powers, in the person of Jonathan Boucher." These questions filled the province with contention. An act regulating clergy dues, some time after, put that question to sleep; the other remained in angry suspense, till swallowed up, with all less disputes, in the vortex of the Revolution.

That event was now nearly impending. It may be remembered, that the duty act of 1767, in which the ministerial scheme of taxing the colonies had been revived, had been subsequently repealed, except as to the article of tea, on which the duty had been retained, "by way, it has been remarked, of pepper-corn rent, to denote the tenure of colonial rights." A new stratagem of the ministry in this matter was followed, it is also known, by "the burning of the tea in Boston," and by the retaliatory measure of the Boston-Port Bill; acts, respectively, which may be said to have made up the issue between the conflicting parties. The convention in 1774, assembled at Annapolis, in June of that year. In the October following, the *tea-burning* at Boston was re-enacted in Maryland, with circumstances of deliberation and defiance that show what a flame was abroad. On the 14th of that month, the brig Peggy Stewart arrived at Annapolis, having, as a part of her cargo, seventeen packages of tea. The non-importation agreement, to which the act of 1767 had given rise, was understood to be retained as to this article, which still bore the badge of usurpation in the obnoxious duty. The consignees did not venture to incur the public indignation by landing the teas, without at least consulting the Non-Importation Committee; but in the meantime, the vessel was entered, and the duties paid by Anthony Stewart, a part owner of the vessel. The people, highly incensed, determined, *in a public meeting,* at Annapolis, that the tea should not be landed. It was proposed, in a subsequent one, to burn it; and at a county meeting which followed, it was decided, that this should be accompanied also by a most humiliating apology from Stewart and the consignees. As the people now threatened to burn the vessel itself, the former, by the advice of Carroll of Carrollton, proposed to destroy her with his own hands. Crowds repaired to the water-side to witness the atonement; the vessel was run ashore at *Windmill Point*, where Stewart set fire to his own vessel, with the tea on board.

All was now preparation for open hostilities. Military associations were formed, military exercises eagerly engaged in, and subscriptions set afoot for purchasing arms and ammunition. The planters were requested to cultivate flax, hemp, and cotton, and to enlarge their flocks with a view to the manufacture of woollens. At this point we must leave Mr. M'Mahon. On the appearance of his second volume, we may resume his narrative from this period, and take the same occasion to notice some other matters in his work, for the discussion of which we have not room at present.

ART. X.

PEALE'S NOTES ON ITALY,

Notes on Italy. By Rembrandt Peale. 1 vol 8 vo. Carey & Lea: Philadelphia: 1831.

To review a new volume of travels in Italy, may seem to many readers an un-profitable task. Since its shores were first hailed by the faithful Achates, it has been the goal of travellers and the theme of authors. Every age has sent its children to visit that favoured soil; and the barbarians who rudely invaded it from beyond its Alpine barriers, have been followed by successive generations of men, less rude indeed from the progress of time, but not less ardent to explore and overrun it. Peace and war have alike urged them on. Its mountains, its valleys, its defiles, its broad and sunny plains, have resounded for hundreds of years with the clash of arms, and glittered with innumerable warriors; bands scarcely less numerous have penetrated every corner, led by spirits inquisitive for knowledge or fond of dwelling on beauties of nature, perhaps unrivalled, and on the certain charms of refined and exquisite art, with which no other land, however favoured, has yet dared to offer a comparison. Nor is there wanting the ample, the reiterated record of all this. Historians, and poets, and antiquarians, and novelists, and travellers, have made familiar every incident of every age—every allusion that can give fresh and delightful associations to every spot. What ruin is there that they have not made eloquent? What mountain, what grove, can eager curiosity, urged on by the enthusiasm of taste and genius, discover, which is not already hallowed—that has not "murmured forth a solemn sound."

Yet, still, we read over the oft-repeated tale; we can bear to hear again and again the history of Roman grandeur; we delight to trace the footsteps of warriors, of statesmen, of heroes, philosophers, and poets, whom we have learnt to regard rather as old friends, as household deities, as companions who have enchanted our youth, and beguiled our later years,—who have given us at once rules and lessons of human conduct, and pleasing visions to delight our fancies and our hearts, than as merely individuals in the great family of mankind. We can bear to dwell again and again on the graphic page which imparts to us the knowledge of those triumphant efforts of taste, of genius, and of art, whose charm time cannot injure, and which become to us the more dear, because they remain after centuries have passed away, with scarcely a single rival.

We were impressed with these feelings when we took up the unpretending volume before us; we can scarcely doubt, that they will be common to many at least of our readers, when they find our page headed with *"Notes on Italy."* To these sentiments will be justly added a favourable impression from the character of the writer, and the circumstances which have led to his tour and to the publication of the present volume.

As early as the year 1786, Charles Wilson Peale, the father of the author, and a gentleman whose name is well known as connected with the infant arts and sciences of America, was the first person to build an exhibition room in the city of Philadelphia. There he displayed to a public, perhaps but little prepared to appreciate them, the first collection of Italian paintings, and there his son acquired in his earliest youth, not only an enthusiastic admiration for the art itself, which he has since successfully cultivated, but an ardent desire to visit the region where he could behold the productions of artists whose genius he had learned to venerate.

Having commenced his studies as a painter under the direction of his father, he went to England, during the peace of 1802, with the design of visiting France and Italy. The renewal of hostilities, however, prevented this, and after availing himself for a short time of the benefits London offered, he returned home. In 1807, he again crossed the Atlantic; the disturbed situation of the continent obliged him to confine himself to France; but in the gallery of the Louvre he could admire, study, and emulate the noblest productions of the pencil and the chisel, collected by that wonderful man, who loved to blend in the triumphs of warlike ambition, the trophies dear to philanthropy, to science, and to art. Mr. Peale returned to his own country, not satisfied however, because Italy itself was yet unseen. It was in vain that an increasing patronage and attention to the fine arts in his own country offered him renewed reasons to remain there; he was as restless as before, and in 1810 we again find him in Paris, and again obliged, by the unsettled state of Europe, to forego his long cherished visit. He returned to his own country; but the fever that still burned as in the ardour of youth, was not allayed, and the idea that his dreams of Italy were never to be realized, seemed, as he tells us, to darken the cloud which hung over the prospect of death itself. For a number of years the duties required by a large family forbade his separation from them; but these at length permitted the gratification of his wishes, and patronised by the liberality of several gentlemen of New-York, at the age of fifty-one he was able to gratify a desire which had not failed to increase with his years. The narrative of his tour, which occupied nearly two years, is embraced in this volume. His main object was to examine the celebrated works of Italian art, and to select, for the employment of his pencil, some of the most excellent pictures of the great masters which are preserved in Rome and Florence; the copies of these carefully made cannot fail to advance, among the artists and amateurs of his own country, a correct knowledge of the fine arts.

With his thoughts and his pursuits directed chiefly to this object, we find in the volume before us, no pretension and little attention to antiquarian research, or classical allusion, which have been so generally called forth by the mouldering monuments, and the familiar scenes connected with the history and poetry of earlier days. Neither do we meet with the elaborate reflections on the political or social state of Italy, in the present day. It is true, the remarks of Mr. Peale are not confined to works of art, for he could not shut his eyes to the scenes among which he had to pass, and he was not uninfluenced by a general curiosity and love of truth;—but they are the notes of a transient observer, whose mind was turned to other things. Yet they are found not unfrequently to convey lively impressions of the state of society and manners, and of the local peculiarities of Italy.

Having sailed from New-York, Mr. Peale arrived at Paris, in the month of December, 1828. After a short stay there, merely sufficient to glance over the principal works of art, and to regret the altered situation of the magnificent gallery of Napoleon, deprived of the matchless memorials of his conquests, he continued his journey towards the south of France. Passing through Lyons, the route continued a long way on the border of the rapid Rhone, upon which he saw but one vessel,—whilst the road presented a constant procession of wagons. Such a stream in America, between two great cities, would be covered with steam-boats. As the road advanced south, it passed through more abundant vineyards, the verdure of the fields became more extensive, and, on each side, were seen vast orchards of mulberry trees, for the support of silk-worms, tributary to the great manufactories of silk at Lyons. As he approached Marseilles, the milder atmosphere gave evidence of a more genial climate, and the altered costume of the women, of a different people—to the caps common after leaving Paris, was now added a piece of black silk, of the size and shape of a plate laid on the top of the head; and, in the immediate vicinity of the town, the women wore black hats, with small round crowns and broad rims. Marseilles is a large and bustling sea-port, with but little to detain those who are in search of the productions of Italian art. Instead of pursuing the route he had intended, by Aix and Genoa, Mr. Peale here embarked in a Neapolitan ship, and, after a stormy and uncomfortable passage of ten days, found himself in the magnificent Bay of Naples. Four weeks were devoted to an examination of the works of art in the various galleries, palaces, and churches;— and most of the curiosities, the objects which attract an inquisitive traveller, were examined. Among the latter may be mentioned the catacombs of *Santa Maria della Vita*, which are thus described:—

> "Descending into the valley of houses, and then rising to the foot of a neighbouring hill, we entered the court yard of a vast hospital for the poor; an establishment made by the French, in which are men, women, and girls, each class being kept separate and made to work. Here an old man presented himself who officiated as an experienced guide, furnished with a lantern and great flambeau made of ropes impregnated with some kind of resin. A little back lane conducted us to a kind of grotto, containing an altar ornamented with several marble medallions, which are said to have been sculptured by the early Christians. This chapel served as an entrance to the chambers of the dead, which consist of long, winding, and intricate passages, cut out of the *tufa* rock; in procuring which, for the purposes of building, these vast subterranean excavations were originally made, and afterwards used as depositories of the dead. During the persecutions against

the early Christians, they were occupied by them either secretly as places of residence, where they might practise their worship unmolested, or, by the permission of their pagan persecutors, as abodes of the most humiliating kind, secluded from the light of day. Here our guide, preceding us with his smoking torch, which he occasionally struck on the walls, so as to scatter off a radiating flood of sparks which left him a brighter flame, showed us the little lateral recesses in which the humble believers were contented to lie, and shelves, excavated in the rock, in which their mortal remains were deposited after death. He pointed out the larger chambers, somewhat decorated with columns and arches in faint relief, in which the priests resided; the places where altars stood; and, in a higher excavation, raised his torch to a rude recess, or sunken balcony above the arched passage, whence the word was preached to the faithful below in a hall of great width. The chambers occupied by the most distinguished characters were denoted by better sculpture, Mosaic incrustations, and fresco paintings. We followed the windings of these subterranean corridors to a great extent, till we reached a hall which was said to be a quarter of a mile in height; but whether contrived for the purpose of ventilation, or as a shaft for raising the stone, we could not ascertain, any more than we could the accuracy of our guide's information, that the bodies of hundreds of martyrs were thrown down there by their pagan murderers, whence they were conveyed by their surviving friends into the niches prepared for them. From these remote parts, passages, now closed, were formerly open, which communicated with other catacombs and villages for sixteen miles round, affording the inmates, it is said, the means of escaping the persecutions which, from time to time, fell upon a sect so obnoxious to the pagan priesthood.

"We found the bones in these catacombs in excellent preservation, and on many the flesh of fifteen hundred years was still of such tenacious though pliant fibre, that it required a sharp knife to cut off a piece. The guide showed us the heads of some of those early Christians, with the tongues still remaining in them, but would not permit us to take one away. Here lived the venerated St. Januarius, whose particular cell was pointed out to us; and to these retreats was his dead body borne after his martyrdom; though some ancient painters represent him walking back with his head in his hands.

"We then visited the church of *Santa Maria della Vita*; it is an old and curious edifice, rich in marbles, and remarkable for the style of the grand altar, which is constructed over another one, as on a bridge, to which you rise by two lateral flights of steps, ornamented with elegant balustrades of costly marbles. The old monk showed us, behind the altar, an ancient painting of the Madonna, resembling an Indian, and a precious door to a case containing some sacred relic; but as we did not seem interested in these, he proceeded to open a door in the side wall, and requested us to walk in. To our surprise it was the entrance to another series of catacombs, in which were deposited the dead within the last two hundred years. These were placed in perpendicular niches in the rock, and plastered up, leaving only a part of the head projecting; the men with their faces out, the women with their faces in, only exposing the backs of their heads, from which the hair had long since fallen. By scraping away the plaster, some of the skeletons appeared in their whole extent, among which was an extraordinary one of a man about eight feet tall. The plaster which covers these bodies, thus showing only one half of the head, was painted so as to imitate the entire figure, clothed as men or women, and sometimes representing them as skeletons in part covered with drapery, with various inscriptions above them. The deeper recesses of these vaults led to chambers where we saw two carcasses of men, deposited only six months since; the flesh not decaying, but gradually drying up. They were naked and seated in niches in the wall, with their heads and arms hanging forward in very grotesque postures. In the catacombs which we first visited, the dead were generally placed horizontally, whereas here, all that we now saw were standing erect. We entered some chambers, however, with numerous empty horizontal recesses."

All the spots around Naples, of particular interest, as Vesuvius, Posilippo, and Portici were visited; crowds of beggars were encountered in all directions; but the people in general appeared to be healthy, lively, and happy. The streets are made gay by the immense number of carriages with which the public are accommodated at a very cheap rate, and people of all ranks are seen splashing along, sometimes to the number of seven or eight, clinging, as well as they can, to a vehicle scarcely large enough to hold half the number. The Neapolitans speak with great gesticulation, using many signs which have a known meaning; and they may sometimes be seen thus conversing across the street, from the upper stories of opposite houses. They are, of course, great eaters of macaroni, which is seen dangling from the shops in all parts of the city; and nothing is more amusing than the humble purchasers gathered around the stalls, stretching their necks with open mouths to suck it in.

Having seen as much of Naples as a long succession of bad weather permitted, our travellers set out in a vetturino for Rome, under the guidance of a snug, young, leather-breeched postilion, who spoke nothing but broad Italian. Crossing the Pontine marshes, where, it is probable, the wintry season prevented the frogs and musquitoes from recalling to their recollection the sufferings of Horace, they first looked down from the heights of Albano on the dome of St. Peter's, glittering in the bright rays of the sun, which just then broke through the clouds. On the last day of January, Mr. Peale found himself comfortably placed in a hotel of the Piazza di Spagna, ready to explore all that the eternal city could offer to his curious research. He remained at Rome till the month of July following.

His earliest visit was to St. Peter's, which he has minutely and graphically depicted. His first sensation he describes as one of surprise at the brightness and elegance of the whole interior, and in part of disappointment at the apparent want of magnitude. This was probably occasioned by the colossal statues, which, being proportioned to the vast pilasters, arches, and columns, seem to reduce the whole to an ordinary scale; and also to the wonderful harmony of all the parts, which prevents the contrast necessary to fill the mind with a sense of a gigantic object. When he had, however, walked over the wide fields of pavement, and compared the human beings before him with the stupendous masses around, he became by degrees convinced of the mighty magnitude, and experienced increased emotions of wonder and delight.

His visit to St. Peter's was followed by a minute survey of all the principal churches, galleries, antique monuments, and ruins, with which Rome abounds, among them, and in the study of the works of the great masters of art, he found five months pass rapidly away.

The houses of modern Rome generally present a good appearance, from the circumstance, that, although built of brick, they are, with few exceptions, plastered with great skill and dexterity to resemble stone, outside and inside. The puzzolana earth forms an admirable cement, and even when placed on the tops of houses it forms a terrace impenetrable by water. The streets are kept rather clean by the employment of convicts, but there is always abundance of dirt around the dwellings of the poor, who inhabit the ground floors, which are used not only for the residence of poverty and wretchedness, but for stables, and shops of every kind. The men, women, and children, however, in these unpromising abodes, are fat, dirty, and merry, and present no appearance of being victims of malaria or despotism. The streets, except the Corso, are seldom straight; but in the evenings they are filled with people, the rich taking a fashionable drive, with the utmost seriousness and silence, the poor lying and sitting on the ground, eating a piece of bread, or a fresh head of lettuce, in general, silent and serious like their betters, but occasionally bursting into roars of laughter, and expressing their hilarity by loudly clapping their hands.

> "As the warm weather advances, every kind of workman who can get out his little bench, apparatus or chair, is at work in the street close up to his house. I have counted nine shoemakers, with their stalls, in front of one house, for the purpose of enjoying light and air. Benches and chairs are likewise occupied by the idle, chiefly old gentlemen, in front of the coffee-houses, especially in the Corso, where they are amused by the continual movement of carriages and pedestrians. In the evening, especially on holidays, tables are spread out with white cloths, and brilliantly illuminated and decorated with flowers, containing various articles of food, whilst a cook is busy on one side with his portable kitchen,

cooking dough-nuts, or other articles, which are eaten on the spot.

"The English and French style of dress, both among men and women, prevails not only in the higher classes, but through all others, and in every part of the city. Huge Parisian bonnets, full set with broad ribands, are seen in every street; contrasting widely with the fashion of the country, which covers the head with a white linen cloth, folded square, and either hanging loose, or kept flat by sticks within them, or long pins like skewers, which bind up the hair. Long waists and stays are universal—the rich wear the fashionable corset of France—the poor, the stays of the country, thick set with bone, covered with gay velvet, and worn outside of their gowns, when they have any on, and tied at the top and back of the shoulders with long bunches of gay ribands. An apron, skirted with many coloured bands, hangs in front of a short petticoat with similar bands, and the shoes have great silver buckles. The taste for large ear and finger rings is universal, and heavy rolls of beads encircle almost every neck—the dark red coral being calculated, by its contrast, to improve their brown Italian complexion.

"The peasants, as they appear in town, differ from these, in wearing coarse pointed wool hats, decorated with ribands or flowers; wretched, old, ragged, or patched clothes; breeches without buttons or strings at the knees; sandals which they make out of raw hide, turning up a little above the sole, and with strong cords bound to their feet, the cord passing around their legs and up to their knees, encircling coarse linen or rags, which they wear instead of stockings. On Sundays and holidays, certain streets, as the *Repetti*, are the rendezvous of labouring men, who are then a little, but very little, better dressed than on other days; always displaying their stout legs in coarse white stockings, their knees still unbuttoned, and their shirt collars open even in cool weather, and, if warm, their jacket across one shoulder, one sleeve hanging in front—the other behind, and shifted to the other shoulder, should their exposure to the wind or current of air require it. I have often stopped to notice these groups, and have been surprised to find them generally silent, but with an expression of content. Occasionally, when a joke would circulate, it was managed with the fewest words. It is only when much excited, that a Roman displays any volubility of tongue or extravagance of gesticulation to disturb his usual air of dignity—whether above or below contempt—whether with much thought or with no thought at all.

"The Romans are certainly a sober people, but the lower classes, though they are not afflicted by Irish, Scotch, or American whiskey, Holland gin, or English porter, yet often indulge to excess in the cheap wine of the country. Every body drinks wine, and to offer water to a beggar would be an insult. It is only used occasionally with lemons in hot weather. At a late hour in the evening, in many streets, may be heard the noise of Bacchanalian merriment proceeding from some deep cavernous chamber, which, seen by lamp-light, shows nothing but coarse plastered walls, a greasy brick pavement, and benches and tables, around which, in the absence of all other comforts, the most miserable enjoy their principal, or only meal of the day, and freely circulate the bottle as a social bond. Besides, on holidays, the wine shops are frequented by groups of men and women, who sometimes exhibit around the door a noisy and licentious crowd. But wine is not always deemed sufficient, and those who are disposed to take a walk about sunrise, may every day see persons with little baskets of *aqua vitæ*, which is swallowed by artificers between their beds and their workshops."

During Mr. Peale's stay at Rome, the election of the pope afforded him an opportunity of witnessing the many gorgeous and striking ceremonies, which attend the elevation of the spiritual father of the church to his temporal throne. These he has described minutely, but with little variation from the accounts given by those who have been at Rome on previous and similar occasions. He speaks of the sudden illumination of the vast dome of St. Peter's, as a sight of singular magnificence; in an instant the whole edifice appeared to throw out flowers of flame, and then, a few moments after, a new succession of lights, still more vivid, by their superior brightness, rendered the first nearly invisible.

From Rome, Mr. Peale went to Tivoli, and spent some days among the lovely scenery of that spot, familiar to every one who has not forgotten the exquisite praises Horace has bestowed on it. He saw and admired the remnants of the temple of the Sibyl, which Claude Lorraine has so often selected to add to the harmony and beauty of his inimitable landscapes; and amid the importunities of beggars, who infest a traveller in Italy in every haunt to which the love of antiquity or of scenery can lead him, and beneath the spray of the cataract—the *polvere del'acqua*, as it was called by the natives—he sketched a drawing of a spot which poets and painters have alike loved to select in ancient and modern days.

On entering Tuscany, he was pleased to find no longer the rags and patches of Naples and Rome, but a peasantry, better clad, and more industrious; the country was in a fine state of cultivation, and the habitations were neat and commodious. It was the season of harvest, and the fields abounded with men and women in nearly equal numbers, and apparently happy as they were cheerful.

At Florence, where Mr. Peale arrived on the 7th of July, he remained until the 22d of April following, thus devoting to that fair seat of the arts more than eight months. His time was zealously employed in the pursuit of his favourite studies; and he made, in the galleries so liberally opened to artists, copies of many of those works which have been considered as masterpieces at all times, which have been deemed the noblest of the spoils of conquest, and have become the guides of aspiring genius, and the test of taste, throughout the world.

The manners of the inhabitants are lively, but in general decorous; and whenever crowds are accidentally assembled, they disperse without tumult.

"In the public square it is common, once or twice a week, to see a quack doctor, seated in his chaise or gig, haranguing the crowd, with the most impassioned language and gestures: at one corner of his carriage is a banner consisting of a hideous portrait of an old monk, from whom he professes to have learned his precious secrets in the healing art; occasionally he displays a book of botanical engravings, gaily coloured, to show his knowledge of nature and his reliance on the bounty of Providence, invoking frequently the name of the Blessed Virgin, and reverently taking off his hat, in which he is imitated by the faithful around him. At the end of his discourse he produces his medicines, which are eagerly bought by the credulous.

"Occasionally, too, a dentist appears, on horseback, with an attendant, likewise on horseback, who, in a similar manner, but with an eloquence more voluble, and language more refined, expatiates on his well known skill and experience; and then, to suit his action to the word, proceeds to draw the teeth gratuitously of any that may present themselves at the left side of his horse, to the amount of five or six. It is surprising with what dexterity he performs the act, without moving from his saddle. Afterwards, if any one wants the assistance of the accomplished dentist, he must be sought at his lodgings."

The number of beggars, though great in itself, is small, when compared to that at Rome. Every place, too, is crowded with persons who pester you with knives, razors, and combs—linens, silks, and cloths—cravats, shawls, and rugs—alabaster carvings, and every thing that can be carried about by hand, which they persecute you to buy in spite of your no, no, which means nothing to them. Experienced Italians send off the dirty fellows with a *"caro mio"* —"no, my dear, I am not in want of it." The streets are kept remarkably clean, and the houses are generally substantial and well built, but less ornamented with stucco and sculpture, than those of Rome. The public edifices are remarkable rather for massive strength than architectural beauty, looking more like fortresses than palaces, and black with stone and time. There are numerous fountains scattered through the city; but, amidst the abundance of bronze and marble ornaments which they exhibit, the stream of water they pour out is extremely insignificant. The coffee-houses are well served, the favourite ices are made with clean ice taken from the streams, instead of the frozen and dirty snow collected in the mountains, which is used at Rome. In all public places of resort, are seen quantities of beautiful and fragrant flowers, the delight of the Florentines; and men are everywhere met who carry baskets of them, which are offered not only to the ladies, but are presented bunch after bunch, with the most persevering assiduity, to gentlemen who are sipping their coffee, eating their ice-creams, or reading the papers.

While Mr. Peale was in Florence, he had the good fortune to witness the powers of the most celebrated improvisatrice of the day, *Rosa Taddei*, of Naples. Her performances took place at the principal theatre, two or three times on each occasion, but with intervals of several days:—

"When the curtain rose, the scene was that of a parlour, with an open piano, at which a professor of music was seated. On the entrance of Rosa Taddei, she was greeted with loud applause by her old friends and confiding expectants. She appeared to be about thirty years of age, and, though small, her uncorsetted chest gave ample space for the important action of her powerful lungs. She was dressed as a private lady. Her pale face indicated a studious life, but her forehead was low and narrow, though her head was broad; her little sunken eye was quick in its movements, and when it looked intently out, to fashion the measure of a thought, was accompanied by a slight contraction of the brow that banished all suspicion of coquetry. Her nose was small, and her mouth would be called ordinary; but when it was about to speak, it quivered delicately with the rising emotion, and varied its expression according to the passion of her discourse.

"A servant now advances to the front of the stage, holding a little casket, destined to received the papers which are handed from different parts of the house, containing subjects proposed for recitation. When about forty of these are received, the casket is placed on a side table. Without reading them she folds and returns them to the casket. This is an operation of some time, and serves to give the appearance of business, and, perhaps, composure to the performer. Advancing to the side boxes and orchestra, she offers successively to different persons the casket, out of which, each time, a paper is drawn and presented to her. With a grave, deliberate, and emphatic voice she reads the theme proposed. If the subject is hackneyed, dull, or unfit, a lamentable and deep-toned ah! synonymous with our bah! is heard from various parts of the house; on which she tears up the paper with an impressive look, which seems to say—such is your pleasure. When six or seven subjects are approved by the cries of yes, yes, she places them on her side table, selects one, and, advancing to the piano, decides upon a musical harmony, which the professor immediately begins to play, and continues delicately; during which she walks in measured steps across the stage backwards and forwards, looking earnestly down, occasionally pausing, sometimes raising her hand to her mouth or forehead. The crowded house is silent as death, and she is only influenced by the measure of the music and the arrangement of her unseen materials of thought. This being completed, she suddenly advances, and begins with a burst of language, in which she continues with unhesitating volubility and moderate action, occasionally uttering some fine expression that draws forth from experienced critics an approving bravo! It was to be remarked, that as she advanced to the termination of every line, couplet, or stanza, according to the compass of the sentiment, there was a dwelling on the syllables and a monotonous chanting, very much resembling the cadence of a Quaker preacher; thereby permitting her thoughts to advance and fashion the commencement of the following line, couplet, or stanza, which was always eagerly and expressively pronounced at its commencement, and as regularly terminated in the thought-resolving chant.

"Among the subjects which she treated, some of which she began with little preparation, were the following:—The discoveries of Galileo and Columbus, and the ingratitude of their country; two Doctors, a Lawyer and Jealous Woman; a Lawyer's Inkhorn; and a Dialogue between the Dome of St. Peter and the Dome of Florence. This last appeared to perplex her a little, and it was some time before she could fashion it to her mind; indeed, there was an expectation, from the frequency of her turns across the stage, and her contracted brow, that she would be obliged to acknowledge a failure; but when she advanced and began in elegant strains to state the difficult nature of the singular task imposed on her, to give tongues to the domes so long silent, and listen to so distant a dialogue between the Duomo, the boast of Florence, and the Dome of St. Peter, suspended in mid air by the divine Buonarotti; and then with increasing enthusiasm, made them recount, in strains of honourable emulation, the great events of which they had been the witnesses, the delight of the audience knew no bounds in the thundering repetitions of bravo!

"Some of the pieces she composed with terminating words, suggested by acclamation from the audience as she proceeded; other pieces were so conceived as to introduce a particular word into every stanza, proposed by any voice at its commencement. It was a singular and interesting exhibition, in which a little feeble woman, during a whole evening, could afford the most refined entertainment to a crowded theatre. Such is the homage paid to mental superiority."

From Florence, Mr. Peale proceeded to Pisa, and thence along the plains or alluvial grounds between the mountains and the Mediterranean, on the road to Genoa. At Carrara, he visited and examined the studios and work-shops, where the various works in the marble of the celebrated quarries are made. This marble is obtained in the ravines of the mountains, from two to five miles distant from the town. It is generally taken from their base, but frequently great masses are tumbled from situations many hundred feet high, to which the labourers are an hour in ascending, and where they work with cords around them, to secure them against the danger of falling. The whitest marble is found only in occasional layers, some at the base of the mountain is most beautifully so.

On entering Genoa, the streets through which Mr. Peale passed, though of moderate width, presented the appearance of much magnificence, being lined with the palaces of the king and nobles. In other parts he remarked, however, but little of the splendour which would entitle it to be called a city of palaces; the houses are in general plain and high, and the passages of communication wide enough only for persons on foot.

From Genoa, Mr. Peale turned again to the east, and, crossing the extremities of the Maritime Alps, passed through the broad and beautiful plain which spreads far and wide on either bank of the Po. At Parma, he visited the plain and simple palace where the Empress Maria Louisa resides, and a beautiful new theatre contiguous to it lately built by her; he saw also the more splendid palace once inhabited by Napoleon, which is at the extremity of the city, surrounded by fine gardens, and contains some good frescoes and fine old tapestry. The pictures which crowd the churches, are not, however, in the best style, but the marbles are frequently rich and well wrought.

Bologna presents the singular character of a city composed of streets, lined, with a few exceptions, with arcades, many of which are of lofty and elegant proportions, and the arches supported by stone pillars with handsome bases and capitals, while others are of plastered brick. These long ranges of columnated arcades, impart great elegance to the general aspect of the place. The public square is ornamented by a magnificent fountain, which ranks among the greatest works of John of Bologna. In the gallery of the fine arts are some admirable pictures of Guido, Domenichino, and the Caraccis; and the Pontifical University is attended by a great number of students, while its halls are well filled by an extensive library, and large collections relating to natural science.

From Bologna Mr. Peale proceeded through Ferrara to Venice. His description of the entrance into that celebrated city of the sea, does not offer the glowing picture which novelists and poets have delighted to paint, but perhaps conveys a more correct idea of the reality.

> "Early the next morning we beheld the queen of the ocean, at the extremity of the lagune, stretching across, and almost united with the mole of fishermen's dwellings, called Palestrina. The steeples and domes were relieved by an extensive range of gray mountains, rising high in the distance, upon the tops of which the snow was bright with the rising sun. For many miles our boat was towed by another boat with oarsmen. At length we reached some old walls and ruinous houses, the outskirts of Venice, and passing these, opened into a magnificent harbour, resembling a great river, lined with good houses, and animated by a variety of shipping and boats in motion. Crossing this great harbour, we approached a point of land embellished by a beautiful edifice as the Porto Franco, and then opened into another great but less spacious canal. In front, the singular but beautiful palace of the doges, and the lesser palace of St. Mark were close by, with a fine terrace or wharf extending along the water's edge. As our boat pursued its way to the

post-office, down the great serpentine canal or river, the magnificence of the palaces, and their peculiar style of architecture, rich in
bold ornaments, balconies, and sculptures, excited us to frequent
exclamations of admiration. What must have been their beauty
when Venice was in her full glory, and these marble palaces were
new or in bright repair? From many which were built of brick, the
plastering was falling off, and others, with broken windows, were
uninhabited: yet, as an evidence of renovation, since Venice has
been made a free port, we passed a large new edifice, rising from
an old foundation, and others undergoing repair.

"The *Gondola*, about which so much is said and sung, is a fer-
ry-boat, very much resembling an Indian canoe, floating lightly
on the water, and rising pointed at each end, the front being ornamented with a large sharp-edged piece of iron, something like a
battle-axe. In the centre are cushioned seats, with an arched cov-
ering of black cloth, where two grown persons and two children
may conveniently sit, or, on an emergency, six grown persons
may squeeze together, either with open door and side windows,
or closed with glass or black Venetian blinds. The boatmen, without a rudder, and only one oar at his right side, stands on the little
deck of his narrow stern, and bearing his weight on his oar, which
seldom rises out of the water, not only urges the gondola straight
onwards, but by dextrous movements, which are practised from
infancy, turns it in all directions with surprising facility and accuracy.

"Having reached the post-office, and assorted our baggage,
we entered one of these gondolas, and returned to the Hotel de
l'Europe, which we had passed on entering the port. I found that
the use of one oar produced an unpleasant rocking of the boat, to
which those are not subject who employ an additional boatman
at the front of the canoe, whose oar, striking simultaneously with
the other, at opposite sides, corrects the evil, and it affords the
advantage of greater speed when long excursions are to be made.
We landed on marble steps rising a few feet out of the water to a
vast hall, in which the light gondola, when only for private use,
may be deposited; first divested of its covered chamber, which
two men lift off the seats and carry up.

"It had begun to rain before we entered Venice, and a mist
obscured the magnificent mountains which we had seen at sunrise stretching beyond and extending far over the low lands of
the adjoining continent. As it cleared up, however, the view from
our elevated balcony, of splendid edifices stretching in various
directions into the broad expanse of waters, was as delightful as
it was novel."

Mr. Peale remained in Venice, only sufficiently long to make a rapid survey of the works of art which it contains, especially the masterpieces of Titian, Paul Veronese, and Tintoretto, which are found in its palaces and churches. Though the necessity of passing generally along the canals, and the narrowness of the streets which do traverse the city to a much greater extent than is supposed, give a gloominess to Venice, yet the place and arcades of St. Mark offer a gay scene not often surpassed. The leisure and excitement of a Sunday afternoon especially, make them lively with the fashion and curiosity of the city; among which the gay modes of Paris are less to be admired than the fine features and rich complexions of the descendants of those men and women, who have served as models for the glowing pencils of the masters we have named. In the evening, the crowd may he seen still to increase, enjoying the soft mildness of the sea atmosphere, and basking in the blaze of the patent lamplight which attracts them round the coffee-houses; whilst a fine band of military music, stationed in the centre of the place, with music-books and lamps, greatly increases the popular enjoyment at the expense of the government. The grand canal, in length two miles, presents on each side a great number of elegant palaces, intermingled with some ordinary buildings, all in a degree blackened and injured by age and neglect. Some of the palaces of the ancient noble families are in a grand style of architecture, enriched with a profusion of bold sculpture, according to the taste of the times, and the peculiar propensity of the Venitians to this exuberance of decoration.

From Venice Mr. Peale again turned across the peninsula. Passing through Padua, Vicenza, and Verona, he reached Milan, where he visited the celebrated works of art, which however do not seem to be numerous. There, however, he took leave of the arts of Italy, and bent his way towards the Alps. Near the village of Arona, he saw and inspected the colossal statue of San Carlo Borromeo, which he thus describes.

> "It is made of sheet copper, and stands on a pedestal about forty feet high; and judging by a ladder which was placed at one side, and the proportions of the persons who ascended it, I computed the height of the statue to be about seventy feet. This agrees with the statement of my companions, who ascended under the skirt of his tunic, and climbed the iron bars which united the circumference of the bishop's garment with the brick core that rises through it. The head, they agree, is about eight or nine feet in height, so that only a boy or a very small man can stand in the nose. Yet it is not only a very stupendous, but I think it rather an elegant statue. My companions were amused with the singular animation which they found in the head of the saint, the dark asylum of a vast number of bats, which darted past them to escape out of a trap-door in the neck."

Crossing the Alps by the route of the Simplon, Mr. Peale reached Geneva, on the 29th of May, and after a short stay, set off for Paris. The dirt and incommodiousness of most of the Italian cities, gave increased enjoyment to his return to the noble quays of Paris, the Boulevards, and the gardens of the Luxembourg, Tuileries, and Palais Royal. After the course, too, which he had made through Italy, it became an object of no little interest to examine the treasures of the Louvre. He acknowledges that the specimens of the Italian painters there preserved, sunk a little in his estimation as he compared them with the best works in the galleries he had visited; but at the same time, he derived increased pleasure from many of the productions of what may be termed the old French school—especially from those of Poussin, Vernet, and Subleyras.

From Paris, he crossed the channel to England. He was astonished at the great improvements of late years in London, especially in the vast amount of buildings and ornamented squares, erected in the place of green fields, and the improvements effected in opening and widening many streets. *Regent street*, lined with splendid shops and dwellings like palaces, including its circular sweep of fluted cast-iron columns, and connecting St. James's park with the Regent's park, encircled with splendid mansions, he thought perhaps unequalled by any thing of the kind he had seen. Among the artists, he found our countrymen, Leslie and Newton, holding a distinguished rank, and he bears especial testimony, not only to the genius and reputation, but to the urbanity and moral worth of the former.

From London he proceeded to Portsmouth, and embarking there, reached America after an absence of nearly two years, on the last of September, 1830.

We have already remarked, that in this volume a reader is not to look for those reflections, either on ancient or modern Italy, which are to be found in the pages of scholars and travellers, who have visited it to revive the memory of former studies, or to gratify emotions which are excited by the contemplation of the fading relics of the grandeur of Rome. Yet, we collect among the notices of Mr. Peale, many remarks which occurred to him in the necessary attention he paid to the antiquities that abounded on his route, from one part of the country to another; and while he was exploring, with the curious zeal for which he is distinguished, all parts of the various cities and towns in which he stayed. Of these his narrative is perfectly simple. He enters into no antiquarian discussions; he quotes no passages of familiar poets and historians; he feels no peculiar glow from standing upon spots, or gazing upon scenes, which would have filled to overflowing a heart imbued with the remembrance of Virgil and of Livy. He paused in the midst of the Forum, but not for him

"Did the still eloquent air breathe`—burn with Cicero."

He wandered among the heights of Tivoli, but though the "præceps Anio" and the "domus Albuneæ resonantis" were still there, they seem not to have excited one thought of him, who not only preferred them to the favoured cities of Juno and Minerva, but gave them as lasting a fame. This is not in our opinion an objection to the volume of Mr. Peale; the task of classical illustration has been well performed in the travels of Eustace, whose book, censured as it may be, will ever be a favourite with scholars; and it has been yet more brilliantly performed by the wonderful genius of that man, who has given new fame in his immortal poem to spots already consecrated by the noblest and sweetest inspirations of the muse. As to most travellers, indeed, we had infinitely rather that all classical allusion was omitted, than have inflicted upon us the long string of hackneyed quotations, and the vapid recollections of schoolboy studies, which go for the most part to make up such portions of their journals. What we find here on the subject of antiquities, is just what we might expect from an inquisitive man of taste, making no pretensions to extraordinary research or information. When at Naples, Mr. Peale of course visited the buried towns of Herculaneum and Pompeii, and has described them with much minuteness, so as convey a very distinct impression of their present state.

"The first house which was shown to us was the *Villa of Diomedes*, of considerable extent, comprising a variety of apartments and gardens. We descended into his wine cellar, where there still remain some of the jars that contained his wine. In this spacious cellar seventeen skeletons were found, probably persons of his family who had sought this place for safety. They were smothered and entombed, with all their ornaments of gold upon them, by the flood of hot water and ashes, which had evidently flowed in through the little windows where light had been admitted, and where the traces of the fluid may still be seen.

"The houses were generally of only one story, though, in a few instances, we found a small stair-way leading to some upper apartments. They consist of a great many small rooms surrounding a court-yard, with a kind of piazza all around, as a protection against the sun and rain. In two private court-yards we were shown gaily decorated fountains, in alcoves or niches, curiously and elaborately ornamented with mosaic and shellwork, the shells being in perfect preservation.

"We looked into many shops, the counters of which were incrusted with bits of marble, of various colours, fitted around the narrow mouths of large earthen jars, which were imbedded in solid brick work, to hold oil and wine. Sometimes there were little shelves, like steps, covered with marble, upon which small articles were displayed close to the window.

"The basilica, or great hall of justice, was an oblong hall of great size, surrounded inside with noble columns, which, from their size, must have supported a lofty roof. At the farther end was an elevated throne, on which the judges sat; and beneath it a chamber, where three skeletons of men were found, fastened by their legs to iron stocks. From the public promenade we entered the tragic and the comic theatres; walked over the stone scats, now moss-stained; looked on the shallow stage, which allowed no scenic effect; stood in the prompter's central niche, and read the names of the managers, recorded in mosaic letters on the pavement in front of the orchestra; but its best sculptural decorations had been removed to the museum."

In the museum at Naples are preserved all the articles taken from the houses at Herculaneum and Pompeii, and they offer specimens of almost every thing that, even at the present day, domestic establishments seem to require. The visiter may here behold the charcoal form of a loaf of bread impressed with the baker's name; a plate of eggs, or rather egg shells, some of which are not broken, retaining their natural whiteness; thread nets for boiling vegetables; figs, prunes, dates, olives, and nuts of various kinds; the golden ornaments of the ladies; vases of glass of various colours; utensils of the clearest crystal; bronze candelabra of singular and beautiful forms; and all the apparatus of a household, exhibiting taste, convenience and luxury. Here, too, are seen the fresco paintings taken from Pompeii. Those first discovered, happening to be found in a part of the city inhabited by trades-men, did not furnish the most elegant specimens of the arts. The judgments which were consequently propagated from one antiquarian critic to another, were unfavourable to the ancient painters, who were pronounced inferior to contemporary sculptors, and ignorant of grouping, foreshortening, and perspective. Subsequent excavations have been made in a portion of the city where splendid temples, halls of justice, theatres, and spacious dwellings, gave occasion for the best employment of the arts. The result has been the discovery not only of statues and sculpture far superior to that formerly developed, but of fresco paintings of great excellence and beauty. Very different from those previously collected, they decisively indicate a high state of painting, as it must have been practised in Greece and Italy at the time the statues were executed, which yet exhibit such perfect knowledge of the human form, and of the principles of grouping. They prove that the ancient painters were perfectly acquainted with the rules of perspective and foreshortening. Indeed, we may fairly believe, from these beautiful works, done on walls, and probably by inferior artists, that on other occasions, as in moveable pictures, their best artists must have painted in a manner to correspond with the high rank of their sculpture, and the extraordinary accounts given of them by contemporary writers.

"These specimens of ancient fresco painting have been cut out of the walls, where they were executed, with great care, and transported here in strong cases, which serve as frames. When first found, they are pale and dull; but, on being varnished, their colours are brightened up to their pristine hues, and exhibit to the astonished eye every stroke of the brush, slightly indenting the fresh mortar, which was given by hands that perished, with the genius that directed them, nearly eighteen hundred years ago, yet appearing as the rich and mellow pencilling of yesterday. Most of them are taken from shops and ordinary houses, and represent all kinds of objects, drawn with remarkable spirit and truth. Many of the better kind served to decorate apartments in which there were no windows, where they must have been executed, and afterwards seen only by lamplight. But the best were found in the porticos of open court yards, or on the walls of dining-rooms or saloons. In looking closely into these, I was surprised to find such spirited execution and knowledge of anatomy, combined with the most exquisite beauty, perfection of drawing, colouring and expression of character."

It is, however, to the works of modern art that Mr. Peale has turned his principal attention. Travelling himself as an artist; seeking for the subjects of his own studies, the masterpieces wherever found; exercising a criticism, not as the picture-dealer who sees in every dingy canvass which bears, truly or falsely, the name of some celebrated master, the marks of pre-eminent genius, regardless of the time or circumstances under which it was executed—nor as the connoisseur or virtuoso, who has to maintain or to gain reputation by the singularity, the rashness, or the accidental correctness of his opinions; but viewing them at once with the devotion of an artist who had long heard of and known the works he was now to see, as the various efforts of genius, sometimes successful, but sometimes also less happy, and having no end to gain but the improvement of his own style, and the gratification of his own taste, Mr. Peale must be allowed the credit of candour, and entire freedom from affectation in the judgments he has passed. At the same time we should not omit to notice the variety, extent, and minuteness of his examinations. No church, gallery, or collection, was passed by, and most of the individual pictures are separately and carefully noticed. At Rome, especially, he admired and copied many of the works of her immortal artists, and in the loggie of the Vatican he gazed on their matchless productions with the enthusiasm of a painter, but without yielding up his senses to the praise of tablets, famous only in name, and disfigured by smoke, damp, and age. The walls of the celebrated Sistine chapel were painted by various artists of merit in their time, but they are now much injured, and offer little worthy of notice; but the ceiling, designed and executed by Michael Angelo, is eminently worthy of admiration, as exhibiting the best productions of his pencil, and as among the few paintings of that great genius not yet destroyed by smoke, and giving evidence of the grandeur of his invention and the boldness of his execution. The *Last Judgment*, so familiar in name to every one who reads the history of art, now excites no attention except from its former celebrity, as it is dimly traced in the dark, through stains of damp and mould, and blackened by smoke. Of his great rival, and in some respects superior, the fate is scarcely different, whilst some of the smaller works of Raphael are tolerably preserved, the celebrated frescoes in the Pauline chapel are so much injured by time and smoke, and the lances of soldiers who have occupied the rooms as barracks, that they excite but little pleasure at first sight. Artists, however, of all nations may be seen continually copying them, some mounted on scaffolding up to the ceiling, some drawing, others painting, and all seeking out with almost idolatrous or rather superstitious admiration, the beauty of every head, hand, limb, and fold of drapery. They obtain permission to copy, without difficulty from the Pope's secretary, when the places are not occupied, or whenever a vacancy may occur; but so numerous are the applications for some celebrated pictures, such as the *Transfiguration*, that they are frequently engaged for years in advance by artists of various nations.

It is, indeed, by foreigners chiefly, that the galleries of Italy are filled. The praise of superiority is no longer due to the painters of the peninsula, and amidst the precious models which they have around them, few have, of late years, maintained or restored the departing glory of their country. Fresco painting, so admirably calculated to call forth and give display to grand and spirited invention, as well as to promote careful and beautiful drawing, by the elaborate cartoons which it requires, has almost ceased to exist as a branch of works of design. Mosaic is still cultivated with considerable success, but it is seldom applied to original works. We may rejoice, however, that this happy art will preserve to future and distant ages, accurate copies of those great productions which have faded, and are still quickly fading, beneath the touch of time.

In the Vatican, there are apartments especially assigned to workers in mosaic, and placed under the directions of the historical painter, Camucini, who is zealous in endeavouring, by means of this curious art, and the great skill of those artists who at present execute it, to preserve the best paintings of the great masters, now imperfectly seen in several churches, and in danger of perishing. In these rooms may be found various workmen, some copying small pictures, for the purpose of learning and practising the art; and others, who are more experienced, occupied with larger works for the churches. In a great hall is a store, arranged on shelves, of the semi-vitreous porcelain, or coarse enamel, in cakes half an inch thick and several inches in diameter. These cakes are of every colour that may be required, all arranged, numbered, registered, and weighed out by an accountant to the workmen as they are wanted to be afterwards broken into bits. Some of the cakes consist of two or more colours, gradually blending into each other; and there are said to be no less than sixteen thousand assorted tints. The large pictures are wrought by being placed nearly erect, with the one to be copied, so that the effect may be compared from time to time; when not more than three or four feet long, they are done on sheets of copper, stiffened with strong iron bars within a rim of metal; but those of a greater size, especially such as are intended for permanent fixture in churches, are executed each on one great slab of stone, from eight to twelve inches thick, which is excavated about an inch deep, leaving a raised border all round. The irregular surface is then nearly filled up with a level mass of cement. On this, when dry, the artist carefully traces the contours of his picture; he then procures from the adjoining magazine an assortment of tints to suit the part he purposes working at; and is furnished with a little table, on which is fixed a chisel, with the edge upwards, in the manner of an anvil, on which, with a hammer, he breaks the semi-vitreous composition into small squares or other shapes, to suit the part to be copied. Along side of this is another table, furnished with a horizontal grindstone on a vertical shaft, made to revolve rapidly by a cord which passes round a larger wheel, turned by a pin at its periphery. This is moved with the left hand, while the right is employed in fashioning the bits of stone into squares, triangles, circles, crescents, &c. of various dimensions. The artist then chisels out of his composition, within the lines of his drawing, any spot he chooses to fill up with his mosaic; which, being inserted, stone by stone, with fresh cement, enables him either to pursue the continuity of an outline, or the masses and directions of similar tints; so that he can work at any spot, and fill up the intervals, or take out any portion of what he has done, and do it over again. The stones are from half an inch to three quarters in depth, and in breadth, of all sizes, from an eighth to half an inch in diameter. After the picture is finished, and the surface of the stones ground down to a level, and perfectly polished, the white cement is carefully scraped out of the interstices to a little depth. A variety of painters' colours, in fine powder, are then each mixed with a small portion of melted wax, and put on a palette. With these, by means of a hot pointed iron, like a tinman's soldering-iron, the artist melts a little of the coloured wax to match the stones, and runs it from the point of his iron into all the crevices—then scrapes off the superfluous wax, and cleans the surface with spirits of turpentine.

In an art kindred to painting, but perhaps more impressive on the imagination and the senses, that of statuary, the Italians of the present age may bear a more honourable comparison with their predecessors. It is true, they cannot aspire to that wonderful excellence, which we are able to appreciate in the few fragments that have descended to us from the great sculptors of ancient times; but, still, the works of Canova, Thorwaldsen, and others, may be added to those of Michael Angelo and John of Bologna, and given as evidence of great powers of invention and a profitable study of the ancient remains. Thorwaldsen, who, since the death of his great rival, Canova, holds the first place as a sculptor at Rome, and whose taste and skill are known in America by a graceful statue of Venus, executed for and in the possession of a gentleman of Philadelphia, is remarkable for his careful cultivation of the antique taste, and the extreme simplicity of his statues. To become an artist, he studied at Rome, with singular assiduity, although contending with the most distressing poverty, till the age of thirty. His practice at the academy was to draw from the life only those parts of the figure which chanced to please him. He modelled in clay numerous spirited compositions, which he was obliged to destroy for want of the funds necessary to put them into marble or even plaster of Paris: and it was owing to the taste, judgment, and liberality of an English gentleman, that he was at last enabled to execute his first work in stone. In his workshop, Mr. Peale was shown a basso relieve to the memory of his patron, who is represented supplying the lamp of genius with oil.

Statuary, however, at the present day, appears to be an art altogether different in its mechanical and practical details from that of former times. The genius of Michael Angelo was frequently fatigued before he could approach in his blocks of marble, the forms his imagination conceived, and he often hastened to chisel out a part as a guide in the development of the whole figure, which was sometimes spoiled by his impatience. Now, however, a sculptor is scarcely required to touch his marble, or even to know how to cut it. He first models the figure in ductile clay, which is kept moist by wet cloths, during any length of time, so that he may give it the utmost perfection of form. This model he places in the hands of a careful mechanic, whose art is to make a mould upon it, and to produce a facsimile in plaster of Paris, the colour of which enables him more readily to judge of its effect, and to add to its beauty. When the model is thus perfected, the artist may either copy it himself in stone, or employ workmen who generally do nothing else all their lives, and who proceed without any of the inventive enthusiasm of genius, but with wonderful mechanical accuracy. The model is marked all over with numerous spots, which are transferred by the compasses to the block of marble; two well defined points may serve as a base for fixing the position of a third, and the workman continually measures as he advances to the completion; and in this he is expert or excellent, in proportion to the attention he has paid to his studies in drawing, modelling, and anatomy. The accuracy with which these workmen copy the model, is such as to induce the ablest sculptors to trust to them their choicest works. Many of the most skilful reside at Carrara; and, to save the expense of transporting large masses of marble, it is becoming very customary to transmit thither the model very carefully packed up, and to have it either accurately copied there, or roughed out for the sculptor to complete. Thorwaldsen, whose models are seldom remarkable for the delicacy of the finish, is so well satisfied with the general accuracy of the work done at Carrara, that statues which he is making for his native country, will be boxed up there and sent to Denmark, without being once seen by him.

As a school of art, Mr. Peale seems to consider the great advantages of Italy, as arising less from her academies, or from any direct facilities which are there offered to the student, than from the treasures of ancient sculpture, and the sublime works executed by the greatest masters, which offer admirable models, and serve to infuse a kindred spirit. In regard to the peculiar excellence exhibited in these, he admits that nothing has more puzzled the professors and critics of art. He thinks that, although much must have depended upon the capacity of the artist, and his means of information, and a great deal on the nature of his employment and encouragement, yet that almost as much advantage has been derived from accidental circumstances. The Italians, who enjoy a clear sky, and witness in their sunsets the most glowing colours, are surprised that the Hollanders, living in an atmosphere of gray mist, should have produced so many excellent colourists. It may be from that very circumstance that they were so. A vapoury atmosphere which reduces all colours at a distance to one hue of gray, serves, at the same time, to render every colour which is near, not only more distinct, but more agreeably illuminated; but, under a blue sky, the shadows are necessarily tinged with blue, and the eye becoming accustomed to vivid colours, too easily rests satisfied with the most violent contrasts, both in nature and the works of art. The atmosphere of England, in like manner, has contributed to produce a good taste in colouring, which was confirmed by the example and authority of Reynolds, who so well understood the principles of the Flemish masters. Giorgione, Titian, and Paul Veronese, were, it is true, Italians, and rank at the head of good colourists; but the situation of Venice, built in the water, essentially softens its atmosphere, and combines the advantages of Holland and Italy. The happy genius of Corregio derived his theory of light and colour certainly not from his visit to Rome.

Accidental circumstances have probably influenced several distinguished artists. Vandyck happened to learn the use of a certain brown colour from Germany, called Terra de Cassel, by which he softened and harmonized his shadows; hence the English artists call it Vandyck brown. Holland, enjoying the commerce of the East Indies, which furnished her with a variety of pigments, likewise produced from her own soil the best quality of madder, from which her chemists and manufacturers procured the richest and most durable dyes. Van Huysum, and other painters of that country, must have learned the use of this and other rich pigments, the knowledge of which they could not entirely keep to themselves, but which were probably known to Andrea del Sarto and the good colourists of Florence. It is not improbable that the fashion of wearing changeable silks, reflecting opposite colours in different angles, may have influenced the old painters to represent their blue draperies with red shadows and yellow lights, as in Raphael's picture of the *Transfiguration*: certain it is that such things being found in the master works of the great painters, which are copied with the most scrupulous exactness, even to the most palpable fault, the painters of the present day in Italy pursue the same system of colouring, with as much pertinacity as they display in their hard-earned accuracy of outline.

Besides, the revival of the art in Italy was by fresco painting, the peculiar nature of which required that the artist should first prepare his compositions in finished cartoons. At all events, it was the practice of painters, derived from each other, and passing from generation to generation, to bestow their chief study on a cartoon executed in black and white chalk of the full size of the intended fresco. Many of these are preserved in the galleries and churches of Italy, and are to be considered among the most precious relics of the art; displaying the finest skill of the master, in composition, drawing, light and shade, and execution. Of these original and spirited drawings, what are called the original pictures are but copies in colour, sometimes executed by the master himself, but more frequently by some of his pupils.

When oil painting was introduced into Italy, and adopted by those who had practised in fresco, the habits which they had acquired led them to practise the methods with which they were most familiar. Their oil paintings were therefore generally painted from drawings, and, hence, the colouring was often from imagination or recollection, which sufficiently accounts for its deviation from nature; although it is frequently spread out with great beauty and airiness. Those painters who, it is agreed, excelled in colouring, almost always painted their studies in colours, by which they had a double chance of success, without vitiating their own powers of vision by the continual contemplation of highly wrought colourless forms, or transcripts in fanciful hues.

We had desired, after these observations on the subject of the arts, which it must be confessed form the topic of chief interest in perusing the volume of Mr. Peale, to add some remarks on the political and moral character of the Italians, as it appears in the unaffected and occasional observations which occur in regard to the people themselves and their institutions. There is in general a freedom from prejudice; a temperateness of expression; a mildness of judgment, and a clear and natural manner of relation, which do great credit to the author, and while they assist a reader in forming an opinion of his own, give strength to that expressed by the writer himself. Our limits, however, do not permit us to do so, and after the expression of this general opinion, we must refer to the volume itself for the evidence of its correctness. In concluding, we may respond to the sentiment of Mr. Peale, when on leaving Milan, he bade farewell to the arts of Italy.

> "An Italian, not exempted from bigotry, discovered a new world for the emancipation of man. May America in patronizing the arts, receive them as the offspring of enlightened Greece, transmitted through Italy, where their miraculous powers were nourished in the bondage of mind. Let them in turn be emanci-

pated, and their persuasive and fascinating language be exalted to the noblest purposes, and be made instrumental to social happiness and national glory!"

THE END.

Lector House believes that a society develops through a two-fold approach of continuous learning and adaptation, which is derived from the study of classic literary works spread across the historic timeline of literature records. Therefore, we aim at reviving, repairing and redeveloping all those inaccessible or damaged but historically as well as culturally important literature across subjects so that the future generations may have an opportunity to study and learn from past works to embark upon a journey of creating a better future.

This book is a result of an effort made by Lector House towards making a contribution to the preservation and repair of original ancient works which might hold historical significance to the approach of continuous learning across subjects.

HAPPY READING & LEARNING!

LECTOR HOUSE LLP
E-MAIL: lectorpublishing@gmail.com

www.ingramcontent.com/pod-product-compliance
Lightning Source LLC
LaVergne TN
LVHW091146180726
843490LV00004B/1328

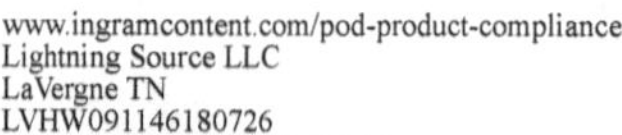